THE SKRIPAL FILES

Also by Mark Urban

Soviet Land Power

War in Afghanistan

Big Boys' Rules
The SAS and the Secret Struggle Against the IRA

UK Eyes Alpha
Inside British Intelligence

The Man Who Broke Napoleon's Codes
The Story of George Scovell

Rifles
Six Years with Wellington's Legendary Sharpshooters

Generals
Ten British Commanders Who Shaped the World

Fusiliers
How the British Army Lost America but Learned to Fight

Task Force Black
*The Explosive True Story of the SAS and the
Secret War in Iraq*

The Tank War
*The British Band of Brothers – One Tank Regiment's
World War II*

The Edge
*Is the Military Dominance of the West
Coming to an End?*

THE

Comhairle Contae
Átha Cliath Theas
South Dublin County Council

LIBRARY SERVICES ONLINE at www.southdublinlibraries.ie

Items should be returned on or before the last date below. Fines, as
displayed in the Library, will be charged on overdue items. You may renew
your items in person, online at www.southdublinlibraries, or by phone.

First published 2018 by Macmillan
an imprint of Pan Macmillan
20 New Wharf Road, London N1 9RR
Associated companies throughout the world
www.panmacmillan.com

ISBN 978-1-5290-0688-9

1 3 5 7 9 8 6 4 2

A CIP catalogue record for this book is available from the British Library.

Printed and bound by CPI Group (UK) Ltd, Croydon, CR0 4YY

CONTENTS

INTRODUCTION

The situation that presented itself in March 2018 was one quite unprecedented in my thirty years as a writer. A former Russian spy for MI6 was lying in a coma, having been poisoned by a nerve agent, and the world's press had descended on a small city in the south of England. The man at the centre of all this was someone I had not only met, but had spent hours discussing espionage with.

He had not been giving me an interview as a journalist. I felt confident he would not have wanted everything blurted out over the airwaves. He had seen me because he knew I wrote books, and wanted to do one about post-Cold War spying. By the strangest turn of fate, back in 1988 I had embedded in a Soviet regiment on operations in Afghanistan that he had previously served in. As our conversations started it was apparent that he knew some of the officers I'd met on this assignment well and this seemed to put him at his ease.

The interviews I'd done with him in 2017 assumed a particular narrative in which a spy swap that took place in Vienna airport in 2010 was central. This was the moment that the former Russian intelligence officer, convicted of spying for Britain years before, had been pardoned and flown to the West.

Roll on several months to March 2018, and everything was looking very different. Worldwide interest in Sergei Skripal had exploded. Who was he? How had he ended up in this incongruous street in an English cathedral city? For a while everyone wondered whether he would survive, then later whether he would simply disappear without ever speaking publicly. Either way, there was fascination in his story. I felt I had to tell it.

Suddenly the wider narrative that I had been researching when pursuing 'Plan A' before the Salisbury poisoning, that of an East–West spy battle that had barely slackened after the end of the Cold War, seemed much more relevant too. The result – setting Skripal's life and the poisoning into this context – is what follows here.

There were many dilemmas along the way, not least whether it was right to do this when there were quite a few issues that I wanted to discuss further with Sergei before pushing ahead. He chose not to speak to me after the poisoning, and doubtless he had many more important matters on his mind. I must therefore take full responsibility for any errors in these pages.

To those who worry that a book like this will inevitably give too much away, you must remember that Skripal was interrogated for two years by the Russian counter-intelligence people, and then put on trial: the outlines of a career as an agent for MI6 that ended fourteen years ago are already very familiar to the Kremlin's secret servants. My aim is to share some of this knowledge with the public. As for those who believe that this text is too coy in places, or the product of some cosy relationship with our own agencies, the Salisbury events should remind you that lives indeed are at stake. There are also many things in this account that Western intelligence agencies would have preferred to keep quiet.

The experience of previous books about the intelligence world and special forces has taught me that there are some people who would rather these stories were never told, and others who regard anyone who talks to those in the secret world as complicit in some sort of conspiracy. None of these judgements are easy, but there has already been an enormous amount written on this case, and there are reams more of it to come. It's that someone who has at least met Skripal and followed the intelligence battles of the last thirty years should be writing this. Who knows, one day Sergei or his daughter Yulia may write a book also.

In order to avoid endangering people, I have observed some basic rules: certain people who appear in this book are given pseudonyms (denoted on their first mention by an asterisk, like this: *John Smith); in cases where intelligence sources might be involved, I avoided asking questions about them, still less speculating or hinting at their possible identity; and I have respected the stipulation made by many who gave me information that it should not be attributed to them.

Having faced dilemmas over telling the story, I then had to write it, producing a manuscript quickly in a number of languages while keeping going with the intensive demands of my day job. In this I am very grateful for the support, understanding, and insights that have come from my editors, principally Christiane Bernhardt and Kristian Wachinger at Droemer Knaur; Robin Harvie and Matt Cole at Macmillan in the UK; and Paul Golob and Caroline Wray at Henry Holt in the US.

Jonathan Lloyd put this international publishing deal together while offering expert advice, as he has done without fail during more than two decades as my literary agent. Thanks are also due to Neus Rodriguez, Anya Noble, and Olga Ivshina for their help with research.

I am also grateful to Esme Wren, Editor of *Newsnight*, for her understanding about how we could report the story for our audience at the same time that I was writing the book.

Finally I must thank my dear wife Hilary, who has come to know all too well that strange, distracted air that comes over me once I become possessed with a book idea. She and our kids have put up with rather too much book-related absenteeism from me, and I am deeply grateful for their indulgence.

PROLOGUE:

AN UNLAWFUL USE OF FORCE

The moment that the Prime Minister rose to her feet was one of utmost seriousness. Benches were lined with members, and a reverent hush descended as she began her statement. Everybody understood the seriousness of what had happened in Salisbury. But what on earth was she going to do?

Theresa May said she was taking the opportunity to update them on the incident, 'and to respond to this reckless and despicable act'. Flanked by her Home Secretary and the Leader of the House, she paid tribute to the emergency services and the fortitude of the people of Salisbury. That was all very well but what everyone was waiting for was what she was going to say about Russia.

She had chaired a meeting of the National Security Council that morning, and been briefed on the latest intelligence, as well as the state of the investigation. 'It is now clear,' she continued, 'that Mr Skripal and his daughter were poisoned with a military-grade nerve agent of a type developed by Russia. This is part of a group of nerve agents known as Novichok.'

The work of government chemists, 'Russia's record of

conducting state-sponsored assassinations', and the assessment that the Kremlin regarded it as quite legitimate to kill defectors had led the UK government to conclude it was 'highly likely' that Russia was responsible for the poisoning of Sergei Skripal, a one-time officer in its military intelligence service, and his daughter, Yulia.

Mrs May went on to offer an ultimatum to the Kremlin. It was one that, as a British diplomat phrased it, 'was designed to be refused'. Either the Salisbury poisoning was a state act by the Russian government or somehow that government had lost control of deadly chemical weapons – which it should not have had anyway under international treaties. Russia was given more than twenty-four hours to respond. If no credible answer was provided, 'then we will conclude that this action amounts to an unlawful use of force by the Russian state against the United Kingdom'.

Many spectators couldn't believe what they had just heard. It sounded like 1914, or if not a prelude to war, certainly like the onset of a serious international crisis. To many on the Labour benches it seemed a rush to judgement based on secret intelligence – the very commodity that had been spooned out in Parliament fifteen years earlier to take the country into Iraq.

In amplifying her point, Mrs May added a load of accusations against Russia that testified to how bad relations had become by the spring of 2018: it had illegally annexed Crimea from Ukraine; it had fomented large-scale violence by separatists in the east of that country; it used nuclear threats against the West; and of course it had murdered a dissident, Alexander Litvinenko, using a rare radioactive isotope as a poison in London in 2006.

But who was this man, this former colonel who was

now lying critically ill, apparently because of a decision made many years earlier to spy for British intelligence? He certainly wasn't a Litvinenko, in the sense of somebody who had campaigned noisily against the Russian president, accusing him of all manner of evil. Sergei Skripal, on the contrary, had virtually no public profile. After coming to Britain in a spy swap years earlier, he had simply disappeared.

Alone among the journalists watching the Prime Minister's statement on 9 March, and the unfolding of a wider crisis, I had not only met Skripal, but spent many hours interviewing him during the summer of 2017. I had kept what I had learned to myself but understood of course that the time would come to tell his story. At that moment though, far more importantly, what I and so many others wanted to know was whether he and his daughter would survive.

The answer to that question would play out in a small room on Level 4 of Salisbury District Hospital. There a man of sixty-six who had been poisoned with a substance so exotic that nobody had ever treated its effects before was locked in a fight for life. In this battle blood tests, pharmacology, and the very best of medical ingenuity would decide the issue, rather than politics and bluster.

Skripal and his daughter were connected to every device needed to keep them alive: the ventilator, with its bag puffing in and out as it pushed air down their throats; the drips feeding them atropine as well as all the other drugs being pumped into their systems; and lines carrying their blood out to be scrubbed before being pumped back in. In order to tolerate all this invasive medical technology and save their brains from the nerve agent, doctors had put them into the deepest of medically induced sleeps.

How had this poor patient, in many ways so typical of

Russians of his generation, an everyman almost, come to be in this mortal struggle and at the centre of a major international crisis? His story is in many ways an allegory. Certainly it guides us through decades of distrust and espionage between Russia and its Western rivals. It was a battle that never stopped after the fall of the Berlin Wall in 1989, simply paused for a year or two, then resumed, growing more intense and merciless with the passage of time. For Skripal, that conflict had produced a personal reckoning twenty-two years before the poisoning, in an altogether happier time and place.

PART ONE

AGENT

1

THE PITCH

It is high summer in Madrid, 1996. Two men are walking in the Parque del Retiro. It's a working day so they are wearing office attire, which just raises the temperature still further.

The older of the pair is a couple of weeks past his forty-fifth birthday, big, with a boxer's physique. He is fair-skinned and looks a little out of place among the Spaniards who flit along the paths pushing their kids in strollers or walking hand in hand. The other, maybe a decade younger, maybe more, appears to be Spanish. He's darker, dressed the way the Madrileños might dress, and outwardly he appears more at home. But at the same time he doesn't quite look relaxed.

The park's thoroughfares tell the story of the pet projects of Spain's Bourbon monarchs and statesmen. There is one section created in the formal French style with neat trimmed hedges and gravel paths; other thoroughfares are a little wilder. In July there are puppet shows and other activities for children, and the place has a real holiday atmosphere. Under the shade of broad boughs Madrid's youth and beauty gather to picnic and canoodle.

There are hothouses, statues, and a boating lake. That

gave a choice of rendezvous and its broad avenues, lined with horse chestnuts, poplars and maples, and narrower paths branching off them, offered ways to embrace the crowds or avoid them. With its myriad identities, el Retiro was perfect for the business at hand.

The bigger man is Sergei Viktorovich Skripal, the 1st Secretary (Scientific and Technical) from the Russian embassy. Actually that's just his cover. His real business in Spain is as a colonel in Russian military intelligence, the GRU. He is operating in Madrid on a particularly sensitive mission reporting direct to the Centre. As for the man he is talking to, *Richard Bagnall (he is calling himself something else of course, a local alias), and as the stroll through the park goes on, he is growing increasingly nervous.

Richard has seen the older Russian several times now and he knows he must make a move. Skripal is coming towards the end of his three-year posting and anyway this little dance has gone on for long enough.

After a while with this sort of thing, if you don't make things plain, the other person just begins to despise you, and heaven knows Richard had thrown out a few hints since their first meeting that April. He knows also that Sergei doesn't have very long. That just adds to the pressure, as if there wasn't already enough of that.

What the passers-by on that summer's day in 1996 ambling along in el Retiro cannot know is that Richard is engaged in a carefully choreographed seduction. There is nothing sexual about it. Rather it is the beginning of a different kind of relationship, one that will last their whole lives, and is freighted with risk. Indeed the 'thing' that this younger man wants to start could quite possibly destroy Sergei's life completely and utterly.

He is no fool, the Russian. He'd toiled for four years at the Military Diplomatic Academy, the GRU's secret training college in Moscow, to prepare him for foreign service as an intelligence officer. Time and again in those airless rooms listening to the instructors, they had been warned about foreign spies and all the different ways that might be used to compromise and recruit them. And they had learned about recruiting their own agents, the tricks of the trade, how to lead a person past a whole series of moral turn-offs until the only road they could follow was to spy for you.

As Richard made his awkward small talk, building up to the moment, Sergei studied him. He looked so young, and so nervous, the GRU officer thought. How long had he suspected this dapper olive-skinned man, chatting away in the park? Certainly after two or three meetings some alarm bells had gone off.

This suspicious fellow had managed to turn the conversation to current events time and again. And once or twice he had strayed directly towards asking Sergei what he 'really did' at the embassy. One time, as they dined together, Richard had left a copy of a book, *Aquarium*, on the table, claiming it was what he happened to be reading and asking what Sergei thought of it. *Aquarium* was an exposé of the GRU by a former officer under the pseudonym Viktor Suvorov.

Skripal knew what he thought of that book. Its author, real name Vladimir Rezun, had defected to the UK in 1978 while serving at the Geneva *rezidentura*. Skripal attended the Military Diplomatic Academy soon after this fateful event, and heard Rezun described as a vile traitor who had betrayed his Motherland for a few pieces of silver. And what had he really known, this Rezun? He'd just been a captain in the GRU on his first foreign posting. Now he was skulking in the West, trying to make some money by exaggerating his own importance. If Richard had hoped to lure Skripal into talking about intelligence work in that Spanish restaurant, it was never going to happen. The colonel simply brushed him off, saying he knew nothing about the GRU.

On the other hand, there were things about this person that seemed to confirm that he was exactly what he said he was: a Gibraltarian businessman who'd made a lot of money in the oil business in Africa and was now looking for a partner in Russia. Sergei had him checked out by the GRU after a couple of meetings. Richard did indeed have offices in Gibraltar, the phone numbers were answered, and his name or rather his pseudonym was known in various places. And of course they'd been introduced by a mutual Spanish acquaintance.

If it was a cover, it was an excellent one, because Richard splashed the cash as you might expect a successful business-man to do, eating at the best restaurants and staying at excellent hotels when he was in Madrid. And the oil fields in the Tyumen or Komi republic of Russia had at that time become a sort of Klondike where people with the right con-nections could make millions – or indeed billions. What Richard needed, he said, was those right points of contact to get his hands on some of that black gold. It was the mid-1990s and everything in Russia was for sale, or appeared to be. Why was it so surprising that someone wanted to get in on the act?

As they strolled in the park they spoke mainly in English. While Skripal could speak Spanish tolerably well, Bagnall had mastered it. His pseudonym, his style of dress and above all his easy manner combined to make him seem quite genuine.

There was something so open and guileless about this guy

also. He had asked Sergei's wife Liudmila and their kids to join them at a flamenco club for an afternoon's entertainment. After he'd met Sergei's family a couple of times, this mystery man had appeared with presents for little Yulia and Sasha. 'The kids loved him,' Skripal reflected.

Arriving from a trip to London, the businessman had given Sergei something. It was a small model of a typical English country cottage. It was the type of thing that you could pick up for a few pounds in a tourist shop, probably made in China for all he knew. But for reasons he couldn't exactly define, Sergei rather liked the brightly painted resin miniature, with its creeping plants, sagging roof, and arched front door.

Richard could drink too – gin and tonics, glass after glass of Spanish wine, then brandy – and to a Russian that gave him a sort of authenticity. This behaviour really didn't sit well with how Sergei expected the British or Americans to carry out a cultivation. Conventional wisdom in the GRU held that these Western intelligence officers would avoid a target's family for a whole lot of reasons. Not least, if your kid tells someone about the curious foreigner who keeps bringing gifts and seems to be your dad's new best friend, the Russian diplomatic compound is going to start taking an interest.

Of one thing, Sergei had become sure: if Richard was a spook, he wasn't a Spanish one. There was no way, given the long history of rivalry over the ownership of the Rock, that a Spanish operative was going to be basing himself in Gibraltar. Might he be CIA? The GRU colonel knew something else in his bones too, that if his persistent suitor was a CIA man, then he wasn't interested. He wasn't willing to take the risks that would be involved in treason for America, if that's what this angst-ridden young man was indeed building up to.

As Richard built to 'the pitch', that moment when a spy finally asks someone to betray their country, the nervous tension, the temperature rose even higher. So much training, thinking, and advice fixates on that moment. It is romanticized by espionage authors and deconstructed in role plays at the Fort, where the UK's overseas espionage agency, the Secret Intelligence Service, or SIS, but more often called MI6, trains its new officers, and now he, Richard Bagnall, who'd only been in the service for a few years, was about to pitch a GRU colonel.

'Sergei, I have a friend who would really value your information on what is really going on inside Russia. He works for the British government. Do you think you can provide that for us? You would be looked after, of course.'

OK, Sergei thought, we have got to the point now. This guy is indeed a British intelligence officer. Yes, he'd be happy to meet again. 'I was ready,' Skripal would say years later. But how had that happened? How had he gone from arch-patriot, paratrooper, and senior GRU officer to somebody who was prepared to sell it all out for MI6?

2

SERGEI'S JOURNEY

It didn't take long for Sergei and Richard to meet again. The second rendezvous was another quick one, but cards had been put on the table. And essentially, terms had been agreed. Yes indeed Mr Skripal was actually Colonel Skripal of the GRU, and his interlocutor was working for the British government. The Russian was willing to trade information for money. And if it all went wrong he needed some guarantees. 'I wanted to know what MI6 would do for me; documents, passport, legalization.'

Richard would have known that back at 'head office', his service's garish new headquarters on the bank of the River Thames at Vauxhall Cross, there were those who looked upon this budding relationship with a little less euphoria than he did, when he raced back from el Retiro that July day to report that he had made his pitch. The Service details an officer to look critically at each new agent recruitment. This person 'plays the role of professional devil's advocate', explains a former intelligence officer. Even on the basis of this initial commitment to Skripal, Her Majesty's Government was exposed to the tune of hundreds of thousands of pounds. In those days when the Cold War was over and the agency's 'customers' were so much less interested than they had been in Russian intelligence, why bother?

In the mid-1990s senior MI6 people were saying that the Soviet collapse had produced so many would-be defectors 'that we had to turn them away'. To qualify for the resettlement package, they had to have something truly remarkable. But Skripal was not a defector, he was something much more precious than that; an agent in place at a senior level in Russian military intelligence. How had he come to be talking to a deep-cover MI6 officer in the first place? Why was he willing to tread this path for a new life away from Russia, since he clearly still loved his country?

Sergei Skripal experienced an archetypical childhood of the early post-war USSR. Born in 1951 in Kaliningrad, formerly the east Prussian fortress city of Königsberg, he grew up surrounded by the legacy of the Second World War. Viktor Skripal, his father, had been an artillery officer during some of the Red Army's titanic battles, and for his sons his stories were still very fresh. Ruins and bomb sites were everywhere, even in the late 1950s and early 1960s when Sergei and his older brother Valery scampered among them playing war. The city had been pummelled by the Red Army during the final months of that merciless conflict, after which Stalin had driven out the native German population and replaced them with his own people.

The years of his childhood were ones when everyone saw evidence of the country's sacrifice all around them, from broken mothers who'd lost all their sons at the front to ordinary men from the neighbourhood who'd received the highest orders and decorations. And although Sergei's parents would have had a tough life, living in a communal flat, these were years where those who had survived the 1940s witnessed rapid improvement in living standards. Those growing up in the 1960s were therefore inculcated in the strength of the Soviet state – both in defeating the Nazi menace and recovering so quickly after the war.

At school Sergei proved to be a good all-rounder, rather than a genius or a dolt, and an excellent sportsman. Given an hour or two alone in the library he came back time and again to books about knights, conquests, and heroism. He particularly liked the one he'd found about Richard the Lionheart. At home he and Valery were fussed over and cherished by their mother Yelena, who inculcated them with self-belief for good measure.

Given his passions it was unsurprising that as high school came to an end Sergei, following in his brother's footsteps, applied for and was accepted into the Zhdanov Higher Military Engineering School. Becoming an officer in the Soviet Army was not a business for those in a hurry. And Skripal spent four years studying the military engineer's trade in his home town. At the end of a course that embraced the theory and practice of military engineering from the creation and removal of obstacles to demolitions, bridge-building, and storming bunkers he had a qualification that had the same status as a university degree.

He was commissioned as a second lieutenant and swore the military oath. Adherence to this solemn pledge would mark the second great emotional commitment of Sergei's life, after his loyalty to family in general and his mother in particular. In the Soviet Army much was made of this covenant with service life. Ceremonies for swearing in newly commissioned officers were usually choreographed at huge war memorials, often with flaming torches or floodlights, bands playing, and families looking on. The second half of this vow laid particular emphasis on the obligations an individual was entering into, and the possible consequences of failing to meet them:

> I will always be ready to come to the defence of my homeland, the Union of Soviet Socialist Republics, at the order of the Soviet government and, as a fighting man of the armed forces, I swear that I will defend it courageously, skilfully, and with dignity and honour, sparing neither blood nor life itself to achieve complete victory over enemies. But if I violate this solemn oath of mine, may the harsh retribution of the Soviet law and the universal hatred and scorn of the working people befall me.

And as his time at the engineers' college ended, and he bound himself, quite possibly for life, to the army, Skripal nudged the other great piece of his future plan into place. In July 1972, he married his hometown sweetheart Liudmila Koshelnik. A family photo taken a few months before their wedding shows her standing next to Sergei, a good-looking young woman with her thick dark brown hair cut in a bob. Valery, who had already graduated, is arm in arm with his own sweetheart, wearing his lieutenant's uniform. Sergei, perhaps knowing he could not compete with his brother's military glamour, is wearing civilian clothes rather than his cadet's uniform.

There is a Russian proverb, 'God loves things in threes', and as any military engineer will tell you, the triangle is one of the strongest structures there is. It forms the basis of cranes, and its repeated shape can be found in the roofs of houses and the construction of temporary military bridges. In Sergei's case, the triangle of faith and mutual commitment formed by his mother, the army, and Liudmila would prove the foundation of his adult life.

Although it might have seemed, with all this in place, that Skripal's path had been set by the time he was twenty-two, he was not content to follow the typical trajectory of a sapper, traipsing with Liudmila from one far-flung garrison to another. For he (and his brother Valery) had decided that the modern form of chivalry and heroism could be found at its highest form in the airborne forces.

Valery, the more dashing of the two, had shown the way, getting into a department of the Zhdanov engineer school that prepared officers for the divisions of the Vozdyushno Desantnye Voiska, or VDV, as these troops are known in Russia. Each of these formations need their own specialists from artillerymen to logistics battalions and of course engineers. So after passing out from the Kaliningrad school, Sergei Skripal progressed to further parachute training and with it, initiation into the elite brotherhood of the VDV.

Having shown his aptitude and fearlessness leaping out of aeroplanes, Skripal was sent to take part in operations in Russia's far east. There a simmering border dispute had produced actual combat between Soviet and Chinese forces in 1969, after which the Kremlin reinforced its frontier garrisons and updated its war plans. There was a further violent clash between the two communist powers in 1972.

Assigned to what was known as a Reconnaissance Diversionary Company, the young paratrooper engineer would in time enter a twilight world sitting in between the overt side of the Russian military and the covert 'special designation' or *spetsnaz* units that undertook more sensitive war preparations. These special forces formed the ground level or tactical presence of the army staff's Main Intelligence Directorate, known by its Russian acronym, the GRU. As he would discover, the special company he had been assigned to was like the last stop on the route from the regular forces of the VDV to the *spetsnaz*.

Skripal was soon drawn into detailed war planning for any renewed clash between the USSR and China. Along which routes would Soviet forces advance into China? Were the bridges, roads, and railways along them suitable? What infrastructure would they have to destroy in order to prevent China opposing this advance? Much of this planning could be done by map and overhead photography – be it from aircraft flying along the border but peering down into China, or satellites. But some of it required closer inspection of the relevant bridges, tunnels, and so on.

So in the mid-1970s the young officer from Kaliningrad became involved in covert operations. He was a member of small groups infiltrated to conduct detailed reconnaissance inside the People's Republic. 'I have been to China three times,' he later quipped, 'never with visa, only with Kalashnikov.'

This potentially highly dangerous work was followed by time spent in Uzbekistan, in Central Asia, at that time still very much under Soviet rule as one of the constituent republics of the USSR. Despite decades of receiving diktats from the Kremlin, initially by Russian royalty, and later by the communists, it had retained an unsettled feel. Sergei, his wife Liudmila, and their little boy Alexander (or Sasha as he was always known in the family), born in 1974 and so a toddler, found themselves in a tight-knit airborne forces community housed in a military cantonment on the edge of the Uzbek city of Fergana.

The town and area around it had been conquered by the tsars during a series of campaigns in the 1860s and 1870s. That advance was motivated by a desire for imperial expansion, great-power rivalry with Britain, and economic self-interest. The Fergana Valley was a fertile oasis nestling in the high mountains of Central Asia. It became a major source of cotton for Russia and later the Soviet Union.

Skripal arrived in this far-off land, posted to 345th Guards Air Assault Regiment, one of the rapid deployment units that gave the VDV particular value to the Kremlin. He and his fellow officers were living through what some have called 'the Golden Age' of the Soviet airborne force. Under the leadership of General Vassily Margelov, who founded then ran the VDV for a staggering twenty-three years, they had gained a reputation in Soviet decision making, and indeed military culture, similar to that of the Marine Corps in the US. Lacking a big seagoing tradition, Soviet Russia did not have a strong force of naval commandos, rather Margelov had given sky-blue berets and striped sailors' shirts to his paratroopers, styling them the marines of the modern age, crossing oceans by air rather than sea in order to protect their Soviet Motherland.

The VDV had spearheaded Moscow's 1968 intervention in Czechoslovakia, had been stood by to fly to Syria's aid in 1973 as Israeli tanks pushed towards Damascus, and used time and again to reinforce military districts experiencing periods of tension. Along with this vital operational role, a powerful organizational culture developed around these airborne forces. From the moment they were sworn in, paratroopers were encouraged to look down on lesser mortals, and their vodka-fuelled celebrations of the VDV's annual day every August were regarded with trepidation by law-abiding citizens the breadth of the Soviet Union from Vitebsk to Khabarovsk, and indeed Fergana.

Physical fitness and bravery became a powerful feature of the VDV's self-image – with its members building themselves up in the gym, perfecting their own form of unarmed combat, and encouraging boxing, a sport in which Sergei Skripal excelled. He competed at national level in the army championships.

As if the gym, troop training, and staff work were not enough, the officers in Fergana and their families also enjoyed a close-knit social life. The military cantonments established by the tsars in the nineteenth century were outposts surrounded by warlike tribes and guerrilla bands. Even in 1976, when Skripal arrived, it had retained that frontier feeling. Most local people were Uzbek and they socialized little with the officers and men of the 345th Regiment.

When days off or holidays allowed, Skripal's young family and those of brother officers would find a quiet spot for a picnic, spreading blankets in the shade, savouring shashlik, sweet melon, and beer. A fellow regimental officer's wife recalled that posting and the time:

> The best years of my life were the late 1970s when we were living in Fergana . . . we often used to eat very late, because the men were working so hard. But we wives would cook together, laughing and talking while we were doing it, and then we often used to eat out of doors in the cool of the evening. We all had small children, and they grew up together. During the day we would go to the bazaar and buy fruit and vegetables.

Returning from an exercise, Skripal had discovered that during one of these trips to the local market some Uzbeks living near the garrison had been calling out lewdly, disrespecting Liudmila and other regimental wives as they passed in the street. Skripal and a few others decided to take matters into their own hands. 'I went with a few paratroopers and found the guys responsible,' he explained, 'we beat them up – after that everything was relaxed.'

Life with the paratroopers in Fergana provided Skripal with a chance to live out many of his childhood ideas of chivalry and heroism. The VDV moreover gave you every chance to be a *muzhik* – a real man. He leapt out of aeroplanes, boxed for the honour of his chosen corps, cherished time with his little boy, and defended his woman's honour. And he was still only in his late twenties. But events were afoot that would end this idyll in Fergana.

To the south, affairs in Afghanistan were taking an increasingly violent and unpredictable turn. The Kremlin had welcomed a coup in April 1978 that had brought communists – or the nearest to them that Afghanistan could muster – into power. These events were watched with intense interest in Fergana. Pretty soon the activities of Moscow's socialist allies in Afghanistan triggered mass desertions in the army and revolt across the mountainous country. Stirred up by radical clerics, many Afghans feared the communists formed an existential threat for Islam and their traditional, largely rural, way of life.

From the outset, Moscow had wanted to empower and indeed arm the 'progressives' to the south. But the question soon emerged, which ones? Within the Afghan ruling party there was intense and violent factionalism. Sending advisers into Afghanistan, and expanding its intelligence network there, the Soviet Union began to see the possibility for a complete disaster – for the Afghan revolution to be overwhelmed by infighting and rural jihad.

Soviet intelligence agencies suspected the country's defence minister, Hafizullah Amin, of being a CIA agent and an adventurer bent on seizing power. They believed he was using his influence in this key post to neutralize officers loyal to the president, and implicitly to Moscow, and replace them with people personally loyal to him. Many of Amin's faction, the GRU believed, were American-trained officers who had benefited from educational programmes offered by the US in the 1950s and 1960s when Afghanistan sought a middle way between the Cold War rivals.

It was the GRU's desire to take a decisive role in Afghanistan's faction fight that would draw then Captain Skripal to the 'dark' side of covert operations and intelligence work.

Assigned a role in a small team of *spetsnaz* operatives, Skripal described to me a trip to Afghanistan under civilian cover. He suggested it had taken place late in 1978, though my own knowledge of Afghan events suggests early 1979 may have been more likely. They flew into the country on a regular service and of course wore casual clothes. Much about this mission remains unclear – not least the place and precise time when the team would strike. However the targets were mainly US-trained pilots, so we might assume the mission took place at or near one of Afghanistan's air bases. Skripal himself was deliberately sketchy about details even when discussing it many years later. As a newcomer to this type of operation, perhaps he was cast in one of the more junior roles. Their objective was to kill several Afghan officers who'd been trained by the Americans.

The GRU brass who assigned them this assassination

mission apparently assumed that its success would scotch the meddling CIA and at the same time neutralize some of Afghan Defence Minister Amin's plans. Suffice to say that Skripal and his fellow operatives carried out their assigned role, killing the Afghans. But that did not stop either Hafizullah Amin's seizure of power in October 1979 or the Soviet Union's full-scale intervention in Afghanistan at the end of that year.

Even by the late summer of 1979, one battalion belonging to the 345th Guards Airborne had already deployed from Fergana to Bagram air base north of the Afghan capital, where its role was to protect Soviet advisers and aircraft. Once the rest of the regiment followed, as part of the full-scale invasion, the 345th became the elite 'fire brigade' unit of the Soviet Army in Afghanistan, fighting in many of the key actions of the decade-long conflict there. With its commitment to combat, the carefree days in Fergana came to an end, and over the course of its campaigns in Afghanistan, the regiment would lose hundreds of soldiers. Many would also be decorated for heroism, some even winning the coveted gold star medal, the Hero of the Soviet Union.

Like any fighting soldier, particularly one who had built up such close personal ties with many of his regimental colleagues, Skripal would have relished the possibility of going into action with them. But earlier in 1979, months before the invasion, he had been summoned elsewhere. He was to undergo a further stage in his metamorphosis from combat engineer to GRU spy.

3

INTO THE DARKNESS

In the Soviet or Russian military system the concept of *razvedka* embraces everything from the reconnaissance of a soldier creeping stealthily into no man's land to a colonel serving in the embassy in Madrid under diplomatic cover. Either way, their mission is gaining information that will be useful to the General Staff, and therefore their country. 'The GRU has two levels,' Skripal explained, 'tactical level, soldiers and *spetsnaz*, and strategic level, the higher-level service.' By his decision to seek airborne training, taking part in reconnaissance missions in China, and finally his undercover task in Afghanistan, he had stepped through the 'tactical' levels of military intelligence-gathering; now, in 1979, near the end of his twenties, he had been called to something higher. The consequences for him and his whole family would be enormous.

At the time he joined it the GRU had thirty-five thousand people, Skripal estimated. A big proportion of these were at the tactical level, the special-forces brigades in various military districts. Others were involved in collecting signals intelligence, operating satellites, and so on. The 'strategic workers' constituted an elite of several thousand within the GRU. In the Soviet Army this service was considered particularly honourable; it was highly selective; and those who went into it had a life of privilege. As far as their friends and families were concerned there was something else too: it was important national work free from the taint of being a '*chekist*', or member of the KGB. Although the secret police established after the Revolution soon changed its name, the acronym VChKP for its first incarnation lived on, in the term 'chekist', and was indeed used with pride by the organization's members during the Soviet period.

Although the foreign-intelligence arm of the KGB contained quite different, and altogether better-educated, people than the bruisers who dealt with domestic dissent, there were many Soviet citizens who could never quite disentangle them. The army, and even the GRU, by contrast, were among the victims of the Great Terror of the 1930s, they were not its executioners. Those entering the world of military intelligence soon learned that it took a particular pride in the fact that it had no KGB 'special department', it was to a great extent trusted by the party to carry out its secret work. The GRU was, in Soviet terms, the frame of reference in which Sergei and Liudmila grew up, a very respectable form of espionage.

KGB people had their own view of this relationship of course, noting that they vetted applicants for military intelligence, and if significant evidence emerged that some GRU man might be guilty of espionage, their interrogators would soon move it. Vladimir Kuzichkin, a KGB officer who defected to the UK in 1971, and whose views were influential in MI6 because he spoke to its officers about their targets for recruitment, summed up the relationship:

The GRU hates the KGB, the KGB has no similar feeling towards its 'distant neighbours' as the GRU is code-named in KGB documents. The KGB adopts a condescending attitude to the GRU . . . it is roughly as an older man might relate to one of fiery temperament who still has much to learn.

That was certainly true of Skripal as he made the journey from his garrison in Uzbekistan to the glamour and sophistication of the capital. He was engaged in something new and immensely exciting – heroic, in his terms, but also honourable in that it did not involve selling himself to the KGB. The process for becoming a GRU operative was neither quick nor without jeopardy. In the first place you had to be invited to take the exam, as Skripal had been in Fergana. If you passed, you went to Moscow, where a whole manner of additional hurdles would have to be cleared before you would even be considered for a posting overseas.

In order to prepare him for tasks as an intelligence officer, Skripal had to undergo another sustained period of professional training, four years of study at an institution called the Military-Diplomatic Academy, on Moscow's Narodnogo Opolcheniya, or People's Militia Street. At the end of the 1970s, when Skripal was summoned there, this establishment and indeed the entire GRU were cloaked in mystery – and a good deal of fear. Officers did not apply, for doing so might trigger uncomfortable questions about how they knew about the academy or the wider organization. Instead suitable candidates were invited to put their names forward. The organization drew people from across the full breadth of the armed forces, from air-defence fighter-controllers to paratroopers, or officers on submarines. Having engaged in secret operations in China and Afghanistan, the invitation to take the mysterious exam probably came as less of a surprise to Skripal than to many.

Vladimir Rezun, writing as Viktor Suvorov, explained the manner of an army officer's arrival at the Military-Diplomatic Academy, his own elevation to the mysteries of the GRU occurring several years ahead of Skripal: 'immediately you will find yourself in Moscow, with a permanent residence permit . . . it is as if you had moved onto a higher sphere, as if you and your relations had suddenly been ennobled'.

For Sergei and Liudmila Skripal this elevation to the higher strata of Soviet military society meant a radical change to their lives. After a childhood in Kaliningrad and years in *kommunalkas*, flats shared with other young families in the Far East or Central Asia, they would find themselves (some years into his new assignment) in their own place in Krilats-koye, a Moscow suburb springing up a few kilometres to the west of the academy where hundreds of flats were set aside for GRU and other army officers. As Sasha neared school age they knew he would be able to go to a good one nearby, and that Sergei's access to special stores reserved for intelligence officers would allow them to taste the good things in life.

In return for this entrée into the world of Soviet privilege, it was his task to devote himself to study for at least four years. If it went well there was a further incentive at the end: the possibility of a posting overseas, an exotic life neither he nor Liudmila could have dreamt of growing up in bomb-shattered Kaliningrad.

The curriculum at the Military-Diplomatic Academy principally prepared its students to operate as intelligence officers, recruiting and running agents overseas. They learnt the full gamut of espionage techniques, from the ancient ones such as secret writing using invisible inks to encoding messages with one-time pads, running counter-surveillance, and how the typical GRU mission house or *rezidentura* operated. They had to acquire a good many 'soft skills' too, including the art of making polite conversation on the diplomatic circuit, and losing some of those typically Russian traits of dress or manner that might make them stand out in the West.

As for the matter of actually recruiting agents, the students received lectures in the difficulties and arts of successful seduction from some of the GRU's legends. Vyacheslav Baranov, a fighter pilot whose time at the Military-Diplomatic Academy overlapped with Skripal's (and whose personal stories would later entwine also), recalled that the instructors said only 10 per cent of officers posted abroad successfully recruited spies, noting, 'persuading a man to betray his country is usually not an easy thing to do'.

Inductees in the GRU's training system soon discovered that getting to the academy, something they might have considered a life-changing achievement, was only a waypoint into further phases of selection and recruitment: between those who would get desk jobs or be posted abroad; those who would go to Third World backwaters or important arenas in the East–West espionage war; and those who once in country would never succeed in making a significant recruitment, thus ruining their chances of further foreign postings, and maybe even getting sent home early from their first tour.

One GRU man, summing up this sense that becoming a successful case officer overseas really made one an elite within an elite, quoted a wartime fighter ace who had become a senior officer in the military intelligence organization:

Our intelligence work scarcely differs from air battles. Soviet military intelligence trains thousands of officers and throws them into battle. In real life they are quickly divided into active and passive officers. Some attain glorious heights, while others fade out on their first foreign assignment.

As time at the academy progressed those officers destined to take flight overseas also had to learn how to carry off their specific cover. The GRU exploited diplomatic roles in trade missions and embassies, as indeed did the KGB, but also sent some of its people abroad as 'employees' of Aeroflot and Morflot, the Soviet airline and merchant shipping companies, in trade delegation posts or as journalists. The most highly trained of all – often requiring ten or more years of preparation – were 'illegals', those sent without official cover of any sort to assume the lives of others in target countries. These were run mainly by the KGB but the GRU also had illegal operations, though theirs were petering out in the late Cold War period.

Skripal had done sufficiently well at the academy to be selected for an overseas diplomatic mission. And as he attended lectures, month after month, year after year, behind the discreet facade of the academy, change seemed slowly to be coming to the Soviet Union. The Moscow Olympics were held – albeit with some political nonsense from the Western powers. Leonid Brezhnev finally keeled over, to be followed as party leader by Yuri Andropov, and then Konstantin Chernenko. It became acceptable even in official circles to allude to the latter Brezhnev period as the 'age of stagnation', as the heady growth of the 1950s and 1960s slowed and popular frustrations began to simmer. The West seemed to be forging ahead and many in the Kremlin looked to their spies to help answer the needs of the moment. What were the political, economic, and technological trends of the future? It would be the job of the KGB and GRU to stay ahead of them – whether that was informing the leadership of the war plans of the Reagan presidency or purloining new inventions so that Soviet industry could copy them.

For Skripal though the last phase of his period at the academy led to a piece of frustration typical in the world of the Soviet intelligence officer. Having completed his training in the arts of espionage, Skripal was informed that he would begin preparations to be posted to Mozambique. Assignments in the developing world were common for officers on their first overseas tour. They weren't as glamorous as some of the prestigious Western stations, but they also tended to lack proper counter-espionage services, and the money available for agent recruitment stretched further.

In preparation for this job, Skripal spent many months studying Portuguese, and reading about Mozambique. Then he was informed that someone else would go instead, his service had other plans for him. Eventually it became clear that his first foreign assignment, under diplomatic cover, would be in Malta.

After a further period of training for life as part of the small diplomatic corps on that Mediterranean island, including lessons in English, he arrived there in 1984 not long before Mikhail Gorbachev assumed the leadership of the Communist Party back home. Skripal would remain there for over five years, an unusually long posting that testified to the Centre's satisfaction with his work.

Skripal's cover at the embassy was as an attaché for sport and culture. That legend meant devoting a good many hours each week to the legitimate work of furthering good relations with the people of Malta.

In the newspapers of the time Skripal makes a number of appearances: arranging the water-polo coaching for a Maltese squad, setting up matches for a Russian football team, and even fostering exchanges between eye surgeons. He's pictured in some of the articles wearing a tan-coloured suit, looking sharp and attentive at meetings with the island's sporting and political figures. It was the one kind of publicity a spy loves; the type that helped build his legend, disguising his real mission in Malta.

As far as the small Malta GRU *rezidentura* was concerned, the place was an important strategic point in the Great Game for the Mediterranean. The island's neutrality in the East–West stand off also made it a relatively benign arena for espionage. He knew that in order to make his mark, becoming a success in his first foreign post, it was essential for him to make recruitments. So Skripal trawled for agents in the island's 'ruling circles' and tried to spot Western diplomats, military people, or spooks and pitch them into the bargain.

One target in particular came to interest the GRU station in Malta: an unusual category of tourist. The Russians had realized that many members of the US military based in southern Italy came over for breaks on the island. In the mid-1980s, Tomahawk cruise missiles had arrived at Comiso airfield on Sicily, the air station of Sigonella was one of NATO's busiest anti-submarine bases, and the US Mediterranean Fleet had its headquarters at Gaeta near Naples.

It was nigh on impossible to recruit Americans near those bases, particularly the Sicilian ones. There was no handy GRU station nearby, and the US Navy as well as the Italians themselves had significant counter-intelligence services watching out for precisely such activity. In a Maltese bar though the opportunities were altogether better. Skripal therefore spent many an evening trying to befriend sailors and airmen, buying them drinks and posing as a regular guy.

It was at this point though that Skripal started to entertain dissident thoughts – at least in the sense of ideas that undermined the ideological conditioning given to him during his first seventeen or eighteen years of serving the USSR. Even before the GRU academy he had been taught to think of himself as a fighter against Western imperialism. He must be ready – and had shown himself so in Afghanistan – not just to hazard his own life but to take those of others in the great struggle that his nation found itself involved in. Arriving on that small island in the West after all those years of preparation, he decided, 'it was a wonderful place, everyone was so close. The diplomatic community was small but very friendly'.

In Afghanistan just a few years before, he had taken part in murders of people – just on the suspicion they were working for the CIA. In Malta, he found himself chatting face to face with members of the agency, and for that matter MI6 or young American sailors, and found them to be perfectly charming and friendly. They were human. They too had little kids they were bringing up. Why hate them?

This was not a dramatic conversion of course, rather it was in the Maltese playground that a seed of doubt was planted. And, a little uncomfortably, he had become aware of it.

The Soviet diplomatic corps was so small that the departure of a GRU officer usually made it very easy to spot the arrival of the next, whatever his or her cover. And for their part the Russians knew who the small number of Western intelligence officers were. When the identity of the few players, and rules of the game, were so well understood, the chances of a major recruitment were minimal.

A CIA officer writing about the absurdity of the Cold War spy game in a (different) small Mediterranean posting noted:

> The officials in those consulates that you could get to come to your home or out to lunch or dinner – the usual opening gambit in your effort to develop and recruit them – were almost invariably undercover intelligence officers themselves. They had agreed to see you because they saw your invitation as the beginning of their effort to recruit you. In short they were trying to do the same thing to you that you were trying to do to them.

And this question of who was really cultivating whom could be enormously stressful for a GRU officer. It was a mind-bending battle of spy versus spy. After all, if some CIA officer reported back to Langley – truthfully or not – that he was making great progress in cultivating a GRU man in Malta, that might be picked up by a Soviet agent working in one of the US agencies and find its way back to Moscow. The result might then be, well, truly awful. In an unacknowledged way the players in Malta's small-town espionage game knew these risks weren't worth it. Rather than engage in futile attempts to recruit spies from major Western agencies, Skripal focused on locals, as well as the visiting US service members, enjoyed a sunshine posting and savoured family life. His daughter, Yulia, had been born shortly before, Sasha was then eleven, and a small island meant nights away from home were a rarity.

There were Sundays at the beach and happy hours exploring the island with its baroque architecture and spectacular scenery. Fresh seafood was abundant along with traditional Maltese delicacies like fish pie and rabbit stew. Add to that the Western food and barbecues at diplomatic functions and it was a lifestyle all very far removed from the ups and downs of garrison life in the airborne forces.

Late in 1989 it was to the island of Malta that Mikhail Gorbachev and George H. W. Bush, the American president, came for a symbolically important summit. Winding up the two-day, rain-soaked event without agreement on specific new steps to ease tension between the rival blocs, the Russian leader went for something symbolic. 'We searched for the answer to the question of where do we stand now', said Gorbachev at the press conference, 'we stated, both of us, the world leaves one epoch, of Cold War, and enters another epoch.' That gave the newspaper correspondents their head-line – Malta became the place where the Cold War was declared over.

Before the decade ended so did the Maltese chapter in the Skripals' life. They returned to Moscow and their flat in Krilatskoye. Like many coming back from a foreign posting they were laden with Western electronic goods, fancy clothes, and happy memories. But Sergei went back to a desk job at headquarters, and one of the more remarkable, if barely sketched out, moments of his career.

Not long after Skripal came home from Malta, another GRU officer returning from overseas, Colonel Vyacheslav Baranov, became the subject of a counter-intelligence operation. Baranov had been working the Science and Technology line in Dhaka, the capital of Bangladesh. In 1989, close to the end of his posting, he offered his services to the CIA.

There was a good deal of hesitancy on both sides of this relationship. The CIA had been battered by the loss of so many of its key Russian sources, people who it would emerge had been betrayed from within the American intelligence machine. For his part Baranov offered the agency some information about the shooting down of a Korean airliner several years earlier, by way of establishing his credentials, but then became nervous about giving them something more substantial. To the CIA officers he presented a riddle – was the ex-fighter-pilot GRU man for real or a 'dangle', someone who was deliberately offered, providing only 'chicken feed' intelligence, as a way of exposing the American operation in Dhaka?

Returning to Moscow, Baranov had been given a protocol for contacting CIA officers at the US embassy. Early in 1990, after a few months of lying low, he started to use the system of signals he had been instructed in – a number to be scrawled in a phone booth or chalk marks left on the wall of a particular alleyway.

Baranov, who later told his story to a US journalist, found the agency people in Moscow both timid and incompetent. They were extremely aware of possible KGB surveillance, as one might expect, but also rather bad at responding to his signals and attempts to contact them. The twin fears of penetration and provocation were evidently playing on their minds.

In August 1992, after an espionage comedy of errors, more than two years in which he had only met a Moscow-based case officer once, Baranov was arrested at Sheremetyevo airport, about to board a plane to Vienna, where he was hoping to re-establish contact with the Americans. Tried in 1993, he was sentenced to six years' hard labour. He served his sentence and eventually left Russia, with CIA assistance, in 2002. During his long captivity, Baranov became obsessed with the idea that a mole in the American intelligence world had betrayed him. At first he thought it might be Aldrich Ames, the CIA man arrested in 1994, but later his suspicions moved to another mole, an FBI man apprehended later. In fact, weighing up the evidence after his release from jail, the circumstances of these two penetrations did not quite fit and a lingering air of uncertainty surrounds the case.

Many years later, Sergei Skripal raised the Baranov case with me as I was about to leave his home. Coming to it cold, I was not then aware of its details. As I walked out of the front door, Sergei said, 'I was the one who discovered him.' He didn't offer further facts, and I did not have the time to press him. Annoyingly, other events then prevented our conversation resuming.

Sergei's revelation presents a number of possibilities: that Baranov's discovery was not the result of a penetration at all, having been flagged up in other ways (for example a suspicious colleague in Dhaka); or that there was indeed information from a penetration but like many such leads it was vague, and Skripal helped pinpoint who it referred to.

In the context of this story though the Baranov story is interesting for a number of reasons. I discussed it, and Sergei's role, with someone who was in the CIA at the time; he could not provide corroboration but did comment, 'that would have built up Sergei's credentials as a loyal officer'. Skripal of course was having doubts, particularly as he experienced the state of flux Russia entered in the months and years after his return from Malta. But as his work on the Baranov file showed, he was at that point still prepared to do his duty, and this may have contributed to the GRU's willingness to post him abroad again, and to a more important station in a NATO country.

The lengthy surveillance of Baranov, his interrogation, and his trial may also have served a warning to people in the GRU that the risks of spying for the Americans were simply not worth it. They were penetrated, and their people in Moscow under intense surveillance. Sergei would have to look for other ways out if he was unhappy in his work and with what he saw happening to the country. And indeed events in the Kremlin were moving towards a dramatic denouement.

The party boss, Mikhail Gorbachev, had thrown in the towel in Afghanistan, pulling out his army by early 1989. At home, in many of the USSR's republics, from the Baltic coast to the Caucasus mountains, the Kremlin's liberal policies allowed an upsurge of nationalism and protest. To the officers at GRU headquarters it was all very worrying. This Gorbachev was loved in the West precisely, they felt, because he was giving everything away. The whole socialist bloc was crumbling.

With the fall of the Berlin Wall in November 1989, matters just seemed to accelerate. Friendly governments collapsed across Eastern Europe and in London or Washington the intelligence analysts began to pick up rumblings in the military and party of a possible coup.

That confrontation between Gorbachev and those who took it upon themselves to protect the achievements of socialism eventually came to a head in August 1991. Columns of tanks entered Moscow while the General Secretary was on holiday down south, and for a few days the 'State Committee for the State of Emergency', a half-hearted conservative junta, claimed to rule the country. Gorbachev managed to fly back to Moscow, the coup collapsed, and the Communist Party of the Soviet Union was banned. In less than a week the entire political work of more than seven decades was obliterated. Within months the break-up of the Soviet Union itself was starting. The country and its citizens were plunged into the most profound uncertainty, and in many cases hardship.

The case of Sergei Skripal's brother Valery provides just one example. When these shocking events unfolded in Moscow, he was serving with the Soviet Army in Kazakhstan. As that Central Asian republic grasped its chance for independence it laid claim to military units (and indeed USSR state property) there as its own. Offered the chance to serve in the new Kazakh army, Valery declined. But the flat he lived in came with his post. He wanted to go to Russia – but would have no job or flat if he did so, and indeed nobody would even give him the cash for a ticket out of Kazakhstan. He was stranded and virtually penniless.

Elsewhere, officers and their families found themselves taking cattle trucks out of newly independent regions, or living for weeks in an airport terminal while trying to get a flight out to Russia. In some places locals tried to take over the flats where these army people lived, and armed soldiers were posted to stop them. It was all very ugly. Imagine this humiliation befalling all those officers who'd sworn to defend their Motherland with the last drop of their blood.

And what would happen to their mother Yelena, still living in Kaliningrad? The independence of the three Baltic republics – Estonia, Latvia, and Lithuania – left it an isolated enclave on the Polish border. Before, travelling home to Kaliningrad had been a matter simply of jumping on a train in Moscow, then heading across the same country. Now there would be international borders. For many, the essentials of life, from somewhere to live to an income that could keep pace with galloping inflation, were all suddenly in doubt. Sergei realized that he was the one best placed to look after his family. It was his duty to help his mother and brother.

In the two years after the failed coup, he watched things go from bad to worse. In October 1991, Russia's new president, Boris Yeltsin, dismissed General Vladlen Mikhailov, the head of the GRU, over suspicions that the general had sympathized with the coup attempt a couple of months earlier. Mikhailov was replaced by a general from outside the intelligence branch, whose 'sole contribution to military intelligence', another Russian officer put it rather tartly, 'was to build new canteens for senior officers of the directorate'.

Although the GRU held up relatively well during the chaos and uncertainty that marked the early months of the Yeltsin era, it was not immune. At the senior level there were sackings and resignations. Going to work there might once have seemed like ascending to a kind of nobility but as free-wheeling capitalism and galloping inflation took hold every officer felt like a member of an *ancien régime* fallen on hard times.

Skripal wrestled with his feelings. For him, the military oath sworn in Kaliningrad all those years ago was paramount. But at the end of 1991 the country he had pledged to defend 'sparing neither blood nor life itself', the Soviet Union, no longer existed. There had been some discussion at the office about swearing a new oath, to Yeltsin's Russia, but Skripal, like many other employees of the GRU, had sidestepped it and his superiors were too disgusted by what was happening to the country to insist. And really if it came to betrayal, there had already been so much of that from Gorbachev and

Yeltsin, who had destroyed the state that he had pledged to serve.

So one morning in the summer of 1992, Colonel Skripal made his way to GRU headquarters and requested a meeting with the deputy director, one of the generals who ran the organization.

The colonel had endured enough. 'I didn't accept the Russian democrats', he explained, 'I didn't want to serve the new government.' Skripal was intent on bailing out of the GRU.

4

MASTER RACE NO LONGER

That summer of 1992, as Skripal reached his decision to resign, Richard Bagnall was completing his training as an officer of the Secret Intelligence Service. Those entering MI6 did not have to endure the four years that GRU officers spent at their academy, preparing for espionage work. Rather, having passed the selection boards, British spies went through six months of training before being assigned their first job in a foreign station.

He joined as a junior member of a fabled service. But at that moment, MI6 was engulfed in the uncertainties of the post-Cold War world – an agency that couldn't make up its mind whether it wanted to go after all manner of new targets, or preferred to take advantage of Russia's prostrate state to avenge itself for past humiliations.

As for Bagnall, his path to this point was indirect. He was an army officer when he joined MI6 a couple of years previously and it was agreed that he should attend the long Russian course at the Defence Languages School at Beaconsfield. This prepared students to 'interpreter standard'. During the Cold War the Beaconsfield course had become de rigueur for certain members of the Intelligence Corps, people involved in electronic eavesdropping, and many of those were posted to the British Military Mission or Brixmis in East Germany where a form of legalized military spying provided young servicemen and women with one of the most exciting postings they could hope for. But with the end of the Cold War, Brixmis was disbanded and indeed deep cuts were falling on the armed forces, yielding a 'peace dividend' for the taxpayer.

Having grown up living a peripatetic existence, with a father sent to postings all over the world, Bagnall had found in his regiment a home, and a focus for fierce loyalty. Packed off at an early age to boarding school he might in a different century have gravitated towards the Church.

However, finding an atmosphere of uncomplicated friendship, fun, and camaraderie in uniform, he dedicated himself to becoming as good a soldier as he could be. Like the Russian who he would meet years later in a Madrid park, the young officer's search for excellence and fulfilment led him into reconnaissance units and then to special forces. Bagnall passed selection for the SAS Regiment, but was rejected during the follow-on training known as Continuation. Given the enormous investment of physical and emotional energy in going for it, it's unsurprising his colleagues registered his deep disappointment.

Skripal and the young British officer had something else in common too. While the ranks of the world's intelligence agencies contain all manner of dissemblers, charlatans, and bed-hoppers, both of these men married young and for the long haul. They were dutiful husbands and fathers.

While the army still promised the young captain a good future, and the likelihood of command, the end of the Cold War pushed him, eventually, to seek something different since his battalion ceased to exist. Evicted by history from his regi-mental home, it was to the Secret Intelligence Service that Bagnall now dedicated his efforts.

It should be unsurprising that things went the way they did in el Retiro in July 1996. For in a way Skripal would come face to face with a younger version of himself. This ardent Englishman was devoted to what he was doing, had the physical and intellectual self-confidence that came from arduous training, and, crucially, still had faith in the system he served.

For 'the Friends', as the service sometimes likes to style itself, their new officer was a good catch. Fiercely bright, he had passed into the Intelligence Branch, the organization's fast stream. A senior MI6 officer who oversaw some of Bag-nall's early work describes him as 'a charming and highly intelligent officer'.

Having completed Beaconsfield, he went through the more formal part of an MI6 officer's training. There's a stan-dard six-month course involving the inevitable classroom sessions, inspirational talks from service legends, and prep-aration in spycraft.

Much of the recruit training takes place at 'the Fort', alias Fort Monkton on the Solent. There the officers get a taste for the more physical side of the business, from scaling fences to lock-picking, unarmed combat, and pistol-shooting. Elsewhere, exercises were carried out against experienced surveillance-section operatives, often on busy streets in London. These were designed to school recruits in counter-surveillance – a skill critical in many places to their survival and that of their agents.

Inevitably, given his long Russian language course, Bag-nall must have devoted a great deal of thought during the sessions on cultivating and running agents to how hard this might actually be. For those giving the lectures understood one of the agencies' deepest and darkest secrets during decades of the Cold War: that for all the talk about recruiting and running sources in the Soviet Union, it was a devilishly hard thing to do.

The surveillance state constructed by the KGB was so pervasive that unless somebody had already made the decision to spy for you, it was nigh on impossible to persuade them. A senior CIA officer who rose to near the top of its Directorate of Operations or Clandestine Service put the issue succinctly:

> Over time I came to believe that the Clandestine Service wasted a lot of energy trying to recruit Soviets during the Cold War. Historically those who really wanted to cooperate with the United States have walked in of their own volition and offered their services, usually for money. I know of no significant Soviet recruitment that was spotted, developed, and recruited from scratch by a CIA case officer.

This extraordinary statement, implying that decades of work by hundreds of CIA officers never brought in a Soviet spy who wasn't already bent on treachery, needs some qualification. The CIA ended up running many agents in the USSR during the Cold War who were not 'walk ins', i.e. who'd simply offered their services. In these cases cultivation consisted of identifying the target's pre-existing doubts about what they were doing and little by little carrying them across the line to treason. Even so, what this highlights is the degree to which the self-image of Western agencies, as steely freedom-loving people turning their ideological foes to treachery, was out of kilter with their actual performance. One estimate in the 1980s suggested that only about 5 per cent of CIA case officers, operating in a wide variety of countries around the world, had ever actually recruited an agent – someone productive of valuable intelligence.

For a keen new SIS officer this business of agent recruitment therefore became a challenge, a test of his commitment and skill in just the same way that SAS selection had been. Temperamentally, he was certainly suited to it. A CIA man who observed Bagnall later in his career described him, approvingly, as 'a most aggressive officer'. And of course for an agency or MI6 type bent on making a name for themselves, the time was ripe. The collapse of Soviet communism had created turmoil and an atmosphere in which many Russians decided it was time to look after Number One.

In the latter part of the Cold War, disenchantment with Soviet ideology had led Oleg Gordievsky, then number two in the KGB's London *rezidentura*, to spy for Britain. He had done so knowing that getting caught might well lead to the death penalty, and when betrayed (by an American working for the Russians) he was summoned back to Moscow. Only a daring rescue operation, smuggling him out of the country, had saved his life. Gordievsky, by virtue of his position, had been able to give Britain's intelligence services a good measure of confidence that there were no significant Soviet moles in their ranks. MI6 furthermore had demonstrated to any Soviet citizen willing to work for them that they could save them, even from execution in Moscow.

With the end of the Cold War, the number of Russian spooks offering to sell their knowledge increased considerably. Following the collapse of the party and Soviet system the KGB itself was broken up. What was formerly its First Chief Directorate (responsible for overseas espionage) became a new service, the SVR. In 1991–1992 all sorts of key SVR people offered themselves to MI6 and the Americans.

In July 1992 the SVR deputy *rezident* in Paris, Viktor Oshchenko, defected to the UK. He had been stationed in London earlier in his career and was able to reveal the identity of a British mole he had been running at the time. More significantly, during that same year, MI6 arranged the exfiltration of Vasily Mitrokhin from Russia.

Mitrokhin had until the mid-1980s been one of the principal archivists of the First Chief Directorate. Over the course of twenty years he had copied the crown jewels of the KGB's overseas espionage registry – the codenames of agents in foreign countries, their activities, and access. Thousands of scraps of paper, with these precious facts scrawled upon them, had been hidden by him in milk churns at his country dacha. The archivist had thought hard about how he might convert this extraordinary treasure trove into a retirement plan in the West. Having made an abortive attempt to offer himself to the Americans, he walked into a British embassy in one of the newly independent Baltic states, where a brief conversation took place with an alert British diplomat who told him to come back one month later.

On his second visit to the embassy Mitrokhin was greeted by two members of MI6 who were old Sov Bloc hands able to question the Russian about his offer. Once in possession of the man and his precious (not to say voluminous) notes, SIS had something of extraordinary value: a vivid insight into decades of KGB operations, giving them information of the greatest value to trade with friendly services around the world.

Add to that the SVR defectors who came across to other Western intelligence services, budget cuts back home, and general disaffection following the collapse of the USSR and it becomes apparent why the Western counter-espionage people radiated self-confidence at the time. As for anyone tempted to spy for Russia, Oleg Kalugin, a lugubrious former KGB general who had once run foreign operations, noted, 'only a very foolish man would work for such a heavily penetrated organization'.

During the early 1990s the UK intelligence services gave journalists quite a few briefings, trying to explain their sense of how the end of the Cold War changed the spying business. I was able to speak both to people who ran MI5's K or Counter-Espionage Branch and SIS's Counter-intelligence Directorate. The job of the Security Service, MI5, was essentially to catch foreign agents in Britain, that of MI6 to penetrate hostile intelligence services or bring about the defection of their key players. In keeping with those times of international flux there were reorganizations and changes to the names of some of these sections. As SIS and the electronic eavesdroppers of Government Communications Headquarters (GCHQ) prepared themselves to come into the light, being placed on a proper statutory footing with parliamentary oversight through the 1994 Intelligence Services Act, they were authorized to communicate, up to a point, with the press.

The picture that emerged during these conversations was sometimes triumphalist. 'We've taken them apart, absolutely screwed them,' an MI6 director told me in 1993. Many saw this as the service's ultimate revenge for the treachery of Kim Philby and the Cambridge spy ring. The senior MI6 man was a specialist who had been Controller Sov Bloc. He made clear that while he felt the SVR was on the ropes, the GRU was different. We spent some time discussing the Oshchenko defection and the director cautioned me against focusing too much on those who had come over to the West. An operation like the Gordievsky one, daring as it might be, 'was a sign of failure' to the professional spy catchers because it established someone's guilt beyond doubt and would lead to a Russian reassessment of everything and everyone that mole had contact with. 'The most successful Russian agents', he said, 'were those who remained in place for thirty years and have now retired.'

This fascinating insight into SIS's work was gained just after a press conference at which the service's chief and the director of GCHQ had for the first time in history opened themselves up to journalists' questions.

Colin McColl, the chief, acknowledged that the old 'mega-threat' was gone and that the agencies were facing 'a difficult time'. The strength of MI6 was just under two thousand and it was shopping for new missions in order to keep that up. Journalists at the press conference asked about the new over-sight arrangements, and tasks such as counter-proliferation (stopping the spread of weapons of mass destruction) and fighting terrorism. There wasn't much interest expressed in Russia by the press, even though it was clear at the time that the professionals still regarded its intelligence services at the time as posing the biggest challenge to the UK of all the foreign powers.

One day in autumn 1993 I was in MI5's headquarters in Gower Street. I was to get a briefing with *Jim, who at that time ran K Branch. As we sat chatting in a proverbially non-descript conference room, cups of tea in front of us, he laid out his view of the spying threats to the UK. It was level-headed – certainly he did not seem in any way nostalgic for the Cold War. Jim noted that there was a 50 per cent drop in the number of SVR officers operating in the UK. Facing budget cuts the SVR had come to a deal with the Foreign Ministry, reducing the number of spooks, and with it the potential for embarrassment with the Western countries that befriended Boris Yeltsin's democratic government.

The fall of the Berlin Wall had led to some obvious possibilities for economies in the spy business. Western agencies no longer had to track the activities of the KGB's fraternal Eastern Bloc services, from East Germany to Poland, Hungary, Czechoslovakia, Bulgaria, and Romania. They had become democracies, most dissolving the spying agencies that had become hated symbols of the old system of power. With the collapse of the ideological confrontation there was a host of people also – from the KGB officers in London who liaised with the Communist Party of Great Britain or trades unionists to the staff of MI5's F Branch who attempted to disrupt them – who were simply out of a job.

Adding to this sanguine picture was his assessment of the Michael Smith spy case. Smith, convicted in November 1993, was the agent revealed by the Oshchenko defection. Jim felt that his arrest and prosecution marked the tidying up of Cold War business rather than the start of something new.

There were however concerns voiced about the GRU. Jim told me that Russian military intelligence had successfully 'resisted the nominal attempts at home to bring it under political control'. While the SVR had cut back, 'the GRU have not reduced abroad', and consequently, Jim said, 'we're more worried about them, they're the least susceptible to political consideration'.

Moreover, Britain's agencies considered the GRU a far harder target for penetration: its ethos had held up. The Americans had a couple of successes. Colonel Sergei Bokhan, the GRU deputy *rezident* in Greece, defected to the CIA in the summer of 1985, but that was because the agency warned him he'd been betrayed. Prior to defecting, Bokhan had been what the Americans called an RIP, a recruitment in place. Getting a GRU officer to spy for you during the Cold War, well, that had been a fearsome challenge. MI6 had found it impossible for decades, an important fact when considering the cultivation of Colonel Skripal.

Collectively, the Russian intelligence people, Jim felt, were, 'still re-defining their objectives and working out their priorities'. The same of course was true in Langley, the Central Intelligence Agency head office, or at Vauxhall Cross, MI6's garish new HQ on the south bank of the Thames. The arrest of Aldrich Ames in 1994 exposed the huge damage that could be done by a KGB penetration – several agents had been executed as a result of his treachery and others, including Gordievsky, compromised. The SVR would start to reconstitute itself, and the GRU was unbroken. There was still a job for the mole-hunters.

And what about instability and the dangers of Russia's democratic transition more generally?

In 1989 MI6 had received a defector from inside a secret biological weapons programme, Vladimir Pasechnik. In an interview he recorded with me for the BBC in 1992 he revealed publicly what he had told the spooks three years earlier, that a secret biological weapons programme had been hidden within an ostensibly civilian enterprise, in violation of an international treaty.

The British had also penetrated the chemical weapons establishment, and as both Gorbachev and Yeltsin moved to renounce these deadly technologies, the Western agencies had detected signs of concealment (from leaders in the Kremlin as well as themselves) and evasion from the Russians. The security of nuclear warheads also remained a great concern during these years.

Balanced against a continued desire to spy against Russia was the sense that opportunities were there to be grasped – and the visionary language of politicians who were heartily glad the Cold War was over. Stella Rimington, then Director General of MI5, travelled to Moscow to discuss cooperation. The FBI director did too and suggested the Bureau open a large office in the Russian capital. There were plenty of Western concerns that the Russians seemed to share, from the possible proliferation of weapons of mass destruction to organized crime, and terrorism.

As the Western espionage agencies braced for their own version of the peace dividend, budgetary cuts, those advocating new 'global issues' gained the upper hand, while the denizens of Cold War espionage were on the back foot. At MI6, that section at the pinnacle of the old spying game, Controller Soviet Bloc, was renamed Controller Central and Eastern Europe, suffering a modest reduction in staff and budget.

Along with the reshuffling of desks came the early retirement of some of the old Sov Bloc warhorses. Those running Eastern Bloc agents had been known in the corridors of MI6 as 'the Master Race'; in the mid-1990s they no longer called the shots.

Russia though remained a target for intelligence collection and in the 1990s John Scarlett had a large role in defining the organization's post-Cold War attitude to it. Having been posted in 1991 to Moscow as Head of Station he was, one year after his arrival, 'declared' to the authorities, meaning that his intelligence role was acknowledged and the emphasis of his job shifted from spying on the Russians to liaising over matters of mutual interest.

A brilliant Oxford history graduate and Russian-speaker, Scarlett had been Gordievsky's case officer during the KGB man's London years. It was the type of assignment that in the SIS of the early 1980s had given that officer an aura of enormous importance. If there were to be growing cooperation on counter-terrorism or fighting organized crime, the Office would need its man in Moscow, and Scarlett was as good a person to embody this change as they could find. Nobody at Vauxhall Cross ever thought this groundbreaking move would be a routine liaison posting, like Paris or Canberra, but Scarlett's experience was to serve as a reminder to many in Whitehall of the unreconstructed nature of Russia's agencies, particularly the FSB, which has the mission of catching foreign agents.

In March 1994, Scarlett was expelled from Moscow, when the Russians publicized the conviction of an official in their defence sales organization, saying he'd been spying for Britain. The word back in P5, SIS's Russia wing, was that Moscow's action was really motivated by pique that MI5 had declined to give a visa to the opposite number that the SVR had appointed to London. If London ruled out an ex-KGB heavy, then they would send Scarlett packing. As this episode shows, conflict was baked in to the relations between MI6 and the KGB's successor organizations from the outset.

Throwing out a declared officer was regarded in SIS as an oddly perverse step since he was hardly hiding his true role, and such a step would make any future cooperation harder. When the Russians tipped off the press so that they could photograph Scarlett getting his flight home, this nettled MI6 still further, its officers having a particular horror of exposure in this way. Once a picture becomes public, intelligence services in the other places you may have been, whether under your own name or deep cover, might then reassess who you'd met and where you'd been, conducting a mole-hunt.

As Bagnall finished his first foreign station job and returned to Vauxhall Cross, he was picked up by the Russian Operations Section. By the mid-1990s, after various reorganizations, all of the key elements in the Russia game, overseas field stations, UK-based operations, targeting, and support sections, were grouped together in an organization called P5. The key purpose of P5, like its equivalents in the production directorate dealing with other parts of the world, was the harvesting of the agency's raw product, intelligence from human agents, known in Whitehall's secret jargon as CX.

The Russia targeting and operations sections had the job of identifying suitable people for cultivation, then choreographing that seduction, and running them as cases, wherever that might take them. They were the hunters. It was these people who, over the course of months, and sometimes years, would build up a file on someone like Sergei Skripal. When coming up with Russian targets, a remark reported by a field station or some giveaway line in an intercepted phone call might be enough to suggest dissatisfaction or perhaps some pressure point like an unhappy marriage or gambling debts. We don't know exactly what it was that caused MI6 to vector in on Skripal, but once he was in the sights of P5's targeting and operations people they would have put a great deal of work into creating the right situation for someone, in this case Bagnall, to meet him and make their pitch.

Once an agent was on the payroll, taken on, say, in Copenhagen as Gordievsky had been, and returned to Moscow, they could be run by visiting case officers from the operations team. These people travelled into Russia using 'non-official cover', and were therefore a good deal less visible to KGB counter-intelligence than Moscow-based SIS types who were under heavy surveillance. There were other advantages also to using London-based handlers, notably that if their agent travelled outside Russia it was easier and more discreet for someone from P5 Operations to meet them than for an officer from Moscow Station to leave the country at the same time as his or her asset. The corollary of course was that when the London-based visiting case officers did come to Russia, they were completely vulnerable, lacking diplomatic immunity, if their cover was blown.

This tight-knit team, only a dozen or so case officers, had once been one of the gladiatorial arenas for ambitious SIS officers, the beating heart of the Master Race. By 1996 it had lost some of its lustre. But even so, what every SIS officer interested in counter-intelligence or K Branch-type across the river knew was that it was in the Russian operations and targeting sections that a case officer could still play the intelligence game at its highest level.

Whatever the improvement in political mood music with Russia, the burgeoning of commercial and cultural ties, the irreducible logic of the old Cold War spy business still held true in one sense. If the SVR and GRU were still trying to recruit British agents then they would have to be countered. Gordievsky and Mitrokhin may have given a belt-and-braces confidence in the 1980s that there were no penetrations in the UK's intelligence agencies, but things never stood still. The mission of ensuring, through counter-intelligence operations, that key British institutions remained clean would have to go on.

As for those tasked to do it, finding an agent remained

a fearsome challenge. And when it came to running one in Moscow, where there were literally thousands of Russian operatives hunting spies, that was among the toughest things you could do. And at the top of this peak of professional ambition and difficulty was that most challenging Russian recruitment target: the GRU.

5

BREAKTHROUGH IN MADRID

It is mid-July 1996, and Colonel Skripal is serving in the GRU *rezidentura*, or station, in the Spanish capital. The military intelligence people, along with the SVR station and the legitimate diplomats, all lurk behind the stern facade of the embassy on the Calle de Velázquez.

This enormous building looks more like the palace of culture or party headquarters in Minsk or Makhachkala than a typical Madrid foreign mission. It had been completely rebuilt starting in 1986 and the workers were just getting around to the snagging five years later when the state whose interests the great edifice represented collapsed. Like many Soviet embassies abroad, the smoked glass, marble, and chandeliers had been brought in from the Motherland. Western 'special services' had shown such persistence during the Cold War, trying to exploit any construction work to lace an embassy with bugging equipment, that the most minute attention had to be given to keeping the place free of listening devices. That included bringing containers of construction material from home.

So why was Skripal even serving there, given his resignation four years earlier? The general, the deputy director of the GRU, that he'd gone to had of course refused to accept it. And unless you had reached retirement age or were badly ill, the army could still make it hard for you to leave. What's more, too many officers around the rank of colonel and major general, the customary seniority for the *rezident* or station chief, had managed to get themselves out. It left the service desperate for experienced men with good records.

Early in 1993, in an attempt to keep him happy, Skripal had been offered the job of *rezident* in Paris. Now that was a place he could have lived well with Liudmila and Yulia (his son, Sasha, was entering higher education by then and would remain in Russia). But someone with better connections managed to snatch that plum from his grasp and a couple of months later he was offered a special mission in Spain. He would be reporting direct to the Centre, bypassing the *rezident*. It was a sensitive task, and he would be his own boss.

So after a couple of months of special training, including a crash course in Spanish, the Skripals were sent to Madrid in September 1993. With the usual posting lasting three years, Richard Bagnall's pitch had come as Sergei and Liudmila were already setting their sights on the return home.

Having heard the MI6 man's nervous play for his services in el Retiro and then met again subsequently to say what he wanted, Skripal knew the pressure was on him to deliver. Having decided he wanted the money and the ticket out of Russia that MI6 could offer, he didn't have long to do it because once he was back home in Moscow any kind of meeting with MI6 would be far riskier. So how could the colonel convince the British of his value and at the same time establish what the intelligence people call 'bona fides', evidence that he was indeed a senior member of an organization that MI6 had spent decades struggling to penetrate?

Skripal had put some effort into this, in the privacy of his flat, naturally. The results, committed to paper and folded into an envelope, were tucked into his jacket as he went to meet Richard once again. The contents were so compromising that if anyone in the *rezidentura* had found them, his guilt would be established in an instant.

The colonel left the Russian diplomatic compound and headed south, for the centre of the city. One of the useful skills he'd been taught during those years at the academy was counter-surveillance, sometimes referred to as 'combing'. This procedure can take many forms depending on whether the officer is going to the meeting by foot, on public transport, or by car. But through doubling back, loitering on deserted platforms or quiet roads, and constantly checking, a skilled officer can spot any surveillance. And while a *rezidentura* had the people and cars to conduct operations to make sure its own officers were not being followed to agent meets, they were limited in number and well known to Skripal.

Bagnall had that day positioned himself in one of Madrid's smartest hotels. It fitted with his businessman's cover, of course, and it was also standard service tradecraft for an agent meet. Sometimes a second officer might be in the reception, or elsewhere near the entrance watching the asset arrive, making sure he or she wasn't being followed. In more hostile environments there might be more elaborate surveillance around the meeting point. In a European capital things could be kept low-key. The advantage of the hotel was that even if some goon from the Russian embassy did tail Sergei to the meet, he would get no further than the lobby, because as Skripal took the lift up to Bagnall's room it would be impossible for anyone to follow without it becoming completely obvious. And what went on in that room would, until the MI6 man reported back to London at least, be known only to the two of them.

After the pleasantries, they sat down, Skripal removed the envelope from his pocket, and drew out a large folded piece of paper. Upon it was an elaborate design drawn with all the precision and care of someone with his lengthy schooling as a military engineer. There were boxes connected by lines, dozens of them. Inside each box, details had been typed for neatness and legibility.

Skripal had produced a complete chart of the organization and command of the GRU. Nobody in MI6 had seen anything like this for eighteen years, since Rezun had defected in Geneva. And of course Skripal's version was better because it had the added fidelity of being compiled by someone who knew many of the agency's senior leaders personally and had been serving in it for more than fifteen years.

The Russian could see Bagnall's pleasure as he scanned the document. The power relationship between them had fundamentally changed. In this business one was now not just the buyer, but held the power to destroy the other completely. Skripal understood and accepted this unequal bargain, reflecting, 'I wanted to do the very best for Richard.' A successful recruitment, one veteran Western case officer comments, 'requires him to believe that you will never do what you have just persuaded him to do, betray everything'. Perhaps Skripal's desire to please his handler derived from an understanding of this, that his fate was now completely bound up with this young Englishman and the organization he worked for.

As for the colonel's document, it was indeed something.

And of course London was delighted. Having an agent in place, in the GRU? MI6 hadn't done that since Colonel Oleg Penkovsky in the late 1950s. He had given astounding insight into the Kremlin's decision-making and weapons programmes at the height of the Cold War. But the risks involved in communicating with his handlers eventually led to his arrest and execution in 1963.

The Americans fancied they had engineered the greatest-ever penetration in Soviet military intelligence. Major General Dmitri Polyakov, codenamed TOPHAT, had been recruited by the FBI while he was stationed in the US in the early 1960s. Returning to the Soviet Union, Polyakov had revealed the identity of illegals sent to the US, pinpointed four American officials who were providing secrets to the USSR, and provided vital reporting on Communist Party politics, nuclear weapons developments, and war-fighting plans.

Polyakov's success was such that he achieved the 'home run' of retiring from the army in 1980 and devoting himself to hunting and fishing at his dacha. It seemed to all intents and purposes like the perfect case: a highly placed mole delivering stunning intelligence for a long period and then quietly fading from the scene, producing no dramas, family repercussions, or leak inquiry in the enemy camp. However years later, Polyakov was betrayed by Aldrich Ames, and executed in 1988 following a secret trial.

Back at Vauxhall Cross, hotfoot from the hotel meet, Bagnall must have been received with acclamation. Skripal had established his bona fides all right. It was game on. Following the usual protocol, MI6's new agent was given a codename: FORTHWITH. It was now up to Bagnall, guided by his bosses, to see how much valuable intelligence he could extract from him.

The next few weeks raced by, each weekend following the same format. After the hotel meet, MI6 had put things on a different basis. A flat had been hired as a clandestine meeting point. It was in one of the better areas of Madrid, not too far from the Calle de Velázquez – part of a typical block where the tenants came and went routinely. It had been agreed that these sessions, there were five or six of them as the Skripals' last weeks in the city sped by, should not be on weekdays. Better to avoid FORTHWITH having to give explanations to colleagues about where he was going.

So what did he tell Liudmila about these disappearances, for hours at a time? There was so much to do, workwise, getting things ready for his departure from Madrid. Best she head off, do some last-minute shopping, money being suddenly more plentiful, and he'd see her later.

SIS officers are trained to begin agent meets with what one jokingly calls 'the Holy Trinity': How long have you got? Where and when will our next meeting be? And if someone discovers the meeting, what's our cover story? As the two men met in this Spanish flat, those issues were swiftly dealt with.

The questioning during those sessions started with the GRU organizational diagram, mining away at the connections between departments and the individuals who ran them. What was this man's background? Who were his allies and who were his rivals? All that might help P5 Operations back in London, as it identified more people for targeting.

Skripal wanted to talk also about the set-up in the 'glass house', the *stikliashka*, or GRU headquarters. 'We don't call it the Aquarium,' he would insist, 'it's called the *stikliashka*.' This physical geography was extremely useful when added to the picture of the personal and organizational relationships.

It might assist one day with technical surveillance of the building, or directing another agent towards a point of interest. After so many years without any real insight into the affairs of the GRU, MI6 was now getting it in glorious Technicolor.

And what about Skripal personally? The service had tracked him through his previous posting and of course had its reasons for thinking he might be suitable for cultivation. But this was their chance to verify some of these things from the horse's mouth.

Skripal was proud of his achievements in Malta, boasting that he had 'recruited six agents, one of them a minister'. His interviews in Madrid produced 'CI leads', pointers for the MI6 counter-intelligence people to follow up. After the collapse of the USSR and his abortive resignation, his attitude to making recruitments had changed.

'I wasn't working as I did in Malta,' Skripal explained to me, 'when I came to Spain I was already thinking of a life outside Russia. I wanted to make business contacts, get some money and then maybe, later, resign.' In his plan, the post-GRU future might consist of keeping the flat in Moscow, but spending much of the year in the warm, convivial surroundings of Spain.

As the Scientific and Technical Secretary at the embassy, Skripal had to maintain his cover, working on exchanges between experts, as in Malta. He also played a part helping the Russian state railway company place an order for Spanish rolling stock. However he spent a good deal of time trying to get into the property business.

With Russians free to travel far more freely, Spain was becoming a popular holiday destination. From the Costa Brava to Puerto Banus, the Mediterranean coast brought them in large numbers. Seeing the direction of travel, Skripal got involved with a plan to build a hotel in Malaga. It was a big project, which he hoped might pay him substantial long-term dividends.

While he waited for the property business to mature, Skripal entered into another trade, something altogether riskier, to become FORTHWITH. In return he received a few thousand dollars for each meeting and of course the promise of an exit route if it all went wrong.

Week followed week as the agent poured out his initial torrent of secret intelligence. The conversation switched regularly between English and Russian. It was a pleasant revelation for Skripal to discover Bagnall's grasp of his native language, something he had never guessed at during the weeks of cultivation. The British intelligence officer had stuck to his cover, wisely keeping that skill to himself. 'If he had spoken Russian,' Skripal joked, 'it would have been like turning up in uniform.'

For officers who had spent months watching him before the pitch, the Russian sitting in that flat also held the key to understanding what was really going on in the Madrid *rezidentura*. The Spanish intelligence services had agreed to the MI6 operation to recruit the GRU colonel on their turf. Passing on some of this information would help keep the relationship sweet.

At the head was the chief of station or *rezident*, Rear Admiral Vladimir Kasatkin. Although the GRU had some-times adopted the subterfuge of having a *rezident* under cover as a chauffeur or in another nominally minor role, Kasatkin was hardly difficult to spot, serving as the senior military attaché. He had been posted to Madrid in July 1993, just a few months before Skripal. Under him were a couple of deputies and some operational officers, the people who ran agents, such as they still had, in Spain. The GRU station also had its own eavesdropping station, used both offensively (trawling for interesting traffic) and defensively (trying to learn the frequencies and activities of those conducting surveillance of the embassy).

All up the GRU had about twenty staff operating in Madrid under Kasatkin. The SVR of course had its own *rezidentura* and team on top of this. So how did the Russians manage to conceal this large intelligence-gathering operation when there were only twenty-seven accredited diplomats in Madrid and around one dozen at their consulate in Barcelona?

In Spain, as in the UK or US, many of the people engaged in intelligence work were classed as 'staff' rather than 'diplomats' so they weren't counted as part of that twenty-seven. This might include the cipher clerks who secured communications with the Centre, as well as drivers, technical officers, secretaries, and so on. While the military attachés' office was the obvious place one might look, GRU officers in Spain also used covers elsewhere. Some of those in the Madrid offices of Aeroflot and Morflot were also members of the military intelligence service *rezidentura*. In the early 1980s two successive managers of the Aeroflot office in Madrid had been declared persona non grata, and expelled for espionage activities.

Following the collapse of the Soviet Union, there had been a general sense of every man and woman for themselves. At this time, in many walks of Russian life officials kept turning up at work in their official jobs while inflation reduced the salary to pocket-money level. To supplement this pay they either devoted much of their working day to looking for business opportunities, like Skripal with the hotel project in Malaga, or found ways to make some cash through their official functions. In Madrid, Kasatkin, who was 'pleasant but ineffective', had allowed things to slide. As a naval officer in his mid-sixties who had started his career as a cadet during the war, the fall of the USSR and its associated humiliations must have been more than he could bear.

Historically one of the main functions of the GRU had been to obtain examples of Western technology for consignment back home. The hunger for such items was voracious, and might include anything from the night-vision devices for a new NATO tank to the latest computer. Over the years thousands of objects, as well as blueprints, handbooks, and other technical material, were sent back for reverse engineering, allowing Soviet industry to make great leaps in everything from missile-guidance systems to new passenger planes.

This whole system of espionage was financed from a budget quite separate from the Ministry of Defence, coming from the Military Industrial Commission, known by its Russian initials as the VPK.

In the post-war history of the GRU there were some examples of VPK funds being embezzled by unscrupulous officers. These men were punished severely when caught. But in the 'democratic Russia' of the mid-1990s discipline was slipping, and in Madrid graft was assuming a more systematic form. According to Skripal, a VPK budget of more than $2m a year had been milked by some unscrupulous officers, overcharging for the items they were obtaining, or maintaining fictitious agents. In order to evade exposure the men concerned had made sure they had top cover back at headquarters – an arrangement that became widely known in the Yeltsin years as a '*krysha*' or roof. In return for giving one of the bosses a cut, you could get away with all sorts of things. And that person at GRU headquarters who was hushing things up, well maybe he needed to keep someone above him sweet also. It was a pyramid of corruption.

This intelligence about people skimming the VPK funds in Madrid was important because it gave MI6 some opportunities. Might it provide also a chance to give the Spanish something back, a favour in kind for the privilege of allowing the British to recruit FORTHWITH?

As they sat chatting in the safe flat Bagnall took Skripal through the people in the *rezidentura*, assessing who might be open to a pitch. The colonel pinpointed *Yuri Burlatov, a GRU officer with the rank of naval captain working under cover in the Madrid offices of the merchant fleet. Burlatov was a central figure in the effort to gather technological secrets. He had served one tour in Spain during the early 1990s and had returned. Skripal was on good terms with the captain, even if they weren't close friends, so much so that Burlatov made the gift of a small pistol to him, prior to his departure for Moscow. Leaving aside the pleasantries, the key point was that Skripal mentioned Burlatov to his case officer – he knew about the VPK money all right.

If MI6 had been hoping to gift the Spanish counter-intelligence leads about GRU agent networks in their country, Skripal may have been a disappointment. During decades of the Cold War spy battle, agencies on both sides had learnt the value of strict compartmentalization. In the age of Philby, Burgess, and Maclean, intelligence officers had been notoriously indiscreet, sharing all manner of classified information, with disastrous consequences. As MI6 sought to rebuild allies' trust it had adopted rigid silos. If intelligence was shared, it was sanitized of detail that could identify its origin. Arguably, the Russians carried things even further.

A British spy for the Soviet Union might have been

recruited by the KGB or the GRU. Within these organizations there were separate compartments, or 'lines' as the Russians called them, for those providing political intelligence or giving technological information. Most secret of all were the illegal lines run by both the KGB (handed on to its successor, the SVR) and the GRU. Often illegals were run and supported by people entirely separate to the *rezidentura* in a nation's capital city. The mole-hunters at MI5 believed that it was this separation of different activities that accounted for the fact that Michael Smith, recruited in the 1970s, was only convicted in 1993. Gordievsky and Mitrokhin had between them produced dozens of counter-intelligence leads, but they could only know what they were cleared to see. It took the defection of Oshchenko in 1992, an officer in the SVR's scientific and technical line, to reveal Smith's role as an agent.

Skripal then, while he could give general information about the personalities in the GRU station, had very limited oversight of their agent operations. As much as anything this was to do with his own sensitive role, semi-detached from the rest of the operation. For when the colonel was posted to Spain it was with a special task in mind. The GRU maintained a network of sleeper agents, illegals, in almost every NATO country. It might be dozens strong or it might just be three or four people who, particularly by the mid-1990s, might have lost any enthusiasm for their secret role. The purpose of these illegal networks was intelligence-gathering, reconnaissance, and sabotage in times of war. In the meantime they led completely normal lives and had no contact with anyone from the Russian embassy. The network would only be activated in time of general war, when it might be assumed that the personnel of the regular GRU *rezidentura* would have been expelled or interned.

So Skripal's task, while extolling new levels of friendship and cooperation in his embassy cover role, and indeed searching out opportunities in the property business during his spare moments, was to prepare the means to sow havoc in Spain in the event of general war. If one was looking for some tangible meaning behind the MI5 Director K Branch's assessment that the GRU was an unreformed outpost of the Cold War, holding out against democratic reforms, then this was a good example. For the GRU had cached radios, weapons, and ammunition in secret sites across NATO countries for use in sabotage operations – and it continued to prepare for war as politicians toasted the new post-ideological era.

As the conversations between Bagnall and Skripal continued each weekend through the height of a Castilian summer, the moment for his return to Moscow drew ever nearer. He had already produced a haul of first-rate intelligence, but for MI6 the idea of having an agent inside the *stikliashka*, GRU headquarters, presented mouth-watering possibilities.

Skripal though had his own views about this, and they were quite firm. He was not prepared to carry on meeting MI6 handlers once he went home. Any professional officer would have understood why – and of course Skripal had experience of the Baranov and other cases. The FSB had thousands of counter-intelligence operatives working all over Moscow. And imagine all the other suspicious eyes, of those working at HQ or the residents of his block of flats, so many of whom were also GRU people. No. It just wasn't worth the risk.

So it was that in September 1996, Skripal and Bagnall bade each other goodbye. They had no idea if they would ever speak again. They had established a strong rapport in just a few months, certainly Skripal had a great deal of respect for the MI6 officer, and considered him a friend. And as far as the

British spooks were concerned there was no point pressuring the Russian colonel to keep meeting. Safety came first, and you had to take a long view with a successful case.

So Sergei, Liudmila, and Yulia got their flight back to Moscow, leaving Spain's balmy climate and numerous pleasures. Russians were starting to travel more, of course, but a posting in the West was still regarded as an enormous privilege and for the Skripal family, sadly, their time in the sun had run out.

Liudmila was taking back so many cherished memories, and a suitcase of Western clothes. Yulia had picked up amazing Spanish during their posting, becoming quite fluent. And what about Sergei, boarding that plane back to Moscow? He knew that he had found a way to provide more for his family, and if he ever needed it, a life in the West. Of course this would go better if he continued to provide something to his new employers. As to how on earth that might happen, agent FORTHWITH and his secret masters had come up with an idea.

6

INSIDE THE GLASS HOUSE

The Russia that Skripal returned to at the end of the summer of 1996 was in a state of near-chaos. Boris Yeltsin had in July been re-elected president, emerging triumphant with the backing of his rich business friends, the people Russians called oligarchs, and of course the Western powers, whose darling he remained.

For many of Skripal's brother officers, both in the intelligence agencies and his old corps (the VDV), however, Yeltsin was a profoundly suspect figure. He was continuing the Gorbachev path of selling everything to foreigners, cared little for the army, whose people lived in pitiful conditions, and was suspected of all kinds of corruption. Under Yeltsin, the army had blundered into a particularly nasty war against Chechen separatists, which he apparently had no idea how to get the country out of.

From the moment that Sergei, Liudmila, and Yulia returned to their flat in Krilatskoye, he was re-immersing himself in the world of the Centre, for half the families there were GRU. The comings and goings of those on foreign postings inevitably prompted conversations while waiting for the lift or heading out to buy vodka from one of the kiosks nearby.

When Liudmila and Sergei unpacked they found places for some mementos of Spain, a picture here or a book there. Among the things they found a shelf for was the little model of an English country cottage that Richard had given Sergei. 'My opinion about Great Britain was very positive,' he said, and one of the reasons was 'this idea expressed in the saying that the Englishman's home is his castle'. And among the hustle and uncertainty of the Moscow they'd returned to, perhaps that little cottage represented not just an abstract notion but a fantasy of a future life.

They also found a space for a souvenir given to them by Richard, when he had entertained the Skripal family at that flamenco place in Madrid. Was it odd to have it? Well, Liudmila, Sergei insists, knew nothing at the time of the true relationship between this 'businessman' and her husband. Given how much his wife and kids liked this new friend from Spain, perhaps it would have been odder if Sergei had insisted that they got rid of it.

If there were worries about the situation that Russia was in, there were also plenty of good things about coming home, of course. Sergei would see his mother, Yelena, much more often. They could get Yulia into School No. 63, nestling among the big tower blocks of Krilatskoye, which had a decent reputation. After the postings in Malta and Madrid they could look forward to some domestic stability as well. Professionally, Skripal was back in the heart of things.

The journey from his flat to the Glass House, *stikliashka* or Aquarium of legend, was several kilometres as the crow flies. Both lay on the western side of the Russian capital. The headquarters of the GRU had been built on an old military airfield, Khodinka, and that had once been the edge of the city. After the war Moscow had grown so much that it had been engulfed by developments and these had stretched far to the west, by the late 1970s encompassing green-field sites such as the one where the enormous development in which the Skripals lived had been laid out. The Metro had been extended to Krilatskoye and when he boarded it for work each morning, his destination was a station called Polizhayevska. That meant heading on one line towards the city centre, changing trains then coming back out on another one, a journey of forty to fifty minutes.

Coming out of Polizhayevska station, Colonel Skripal would cross the road, heading up Kausien Street towards the office complex that GRU officers around the world looked to for their daily purpose, praise, and promotion. Approaching the nine-storey main office block (its glazed appearance gave rise to its nicknames) he would negotiate the main entrance to the complex, which formed an opening in a two-storey-high office square construction that enveloped the tower and its entrance courtyard. This low-rise building, bristling with surveillance cameras, and wrapping around the central block like a medieval enceinte protecting a keep, had been nicknamed the Fort.

While the big shots who ran the directorates, and the boss himself, had their offices in the main tower, Skripal's desk was on the second floor of the Fort, close to a walkway leading into the main offices at the same level. His new job was in the 1st Directorate of the GRU, running the personnel department. At this time, he says, there were fifteen hundred people working at the military intelligence headquarters. As Skripal settled into this new role he had the advantage of a powerful ally.

General Valentin Korabelnikov, the 1st Deputy Chief or Number Two of the organization, was five years ahead of Skripal on the career ladder and a twenty-year veteran of GRU. As 1st Deputy his job was to oversee the intelligence-producing directorates of the organization but in the months before Skripal's return he had spent a great deal of his time in Chechnya trying to gain the upper hand over the separatists there. When Dzhokar Dudayev, the man who had led the Caucasian statelet to independence and strife, was killed by a missile strike in April 1996 it provided the Russian military with a welcome win after months of dismal news (and thousands of fatalities).

Dudayev was killed by an impressive intelligence-led operation. While he was talking on his satellite phone, the GRU locked onto the signal, and an Su24 fighter-bomber circling high above the mountains fired a missile targeting the car he was sitting in. General Korabelnikov took credit for this strike, and returning to Moscow, assumed acting control of the intelligence agency (its director at the time being on sick leave), a post in which he was confirmed in May 1997.

During his previous time in the Glass House, Skripal had got to know Korabelnikov. He considered the general to be approachable, highly educated in his profession, and very smart. Happily for Skripal – and indeed eventually for MI6 – the coming man in the GRU had some reciprocal respect for the paratrooper colonel from Kaliningrad.

In his role as personnel director, Skripal sat on what the GRU calls its 1st Commission, a management board dealing with the overall running of the organization. In this way agent FORTHWITH became privy to the affairs of the whole concern. And there was more.

Throughout the Cold War years, the GRU had been able to keep out the KGB internal-security types who could be found in virtually every concern in the country. From colleges to factories or institutes, the 1st or 'Special Department' had been responsible for maintaining ideological purity. In civilian life the term '1st Department' was more common, and people tended to refer to KGB as *chekists*. The *osobii otdel*, or Special Department, performed the same role in army units, where it had the formal function of counter-intelligence. The people who belonged to it, nicknamed *osobists* by soldiers, poked their noses into all kinds of business and were widely despised as a result. This was particularly the case in the airborne forces, where Skripal had acquired some of this contempt.

Everywhere else in society, the KGB had been used to control people, asserting its role as 'sword and shield' of the party. But the GRU was entrusted with such sensitive secrets that it had been given a special dispensation. It was reckoned capable of looking after its own leaks. If there were to be mole-hunts in Russian military intelligence, they would in the first instance be investigated by its own security section, and this sat in the organization under the personnel department which was, as of October 1996, under the command of Colonel Sergei Viktorovich Skripal.

He had learned a good deal during his previous spell at the Centre about catching spies, not least from his involvement with the Baranov case. That was why he had insisted to Richard Bagnall that there would be no meetings once he returned to Russia, and also why he knew that it would be quite impossible for him to leave the country while he sat at the GRU's top table. Self-preservation would have to trump communication. Skripal was hoping in any case for promotion to major general, if he played his cards right.

As the months progressed, the army's concerns about the Chechen situation had intensified. Much of this drama played out while Skripal was serving in Spain.

It began with the wiping out of an entire motor rifle regiment as it entered the Chechen capital, Grozny, in late 1994. In June 1995 an unknown number of Chechen militant fighters, probably in excess of a hundred, struck well outside their troubled enclave, taking over a hospital in the southern Russian town of Budyonnovsk, and with it hundreds of hostages.

After a couple of days' stand-off there was a series of assaults in which one by one each of Russia's main security organizations displayed its incompetence. Alpha Group (formerly the KGB's elite assault force) failed, as did the army, and the Ministry of Interior special troops.

The cost of this was truly shocking. Around a hundred and thirty hostages were killed (the numbers are still disputed) and more than four hundred wounded, many of them cut down by the military's bullets rather than the terrorists. When the guns fell silent with the hostages still under Chechen control, the Russian government negotiated a deal whereby the kidnappers returned to Chechnya (triumphant), the Russian military announced a ceasefire, and peace talks began. During the talks Dudayev was killed by the GRU operation.

It was in November 1996, as he settled into the personnel department, that papers were signed outlining the new relationship between Chechnya and the Russian state. The whole venture had been the most awful disaster. There were more than five thousand dead Russian soldiers, tens of thousands of Chechens, and Grozny had been utterly flattened. At times during the Russian assault, twenty thousand artillery shells a day had been fired into the Chechen capital. But there was also something bigger at stake, so soon after the withdrawal from Afghanistan, collapse of the Warsaw Pact, and of the USSR itself.

For officers of Skripal's generation the loss of the old Soviet republics (following the failed coup of 1991) had already robbed Russia of its protective shield in Europe, the Caucasus and Central Asia. But now, having been out-manoeuvred by a bunch of Chechen fanatics, he could see the next line of defence, the autonomous republics of the north Caucasus, crumbling too. Almost everyone of his generation and military background looked upon these events with alarm and some anger.

In this security turmoil Yeltsin had faced the other way as the KGB, broken up after its involvement in the 1991 coup attempt, started to reconstitute itself. Its 2nd Chief Direct-orate, previously responsible for the domestic surveillance state, evolved through being a security ministry and counter-terrorist service into, in 1995, the Federalnoye Sluzhbe Bezopasnosti – the FSB, or Federal Security Service. It took possession of that forbidding building in Moscow's Dzerzhin-sky Square, the Lubyanka. There, with the toppling of KGB founder Dzerzhinsky's statue in August 1991, the revolution reached its symbolic climax.

In was in 1996–1997 though, as Skripal established himself in his new job and his patron General Korabelnikov was ascending to the helm of the GRU, that the FSB started to make its presence felt again in all sorts of ways. The Chechen conflict had produced acts of terrorism in Russian cities and, understandably, there was a public desire to see some kind of effort to counter the bombers. But the end of communism had produced all sorts of other changes too, ones many people welcomed, like seeing Western companies open operations in Russia, much more foreign travel, and interactions of many other kinds with foreigners.

The FSB, little by little, began to reassert itself. In some places, familiar faces, those burly *chekists* in leather coats, reappeared in the old 1st Department offices, particularly of institutions engaged in any kind of sensitive dealings with the West. Prosecutions started, like that of Alexander Nikitin, a former naval officer, that seemed to sit badly with Russia's newly espoused democratic principles. He was arrested in 1996 and charged with treason. His crime was gathering information about nuclear contamination for an environmental group. It took him until 2000 to get acquitted.

As the Nikitin case rumbled on all sorts of new FSB files were opened: on Russians working with Western NGOs; on people doing business in certain areas deemed sensitive; and on journalists covering certain topics, notably the Chechen conflict. The KGB veterans who had slipped back into positions of command throughout the FSB saw these contacts with foreigners as part of something much more sinister, an epidemic of actual espionage enabled by the dissolution of the iron curtain.

How bad was it? FSB Director Nikolai Kovalyov said in 1996, 'There has never been such a number of spies arrested by us since the time when German agents were sent in during the years of World War Two.' He said that four hundred foreign agents had been uncovered during 1995 to 1996.

This campaigning by the FSB betrayed an obvious agenda

to many at GRU headquarters. General Korabelnikov and his people pushed back against it – they could see the dangers not least to their own operations as a strategic intelligence service. The GRU boss took the highly unusual step of publicly opposing the FSB's spy fever.

'I would not say the Russian Federation is crawling with spies', he told a journalist from *Izvestya* who questioned him about the 'unmasking' of journalists, physicists, and ecologists as agents of foreign powers, 'spies and traitors have always existed. So long as there are secrets, there will be an interest in accessing them and benefitting from their contents. The most worrying thing is that traitors do exist within the ranks of the government and specialized structures [i.e. intelligence agencies]. Upon receiving any information suggesting a threat of betrayal on the part of any agency, structure, or individual, we are obliged immediately to report this information to our leadership.'

This hinted at the secret struggle between the military intelligence people and the FSB that had been going on almost continuously since it was formed in 1995. Skripal, as a protégé of the general, was deeply versed in these intrigues. Korabelnikov's last sentence though underlined the serious consequences that could be expected for anyone discovered spying in the GRU.

At the same time as this re-emergence of the old KGB or *chekist* mentality alleged a wave of spying on a level unseen since the days of Hitler, the opposite trend, that of Yeltsin ploughing on with reforms designed to please Russian reformers and their Western backers, had not yet exhausted itself. It was a measure however of the relative strength of liberal and conservative forces that when a member of the Duma (Russia's parliament), Galina Starovoitova, suggested a law banning former KGB people from holding public office, she got little support. Another, more important step in liberalizing the country was the shelving of the death penalty, including for high treason and espionage.

During the Cold War, Soviet CIA or MI6 agents in the USSR had feared trial and execution. The statute used was Article 64 of the Russian penal code. 'Treason', it stated,

> that is, an act intentionally committed by a citizen of the USSR which is damaging to the independence of the state, territorial inviolability, or military power of the USSR; defection to the enemy, espionage, communicating a state or military secret to a foreign state, flight to a foreign country or refusal to return from a foreign country to the USSR, assisting a foreign country in carrying on hostile activity against the USSR, or plotting with a view to seizing power shall be punishable by deprivation of freedom for a period of 10–15 years; the confiscation of property; or death, with the confiscation of property.

It was Article 64 that was used to execute Colonel Oleg Penkovsky and perhaps a dozen of those sold out by Ames's and Hanssen's betrayals, including in 1988 agent TOPHAT, GRU General Polyakov. In its phrase that 'refusal to return from a foreign country' constituted treason, even defecting ballet dancers had come to fear death at the hands of KGB assassins. Polyakov's execution by firing squad, as far as I've been able to establish, was the last execution of a Soviet asset of a foreign intelligence agency, or if you prefer it 'traitor'. It happened, one should note, three years into the reformist rule of Mikhail Gorbachev.

Oleg Gordievsky was also sentenced to death in absentia under this statute, and lived in the UK under MI5's protection using an assumed name. In his first TV interview after defecting he wore a disguise to alter his appearance. Even under Gorbachev, British attempts to reunite Gordievsky with his family, by allowing them to leave Russia, were thwarted by the KGB.

Certainly, Article 64 carried a particular dread for any Soviet citizen considering defection, let alone spying for a Western agency. At the end of one of his books published in 1984, the defector Vladimir Rezun wrote a postscript, 'For GRU Officers Only'. It sets out his reasons why he felt fleeing the Soviet Union was justified but then, in words that he might have been addressing to Skripal, continues:

> If any GRU officer now finds himself in the same dilemma – to go or to stay – I advise him to think over his decision a hundred times, and then again. If he is thinking of fleeing to the West then my advice to him is – don't do it. Article 64 will be waiting for him, as will the shameful epithet 'traitor', and an agonizing death, maybe even on the frontier itself.

But in June 1996, Yeltsin had suspended Russia's death penalty, setting it aside by presidential decree followed by changes to the law. The last Russian to be executed, by judicial process at least, was Sergei Golovkin, a serial killer, who was dispatched in August 1996 after his appeals were exhausted. What was Yeltsin's reason? He and some of his reform-minded legal advisers wanted to move close to Europe and its political institutions. They had been advised that they could not do so if Russia retained the death penalty. So it was suspended and has been ever since.

When the old penal code of Soviet Russia was replaced with a new one in 1996, treason remained a crime of course, under Article 275, but it was not a capital one. The penalty stipulated was 'deprivation of liberty for a term of twelve to twenty years with confiscation of property or without such confiscation'. The death penalty remained in abeyance although still possible in theory under the statute for aggravated murder and genocide.

As for those already jailed for espionage, quiet representations were made in the case of several who had been serving Western agencies. Some of these men were released and then made their way abroad.

These developments and the general improvement in relations with the West may well have encouraged Skripal and others to believe that if discovered, their crime of espionage would not be viewed as seriously as in the Cold War. Certainly there were hawks in the FSB, and quite possibly the GRU, who regarded Yeltsin's shelving of the death penalty as removing a key disincentive to working for a foreign government, yet another sign of everything going to hell in a handcart.

The view of Yeltsin within these security agencies was often one of scorn. There were episodes of public drunkenness, hopelessly trying to conduct a band while on a visit to Germany in 1994, or slurring his words and declaring the press 'a disaster' while visiting the US the following year. Security people also knew about unedifying episodes that had been hushed up, for example that Yeltsin had been so drunk one evening during that 1995 American trip that he had ended up on the street near the White House, trying to order a pizza while wearing nothing but his underpants.

This disgust with the president was, by the summer of 1997, taking a new political form. Lieutenant General Lev Rokhlin, a decorated veteran of Afghanistan and Chechnya who had become an MP and chairman of the Duma's defence committee, launched a new All Russia Movement to Support the Army. Feeding on widespread resentments, from the humiliating outcome in the Caucasus to the poor living conditions of military families and pensioners, Rokhlin soon garnered support from all sorts of quarters, including some former KGB and military leaders who'd backed the 1991 coup. His campaign became a potent source of difficulty for Yeltsin because Rokhlin, who was soon calling for the ousting of the president by constitutional means, had both a parliamentary platform and the immunity from prosecution that went with it.

In the summer of 1997 then, as Skripal was back in the heart of the GRU, talk of coups – constitutional or otherwise – was again the order of the day in Moscow, following failed attempts to seize power in 1991 and 1993. The struggle also between the army and the re-emerging FSB that was an important theme of his last years in military intelligence was something that concerned him deeply, and he felt he should share it with MI6. 'I wanted London to have a more or less correct picture of what was going on in Russia,' he said.

His daily work was also giving him all manner of information that he knew London would pay for. Running the personnel department he knew the details of who was in which overseas GRU station and what their functions were. He knew who was being prepared to go out in order to take over too. All of this was valuable information for the counterespionage services of Western countries. In times of reduced budgets, how many Russians could they afford to follow around or listen in to? If you knew who in a particular *rezidentura* was truly important, well, that was valuable knowledge.

He would also have been acquiring some information about the GRU's own agent networks, though given the strict compartmentalization of intelligence observed in the Glass House this would have been little more than hints or scraps. Each one of these though might provide a counter-intelligence lead for MI6 or its partners in the CIA.

There was much then that Skripal wanted to share, but equally he was quite clear in his own mind about the risks he was not prepared to take in communicating with MI6. It had been drummed into them time and again at the academy: an agent's communication with his or her handlers is one of their principal points of vulnerability. Dead drops could be placed under observation, agents or couriers could be followed, and emails or other electronic means intercepted. None of these traditional methods of tradecraft was foolproof. You could use short-wave radios and one-time pads for encryption, as a generation of Soviet agents had, but if these were discovered in your home in Russia you would get a one-way ticket to the Gulag for sure. Hadn't the boss of the FSB said that the country was facing its biggest wave of foreign spying since the war?

As for Liudmila or Yulia, well of course their reality was different. They were ruled by the school year and the seasons, like normal people were. And as 1997 wore on, missing Spain as they did, they decided to head back there, taking a holiday with some other friends from Moscow. Sergei knew that he could not accompany them. Officers working at GRU head-quarters simply couldn't do that.

So with hugs and kisses he saw his wife and daughter off. They flew to Alicante and checked into their hotel.

There, after a decent interval, Liudmila got a call from an old friend, Richard Bagnall. He dropped by to say hello to her. He arrived with a gift, something for Sergei. And Liudmila had brought something from Moscow for him also. Sergei had sent Richard a book, a Russian novel, a small token of his friendship perhaps, but one that he knew would mean so much to his friend from MI6.

7

THE VIEW FROM VAUXHALL

Returning to London from Alicante, Richard Bagnall waited for the technical experts behind the green-tinted, triple-glazed windows at headquarters to do their stuff. Inside the book sent to him from Moscow was page upon page of secret writing. During long hours in the privacy of his flat, Colonel Skripal had turned one of the tradecraft tricks he'd learned at the academy against his GRU employers; writing in invisible ink. In this way he had crammed his years' worth of secret reporting to British intelligence into the volume he'd given Liudmila to take on her Spanish holiday as a present for Richard.

Skripal insisted to me that he had not shared his secret life as an MI6 agent with his wife – not at the time at least – and that she was unaware of the critical role played by the apparently innocent volume she had taken out of Moscow. However the 'present' that Bagnall sent back with her to Moscow consisted of thousands of dollars in cash. Perhaps Sergei had claimed it was payment for consultancy work he'd done for their friend from Madrid days. If Liudmila had her suspicions she did not press Sergei too closely, the wife of a spy soon learning that what you do not know, you cannot reveal.

In using secret writing, Skripal had chosen one of the most ancient techniques known in espionage, certainly one going back thousands of years. Early experiments with lemon juice, vegetable extracts and milk produced inks that became visible when a page was warmed by a candle or other source of heat. The techniques had been used to get messages into besieged cities in the ancient world and were revived by European spymasters during the Renaissance.

Early in the twentieth century more advanced com-pounds, derived from silver, cobalt, and other elements were tried. Some of these required a chemical reagent to be applied to the page. During the Cold War both the KGB and Western agencies developed highly tailored invisible inks that could only be revealed at their destination by equally specific chem-ical formulas, thus defeating a casual inspection using heat, ultra-violet light, or one of the silver-based reagents.

Whatever the process used by the Vauxhall Cross boffins to reveal agent FORTHWITH's reports, this first book yielded a large amount of information ranging from Skripal's views on the emerging GRU–FSB rivalry to the posting plans for European intelligence stations and CI leads, i.e. clues to be given to the mole-hunters in Western counter-intelligence organizations.

The treatment given to these pointers towards the iden-tity of GRU assets varied according to the specificity of the information. It might be vague, such as evidence (to use a hypothetical example) that 'a man in the French finance ministry' was a Russian mole. These might cause spy-hunters months of fruitless head-scratching. Even when in receipt of far more specific information, the results rarely produced any kind of formal police enquiry. A CI lead was by its nature problematic as evidence, particularly if it could not be used without endangering the source.

It was the late 1990s, most Western politicians believed the Cold War was well and truly over. Prosecuting Russian spies would be embarrassing, and anyway these espionage cases were notoriously hard to prove. In the rare examples where prosecution had been tried, such as MI5's 1993 case against Michael Smith, or a couple of FBI ones in the USA, there had often been an element of entrapment: a Western agent impersonating a Russian handler in order to lure the suspect into breaching the law.

Skripal's reporting was sent out by MI6 in various forms. Suitably sanitized to disguise the source's precise role, some went out in the form of 'CX', sometimes called the Blue Book in Cold War days, a bulletin of secret intelligence sent to other agencies and government departments with a suitably high security clearance. In many cases though FORTHWITH's product was put out as a specific message from Vauxhall Cross to another service. A short report announcing the imminent arrival of the new GRU *rezident* in Berlin, for example, might be shared with the Germans but few others. In all of these examples of dissemination, the need-to-know principle ruled. The best way to preserve an agent was to keep knowledge of his or her reporting as restricted as possible.

Some of Skripal's reports were 'extremely well received by the Security Service', a Whitehall figure told me. FORTHWITH had helped pinpoint GRU assets in the UK. Since no prosecution resulted we can only imagine that the individual(s) he unmasked as spying for Russia or subjects of cultivation by the GRU were disrupted in other ways: by being explicitly warned;

professionally sidelined or dismissed; or fed disinformation by British intelligence to send back to Moscow. However, not all of Skripal's CI leads were quite so valuable.

Work on the information he had provided about his agent recruitments in Malta did not produce any prosecutions. Indeed it may only have revealed a couple of US military personnel who were actually counter-intelligence operatives leading the GRU man on. As for the Maltese, little informa- tion could be found that suggested active treachery.

What seems to have emerged from the investigation of Skripal's Maltese contacts was a pattern that became very familiar to Western counter-espionage officers in the 1980s and 1990s. Since ambitious SVR or GRU officers were pres- sured to make recruitments in order to remain in their coveted overseas postings or get another job abroad after a few years back at the Centre, 'a culture of systematic exag- geration emerged', says one MI6 officer. Westerners who had met the Russian intelligence officer a few times and were happy to keep in touch were reported back as agent recruit- ments, but most often were not producing anything that could be characterized as secret intelligence.

Skripal's reporting became an important element in MI6's picture of what was going on inside Russia. He was, after all, the first GRU agent in place that they had recruited since Penkovsky in the late 1950s. Two factors, however, limited what they could expect from him. In the first place, Skripal's healthy self-preservation instinct meant that his gifts of books to Richard arrived only occasionally. Indeed when Liudmila presented him with a second volume, during a holiday in Malaga in 1998, this seems to have been the only other use of this channel of communication. Each of these volumes may have been packed with secret writing, but there were only two deliveries of this kind during FORTHWITH's years inside the Glass House.

The other factor that had emerged by this time was abundantly clear to the colonel's colleagues at the GRU Centre. He had developed diabetes, producing some lengthy bouts of sick leave before treatment brought his symptoms under control.

Skripal's illness contributed to personal disappointment in this final phase of his career. On three occasions he was passed over for promotion to major general, something which, by rights, he felt should have been his as head of personnel and a member of the GRU's 1st Commission. Receiving a general's shoulder boards might have allowed him to serve for longer.

While Skripal's recruitment remained a source of considerable professional pride to the Secret Intelligence Service he was just one of several agents in place, and this period, the late 1990s, coincided with a new impetus being given to source recruitment in Russia. After the fall of communism the attitude of the Russia specialists in Western intelligence organizations started with guarded optimism, evolved into suspicion, and was by the late 1990s becoming a great concern. Politicians, by and large, remained much more upbeat, regarding the democratic transformation of Russia as an emphatic win for humanity and stability, even if it was still very much a work in progress. A gap had therefore opened up between the leaders in the UK, Germany, and the US and their secret servants. Since nobody wanted a return to the Cold War the spooks were left discovering developments that disturbed them, exchanging highly classified papers about them, and then essentially remaining silent while Western companies sought to exploit the Russian Klondike. In this context – because of its later relevance to the Skripal story – it is worth looking a little at the issue of chemical weapons.

As the Cold War ended, Soviet experts were working on new nerve agents under a secret programme. In part these were seen as a retaliatory step to the US fielding of new bombs containing a binary (or two-part) version of the VX nerve agent. In the early 1990s a dissident scientist and former head of security at the Soviet chemical weapons organization had revealed the existence of these new compounds, which he said were being developed under the name 'Novichok'. This was awkward because an international treaty ban, the Chemical Weapons Convention, was in its final stages of drafting, and it didn't specifically cover these new agents. This ambiguity would be resolved at a later date by the international chemical weapons watchdog.

Initially MI6 and the other experts in Whitehall saw the emergence of Novichok as the result of inertia on the part of labs and factories where thousands would be made unemployed by the new treaty. The secret agencies went along with the public line that President Yeltsin was being kept in the dark about these developments, maybe scammed by unreformed members of the military-industrial complex. Politically, that was a better alternative than the British or US governments calling out the Russian president publicly.

By the mid-1990s evidence had emerged that some people connected with the chemical weapons industry had been trying to sell their services to Syria, with the idea of producing new nerve agents there. For a time, when they were charged by the FSB in 1996, this actually appeared to be an area where UK cooperation with Russian intelligence might be possible. Avoiding proliferation of such weapons was a mutual interest, after all.

But by the late 1990s there had been a distinct shift in the intelligence analysts' interpretation of developments in Russia. Germany's foreign intelligence service, the BND, managed to bring a defector out of the chemical weapons establishment, complete with a small sample of a Novichok nerve agent. His secret flight to the West produced intelligence that was circulated in 1998, the year after Russia signed the Chemical Weapons Convention. The BND shared its Novichok sample with labs in Sweden, the US, UK, Netherlands, and France. Thus it was at this time that the British chemical weapons labs at Porton Down in Wiltshire first got their hands on the substance about which they had heard so much.

This development was doubly disturbing: first, it became clear that the new Russian nerve agent was undetectable by standard NATO equipment; second, it suggested that research and testing of quantities well above the minute amounts permitted under the new treaty (for the purpose of developing protective measures) were likely still going on in Russia. If Yeltsin's people had signed up to the Convention with no intention of keeping it, or perhaps believing that it didn't cover their latest research, then this was worrying. In later years additional sensitive intelligence about the Novichok programme would reach the Western agencies. But in 1998 it formed just one strand in a web of secret reporting out of Russia that was raising concern among the experts.

It was around this time, while Skripal was serving in GRU headquarters, that steps were taken to up MI6's game against the Russians, making it fit for the post-communist era. This did not result from a particular bureaucratic moment or decision, rather it was guided by two particular individuals who were key to redefining what MI6 was doing in Russia, and how it was achieving its goals.

The first of these was John Scarlett, who was expelled from Russia in 1994 and went back to a desk job in London, and was now Controller Central and Eastern Europe. Although he was also dealing in this post with the emerging Kosovo crisis in the Balkans, Russia remained a key concern. Scarlett was one of those secret mandarins who, far from seeing a contradiction between friendly relations and spying, believed that it was essential to keeping exchanges between the UK and Russia honest. With his clipped delivery and intense manner, the Controller was able to convince many in Whitehall of the need both to focus on the Russian target, as Yeltsin faltered, and to organize the means to improve collection there.

At about the same time, *Harry Murdoch was appointed under Scarlett to be Head of the Russian operations and targeting elements of P5 at MI6. Murdoch was the type of bespectacled, donnish figure familiar from spy fiction. An Oxford graduate and Ph.D. to boot, his earlier career in MI6 had taken him to the Middle East. Consumed by work, and afflicted by the unpredictable life of a spy, Murdoch had not married.

In his late forties when he was placed in charge, Murdoch did not suffer fools and 'upset a lot of people by demanding an altogether higher performance from them', says one Vauxhall Cross insider. 'He is an astonishing judge of character,' observes another, 'he could weigh up people's strengths and weaknesses straight away, and was rarely wrong – I'm just glad he never wrote *my* annual report.' Murdoch's role was to deliver more penetrations over a broader range of targets, and as one observer remarks, 'he is an excellent operational officer who operationalized everything'.

The old idea of a Soviet bloc 'Master Race' in MI6 was finally laid to rest. Instead Murdoch dispatched Bagnall and the others in his team of agent runners pitching their way across Europe, Russia, and wherever else in search of the people who could give profound insight into what was really going on.

In the early 1990s SIS tasking on Russia had been narrow in its scope, covering counter-intelligence targets to make sure there were no high-placed Russian moles in Britain, the hidden chemical and biological weapons programmes, and certain issues that worried Whitehall decision-makers relating to nuclear-warhead security as well as the security of the command system for these weapons. By the end of the decade the Russian target was being looked at very differently. So it was around this time that SIS began using partnerships with the nascent services of some former Soviet republics, notably the Baltic ones, to up its game.

It was all very well to think defensively, going for the SVR and GRU, but Murdoch wanted to know more about the FSB also, as it sought to reconstitute its power within Moscow. And with many of its Russian assets now reporting powerful connections between the FSB, organized crime, oligarchs, and politicians, the net would have to be cast wider. You only had to read the Russian press to see all manner of conspiracy theories about state organizations becoming criminal enterprises, but if this was true, what were the wider implications for UK foreign policy?

During this time, people were to approach many targets as they travelled in former Soviet republics or Eastern Europe.

Some of the old Master Race war horses who had held on in the agent-running section for rather too long, living on past glories, were also moved on. At this time also, MI6's P5 sections also stepped up operations designed to capitalize on the new freedoms enjoyed by Russians, allowing them to target and run people at a far lower cost. A consultancy could be set up in the UK or another Western country, and a visiting Russian businessman asked if he'd like to submit reports in return for cash. He could just fax them over, or, as the technology evolved, use email. In this way, British intelligence might tap into all sorts of expertise, whether it was someone working in defence exports or the oil business. The FSB's suspicion of NGOs and Western businesses would, in this sense, become a self-fulfilling prophecy.

Events in Moscow, meanwhile, were moving by the summer of 1998 to an important moment, a turning point in the battle between reformist forces and post-communist orthodoxy.

In the early hours of 3 July 1998, masked men entered a dacha in Klokovo, south-west of Moscow. There they found retired general Lev Rokhlin and his wife Tamara, both of whom had been drinking. Rokhlin had been forced out of the chairmanship of the parliamentary defence committee some weeks before, but he and his movement to support the army remained a potent threat to President Yeltsin. The retired officer had talked of impeaching Yeltsin, but the president characterized him and his supporters as planning a coup.

So that warm summer's night in 1998, the intruders shot the general in the head. More than ten thousand people attended his funeral in Moscow. In the days that followed, Rokhlin's wife was framed for the crime and charged with murder. That was a neat twist, since in the years it took for the case against her to collapse people did not look elsewhere and other leads were not investigated.

Some time after the crime, Murdoch's section at Vauxhall Cross received some revelatory intelligence about the murder. There were allegations flying about Moscow that a shadowy ex-KGB type in Yeltsin's presidential administration, one Vladimir Vladimirovitch Putin, had arranged it. Three weeks after Rokhlin's murder, Yeltsin appointed Putin as Director of the FSB. In the view of MI6's source, a grateful president used this promotion to reward Putin for taking care of the Rokhlin business.

During its period with Putin at the helm (it was just over a year), the FSB became more assertive, the political murder rate increased, and Russia began lurching towards a new war in Chechnya. Four and a half months after Rokhlin's murder, assassins claimed the life of another Duma member, Galina Staravoitova. At the other end of the political spectrum to the general and his movement, she was the liberal who'd tried to move legislation banning former KGB men from power.

Few politicians in Western countries followed Russian affairs in any great depth. Some, briefed by their intelligence agencies, understood that allegations of corruption swirled around Yeltsin and his family. But publicly most stuck to the line that democratic Russia had become a friend, and this was no time to threaten that amity.

In Vauxhall Cross concerns of this kind had strengthened Scarlett and Murdoch's hand in pushing for more resources, and getting the CX reports produced by his section taken more seriously around Whitehall.

Even early in 1999 it had become apparent that change could be afoot in Moscow. Growing doubts were being expressed about Yeltsin's health and fitness to run for re-election in 2000, and a power struggle to succeed him was beginning. Many fancied Yevgeni Primakov, another former KGB man, and after the 1991 coup, director of the newly created foreign espionage arm, the SVR.

In April 1999, a tape allegedly showing Russia's chief prosecutor, Yuri Shkuratov, cavorting naked with prostitutes found its way onto Russian TV. It was a classic example of *kompromat*, blackmail material gathered (or as was claimed in this case, faked) by the old KGB to destroy someone or control them. It ruined not only Shkuratov but also the fortunes of his good friend and political ally Yevgeni Primakov, who withdrew from the presidential race.

How had this *kompromat* been created and found its way to the TV channel RTR? Remarkably, a journalist was told by someone working at the station, the tape had been hand-delivered 'by a man who looked like the head of the FSB'. Whether or not it was him, Putin followed up his special delivery by publicly calling on Shkuratov to go.

Visiting the newspaper *Komsomolskaya Pravda* in May 1999, the FSB boss was asked by journalists about rumours of coup plots. Was he planning one?

'Why would we need to organize a coup d'état?' Putin replied. 'We are in power now. And who would we topple?'

'Maybe the president?' a reporter replied.

'The president appointed us,' came Putin's answer. It looked to many like he was already in control. Just a few months later, in August, Yeltsin installed Putin as prime minister, putting him in a position to succeed him as president.

What followed later that summer produced anguish among Russian democrats and paved the way for Putin's succession to the presidency. A series of bombings of Russian apartment blocks, claiming hundreds of lives, was blamed on Chechen separatists, triggering a large-scale military operation into the breakaway republic.

The discovery of what looked like preparations to bomb another building, in the Russian city of Ryazan, late that September produced a widespread conspiracy theory. Initially announced as another thwarted apartment atrocity, it was soon linked to the FSB, whose spokesmen said it had been a 'training exercise'. Opponents of Yeltsin (and later Putin) would charge that the Ryazan incident proved the bombings that shocked Russia so deeply had been carried out by the FSB in order to justify a new Chechen war.

This book is not the place to dissect this theory, which I have never found particularly convincing, but it was to become an important part of the case made against the FSB and Putin by some people who are important later in our story, and the apartment bombings defined the moment that Colonel Sergei Skripal finally left the army and the GRU.

For it was in September of 1999 that Skripal, then aged forty-eight, was retired. He later explained to me that he had accumulated thirty-eight years' pensionable service, the months he had spent in Afghanistan, and years in Malta and Madrid counting as double time and time and a half. However this pension had been reduced by inflation to a pittance, and in any case Skripal had no intention of sitting idle.

A few months later, he got a job in local government, in the Moscow region administration. He started a private business with some old comrades from the army engineers, selling demolition services for the construction industry, and, it seems, offered his skills as a 'fixer' with local government connections to some contractors who were building a big housing development in Lobnya, north-west of the capital, near Sheremetyevo airport. By blurring the lines between his official and freelance work, in a way that was quite typical in 1990s Russia, he was able to bring in a decent side income.

But what of his relationship with MI6? Would they still even want to deal with him? Quite clearly they did, not least so as to have more detailed conversations about his three years at GRU headquarters. His two lengthy reports to London, sent via Liudmila in the form of secret writing, had naturally prompted many questions from British intelligence analysts, queries they had been unable to ask until that moment.

For Skripal had decided that it was now safe for him to travel. Crudely, he knew he still had value to the British. He told me that he had held some information back in his 1996 Madrid meetings and reporting from Moscow. Better not to give them everything at once, for even spies have to consider their longevity.

So, early in 2000, Skripal decided the moment was ripe for him to enjoy some winter sun, and some of the pleasures of Spanish life he'd been missing. It was time for him and Liudmila to take a break. They boarded a flight from Moscow to Malaga, part of the typical crowd taking advantage of low-season prices.

There, in a Spanish hotel, they were delighted to see Richard Bagnall once again. He'd met up with Liudmila a couple of times, but had not seen Sergei for three and a half years. He asked after Sasha and Yulia, and warm greetings were exchanged as well as toasts drunk.

In private, Sergei and the MI6 officer had business to transact. For his part, Richard had important news from Vauxhall Cross, and there was someone else he wanted the Russian to meet.

8

BACK INTO THE LIGHT

For a couple of days in Malaga, Skripal met and discussed things with his British friends. For him it was a pleasurable trip; there was winter sunshine, good food, and wine, he enjoyed chatting with Richard, and of course he was being well paid for his time. But the presence of the other SIS officer, *Stephen Jones, was a harbinger of the news from London.

After five years in the Russian agent-running section, Richard was moving on. Whereas many CIA or MI6 officers go their entire careers without making a meaningful recruitment, Bagnall, so people in British intelligence say, had successfully pitched several Russians. But MI6, like any other branch of the civil service, has its career structure, and as a fast-stream officer who'd notched up these recruitments he was being given his own overseas station to run. Malaga was a handover meeting, and Stephen was taking over as Sergei's new case officer.

Agent-runners the world over worry about handovers. While it's true there are examples of the relationship between a case officer and his 'Joe' lasting decades, that's rarely the way. The anxiety in any service is that the asset, who has been living a double life, often taking great risks, will see the departure of his or her old handler as a natural moment to break the cycle of deceit, stress, and subterfuge.

In Skripal's case there was no danger of this. He sized up Stephen, seeing someone closer to his own age than Richard's, more typical perhaps of what he had always expected of an MI6 officer. Stephen was a fluent Russian speaker, naturally, and a graduate of one of England's great universities, a quiet professional. A colleague describes him as 'careful, diligent, and a member of that core group that stayed on the Russia side of operations for much of their careers'.

During their early meetings Stephen Jones's job was to take Sergei back through his reports from Moscow, filling in areas where the analysts in London had further questions, expanding on points that now seemed to be growing in importance as a new Russian president was assuming power. If the FSB was triumphant, extending its powers and getting an old *chekist* into the Kremlin, what were the chances of a military coup? How was Skripal's old patron, General Korabelnikov, faring at the GRU? If Skripal had worried that they might lose interest now he'd retired from the service, he was soon reassured that this was not the case.

Richard Bagnall meanwhile disappeared from the scene as far as Skripal was concerned. The Russian agent had no idea whether he would ever see him again. That was a shame. But they were professionals and such were the exigencies of the service. Even so, Skripal felt they had established a strong bond, a friendship that went beyond the purely professional.

In May 2000, Vladimir Putin was sworn in as President of the Russian Federation. One of his first acts in office was to place the FSB under his personal control. The Second

Chechen War was in full swing, and Putin had come to power promising to smash the rebels. There were foreign spies to be caught also, so Putin knew he would need the agency operating to full effect.

In Western countries, leaders welcomed his appointment. For many this went beyond extending the diplomatic courtesy due to a peer who has just won an election. Yeltsin's final years had been an embarrassment, so after the political tumult and violence of the 1990s it was a relief that power had passed by constitutional means. The transition also marked the start of what would become a repetitive hallmark of policy towards Russia in this new decade: there might be many things going on there that Downing Street or the White House didn't like but this gave the chance for a 're-set'.

Late in 1999, President Bill Clinton, speaking by phone to British Prime Minister Tony Blair (in transcripts only released years later), said, 'Putin has enormous potential, I think . . . he's very smart and thoughtful. I think we can do a lot of good with him.' Blair attracted political flak for visiting Putin in St Petersburg shortly before the 2000 Russian election, as Russian troops were fighting their way into Chechnya. 'The Russians have been subjected to really severe terrorist attacks,' Blair said in defence of the visit, noting, 'it is still right that Britain has a strong relationship with Russia'. BP had started investing big in Russia in 1997, and a host of other major companies were looking for opportunities there.

Other nations wanted to get in on the act too. And if doing business with the Russians meant boosting Putin's international standing, so be it. Asked on German TV whether the Russian president was an exemplary democrat, Chancellor Gerhard Schroeder replied, 'I believe him, and I'm convinced that he is.'

Putin, however, believed in his own very specific form of democracy, one guided by Russian values. He considered that these were best embodied by people with similar backgrounds to his own. Campaigning on a promise to bring in 'a dictatorship of law', this pledge was soon used to put the squeeze on the oligarchs who had surrounded Yeltsin. They faced arrest and imprisonment, and some started to choose exile rather than face politically motivated proceedings.

The new elite were those who shared with Putin a background in the KGB and/or the St Petersburg (formerly Leningrad) connection. Intelligence reports told of the supremacy of the 'Ozero Circle', the group of Putin's mates who had come together through their ownership of plush dachas on Lake Ozero near that city. Nikolai Patrushev, who succeeded Putin at the helm of the FSB, was a typical example of this group. Extolling the virtues of his officers, he said they were not motivated by money, nor by decorations, rather, 'their sense of service, they are, if you like, our new "nobility"'.

Key Putin placemen were put in charge of other criminal, security, and defence agencies too. They became known as the 'siloviki' or powerful ones as they came from what Russians called the 'power ministries'. This new elite saw themselves as the salvation of Russia, the people who would bring order to the chaos unleashed during the Yeltsin years. This sense of manifest destiny was expressed by one of this new elite, a former KGB man called Viktor Cherkesov, who Putin appointed to crack down on drugs:

> We [siloviki] must understand that we are one whole. History ruled that the weight of supporting the Russian state should fall on our shoulders. I believe in our ability,

when we feel danger, to put aside everything petty and to remain faithful to our oath.

Tied to this world view was an emphasis on conflict, one in which the Chechen war, spying, or the latest NATO encroachments in what the Kremlin regarded as its natural sphere of interest all came together in a vivid tableau of Western aggression motivated by anti-Russian prejudice. It was the job of the *siloviki* to stand firm in the face of this, for the salvation of Russia, and to root out those who would play the role of Judas, selling out their Motherland for foreign money.

One courageous journalist took Putin to task in 2001 because of the growing violence against Russian reporters. He was reassured by the president, 'You know Aleksei, you are not a traitor, you are an enemy.' What was the difference, and how on earth was that supposed to come as some sort of comfort? Putin explained:

> Enemies are right in front of you, you are at war with them, then you make an armistice with them, and all is clear. A traitor must be destroyed, crushed.

In these statements, by people like Patrushev, Cherkesov, and Putin, the mindset of Russia's new elite was expressed succinctly – and Sergei Skripal would have understood it very well. The GRU were an integral part of the security state, after all. His own decision to betray the organization was expressed to me repeatedly in terms of 'the oath', and in his mind the fact that the entity he had sworn allegiance to, the USSR, no longer existed had absolved him from it. Similarly, while he would have understood Putin's hatred of treachery, Skripal considered that it was not possible to betray an allegiance to something that now existed only as a memory of happier, less conflicted, times.

For MI6, trying to understand these new power realities in the Kremlin, agent FORTHWITH still had value. He got to know his boss at the Moscow regional council, General Boris Gromov, the last commander of the Soviet 40th Army in Afghanistan, and an important *silovik*. And of course he remained part of a tight network with his former colleagues.

It was Putin himself who said, 'There is no such thing as an ex-KGB man,' and the same applied to the GRU. When I asked Skripal what sort of intelligence he had provided during the early 2000s he gave this example:

> So say I would go to a party, and I would ask one of my friends, 'How is Viktor Ivanovich?' They would say, 'Oh he is excited, he is going soon to Paris,' and this way I would know he was the new *rezident* there and could pass this on.

These titbits were passed from FORTHWITH to Stephen during meetings held in a number of European countries. The FSB was consolidating its power step by step, in 2003 for example absorbing the frontier forces and much of Russia's civilian electronic eavesdropping capability. The GRU though remained a distinct centre of power, one independent of Putin and his 'Ozero Circle'. Skripal was well aware from former colleagues how nervous they were about the FSB's growing dominance, and the threat to the GRU's autonomy. During this time, Skripal told me, there were mutterings in the military about launching a coup against Putin, something he was able to tell Stephen about.

Following their introduction in Malaga, there were seven or eight meetings between 2000 and 2004, usually under the cover of Skripal family holidays but sometimes 'business trips'. The drill was usually the same, Stephen would relay the time and place (invariably a hotel room) and Skripal would turn up for a debriefing.

Skripal's respect for his new handler grew with each meeting. He would go through the answers to each of the questions twice, once in English and again in Russian, methodically ironing out any ambiguities. The Russian considered him 'a very professional officer'. No doubt the care with which Jones took down this information reassured Skripal of its continued value.

The MI6 case officer met Skripal during these years in Spain, Portugal, Malta, Italy, and Turkey. It seems that SIS paid Skripal by the meeting, usually around $3,000. While he tried to be as useful as possible in gathering the specific information that Stephen Jones asked him for, occasional thoughts must have crossed Skripal's mind about how long MI6 would continue to find the relationship worthwhile. For while he retained unique insights into the GRU, there were things happening internationally that were causing dramatic changes in the intelligence business.

The al-Qaeda attacks of 11 September 2001 cost thousands of lives and brought about tectonic shifts in international security. President George W. Bush declared a 'Global War On Terror', mobilizing the USA's military, diplomatic, and intelligence resources to the goal of hunting down the jihadist leaders 'dead or alive'.

This call to action was felt across the secret world. Having lost their 'mega-threat' with the passing of the Soviet Union they were given a new one – only more so. Richard Dearlove, Chief of the Secret Intelligence Service at the time, later revealed that whereas the Soviet Bloc (the USSR and its East

European allies) had never consumed more than 38 per cent of MI6's resources at the height of the Cold War, counter-terrorism soon grew to more than 50 per cent of the UK agencies' activity. Dearlove, himself responsible for overseeing this great refocusing of effort, later commented that 9/11 'cast a very dark, long, and enduring shadow' over the intelligence world. It made them complicit with torture, involved rendition of suspects to 'ghost sites', and spawned a major programme of assassination by US drone strike.

In the context of this story though Dearlove's remark goes to another enduring consequence of 9/11: the relegation of work against Russia to a lesser priority and the emergence of Vladimir Putin, for some years at least, as an ally in the counter-terrorist battle. For those involved in Whitehall's secret world there were all kinds of implications to this. Harry Murdoch, who for a few years had galvanized MI6's Russia operations, was sent back to the Middle East and became a key figure in its counter-terrorist effort. And reports from assets like FORTHWITH, alias Skripal, were suddenly of less interest. 'Unfortunately for him,' a Whitehall type who lived through the early 2000s comments, 'Skripal was a fantastic agent, but at the wrong time. After 9/11 his product ended up being only of interest to a handful of CI [counter-intelligence] nerds.'

That comment goes to an essential truth about the post-9/11 period. While some Western intelligence people argue with my characterization of their Russia work having 'lower priority', suggesting it didn't suffer because the total resources available to the agencies expanded greatly to take on the counter-terrorist task, it can hardly be disputed that the political focus had shifted to the jihadist threat. When President Putin flew home from a visit to London in December

2001, Tony Blair described the UK–Russia relationship as 'unprecedentedly close'. He announced efforts to intensify intelligence collaboration.

As for President Bush, who relied on Putin's cooperation to facilitate US operations in Afghanistan, the turnaround was even more dramatic. The two leaders now had a common cause against the jihadist foe, and Putin was able to portray his campaign in Chechnya as part of the same struggle. 'He has confronted some serious attacks in his country,' President Bush remarked, 'I know the strain, I know the agony, I know the sadness that comes with seeing innocent people lose their lives, and we have shared that.' In terms of Russia's wider situation, Bush praised 'an amazing transformation . . . I applaud President Putin'. The CIA, like MI6, was tasked to intensify its cooperation with Russia.

To many in the spying business, Putin's masterstroke was to convince the Washington policy elite that they could not be pursuing multiple agendas. 'In the 1980s we did arms control deals while at the same time we were killing them, in Afghanistan,' a senior CIA officer explains, 'but now the Russians always want us to believe that all these policy areas are linked, so we never hold them accountable.'

This was all the more regrettable for the Russia House at Langley because Bush, during the early months of his presidency, had shown himself willing to 'go big' on the Kremlin's spying operations. Soon after Bush's inauguration in January 2001, the FBI mole Robert Hanssen was arrested, and it emerged what extraordinary damage he'd done to US intelligence operations during years of spying. President Bush expelled fifty Russian diplomats, six of whom had been directly involved in running Hanssen, as a way of showing his displeasure. This readiness to be much firmer in the face of Moscow's spying operations was to prove short-lived, though. 9/11 imposed new imperatives. Keeping supply lines to Afghanistan open meant American diplomats wanted to look the other way when it came to SVR or GRU activity.

For the American or British agent networks in Russia, however, the risks remained the same, even if the bureaucrats in Washington or London were less interested in the product. While the reports coming from penetration operations in Russia were to some extent sidelined, as a consequence of the focus on Middle East terrorism as much as anything else, and the will to prosecute counter-espionage cases in the UK or US evaporated ('diplomatically embarrassing'), the same was not true in Russia. For as Putin had explained to that Russian journalist, enemies you can accommodate or deal with. Traitors must be crushed.

Alexander Zaporozhsky was a case in point. He had been an extremely valuable CIA penetration while serving as deputy chief of the SVR's North America desk. It was rumoured that he might even have been responsible for the exposure of Robert Hanssen. Zaporozhsky had been recruited by the Americans during the free-for-all of the mid-1990s, quitting the SVR a couple of years later, in 1997, before being exfiltrated to the US.

Just two months after the 9/11 attacks, the SVR man, who lived near Baltimore, had been chatting over the phone to friends in Russia who suggested that he join them for a big celebration they were planning. Was that wise? The CIA advised him against travelling back to Russia, but Zaporozhsky's contacts were quite persistent and assured him that he would be perfectly safe. After all, the international mood had changed dramatically, cooperation was the new order of the day between these agencies. What the hell, he would make the trip.

Flying in to Russia late that November, Zaporozhsky was promptly arrested by the FSB. He was put on trial in 2003 for espionage, found guilty, and given a long sentence. Packed off to a labour camp, he will return later in this story.

The Russian authorities had also decided in 2002 to try in absentia Oleg Kalugin, the former KGB general residing in the US, and Alexander Litvinenko, an FSB officer and ardent Putin critic who had gained political asylum in the UK. These two trials, ending within days of one another, 'sent an icy chill through the system', says someone working in Vauxhall Cross at the time: 'This willingness to go after those in exile underscored the priorities of the new people in charge.' With the Putin circle reliant on the power ministries for their grip on power, hardliners held sway, says a CIA type who notes, 'they are out for blood when it comes to counter-intelligence – they see that [Western spying] as an existential threat'.

Skripal meanwhile continued travelling to his meetings with Stephen Jones during the years that followed the 9/11 'new page' in relations. In this sense, intelligence professionals on both sides continued to wage their secret war. It looked like business as usual. But the difference was that the priority given to it by Western spooks had lessened, along with the will to prosecute Russian penetrations. It's possible that the relative improvement in the climate of international relations may have convinced Skripal that the danger involved in what he was doing had diminished but if he was labouring under any illusions of this kind, they were shattered in 2004.

He flew that October from Moscow's Sheremetyevo airport to Izmir in Turkey, then took a cab to the Hilton Hotel in the centre of town. From there it was a short walk to the pleasant promenade beside the Aegean, a few decent restaurants, and the luxury hotel where Stephen Jones had checked in. There the MI6 case officer delivered an unwelcome bombshell.

Earlier that year, word had reached the British of the panicked flight to Spain of a Russian woman, *Irina Burlatov, and her two young daughters. Immediately upon arrival in the airport they asked for political asylum and were soon interviewed by an officer of the Guardia Civil who, realizing the importance of these circumstances, alerted the national intelligence service.

Irina was the wife of Captain Yuri Burlatov, the Madrid *rezidentura* GRU officer who Skripal had pinpointed in 1996 as having been involved in the diversion of official funds. The British had passed this on to their allies, and, presumably using this *kompromat*, the Spanish recruited Burlatov. Upon the completion of his tour a few years after Skripal, the captain had also returned to work in the Glass House in Moscow. Anglo-Spanish cooperation had thus delivered a great intelligence bounty: they had maintained penetration of GRU headquarters across several years through these two assets. But something had gone dreadfully wrong.

In the spring of 2004, Burlatov had been arrested and subjected to harsh FSB interrogation then delivered to a military hospital for a psychological check-up. When she came to see him on a visit, Irina found her husband dead in his hospital bed, showing marks of strangulation and with some fingers cut off. The official explanation was suicide, but by the severing of fingers a grisly message was being sent. Traumatized, Irina had swiftly taken the decision to leave for Spain. Understanding their debt to her husband, the Spanish granted her asylum and compensation for his secret work.

This dreadful drama had played out shortly before the Izmir meeting. While Skripal had his suspicions about Burlatov's possible recruitment, and the two had remained professional acquaintances in Moscow, he had not, for the good of the two of them, ever delved into detail about whether the captain had also become an agent. MI6's Russia operations people decided, though, that Skripal had to be told about Burlatov's exposure and arrest. They likely spared him some of the awful detail that Irina had told the Spanish but the key point was that if one asset had been exposed, it was quite possible that Skripal had also been. Stephen asked the Russian if he wanted to be exfiltrated, or simply not return to Moscow. Ways could be found to bring Liudmila and Yulia. His son Sasha was already out of the country.

Skripal thought it over. He didn't consider himself under particular risk. He hadn't noticed anything suspicious, and his unfortunate colleague might have been discovered in various ways. No, he would return to Moscow. It was a bad decision.

As he made his way back from Stephen's hotel to his own there were plenty of people on the tree-lined street. After the long summer, Turks and foreigners alike were enjoying the autumnal evening cool. Skripal might have fancied his counter-surveillance skills, or been over-confident perhaps after eight years of this double life. But he was being followed, and had not detected it.

PART TWO

PRISONER

9

INSIDE LEFORTOVO

The block where the Skripals lived in Krilatskoye, west of Moscow, had risen in the early 1980s, thrusting confidently skywards just as the party's gerontocracy faltered, power passing between four leaders in the few years it took to build the estate.

The Skripals' flat was in a seventeen-storey tower where hundreds of families raised their kids, brought home their monthly roubles, and prayed that the elevators didn't pack up. Yulia had gone to School No. 63 nearby, the shops were a short walk away, and there was even a neighbourhood police office in the next block. And it was to that local Militsia post that Skripal made his way on 15 December 2004.

The colonel's permit to keep firearms at home was up for renewal. And since he kept the little .22 pistol that Yuri Bur-latov had given him in Spain it was best to sort things out. But he barely made it through the door.

Masked men leapt on him, twisting his arms behind his back, then pulled his coat down around his shoulders to immobilize him further. Nobody wanted to take chances with a prize boxer. The FSB men then snapped on cuffs and hooded him. There was one guy filming, and before they put the bag on his head they made sure to get some nice footage of him squirming. Then they bundled him into the dark blue minivan that had just pulled up. He had been lifted by the FSB.

The journey from Krilatskoye took the best part of an hour. Trussed up in the FSB's van, the prisoner was sped east, across the Moscow River, and on to the Third Ring Road, heading around the north of the city. From there it was a short stretch up the Lefortovsky Ban to a place that has brought dread to generations of Russians.

Skripal was booked in as a prisoner at Lefortovo. Everybody understood that once you were at Lefortovo you were entering a netherworld.

Lefortovo was finished in 1881, and immediately assumed the character of a political prison. That's not to say there were not some straightforward villains among its inmates, as Skripal would soon discover, but that its most noted prisoners had always been those accused of political crimes: dissent, espionage, and treason.

The Tsars' secret police, the Okhrana, had used it to beat confessions out of student radicals, but it was really under the Bolsheviks that it became a key part in the industrial process of torture, confession, and liquidation. It was the Cheka's facility, then the OGPU's, the MGB's, the NKVD's, and finally the KGB's. The acronyms had changed but the process had continued, generation following generation, the cycle of political crime and punishment. The fabric hadn't altered much either, four storeys of solid brickwork and the curious layout of the cell-blocks, forming a 'K' on one flank of the central prison admin building.

In 1996, the new thought police, the FSB, had taken charge of the jail. Back in the 1930s many an inmate had been dispatched in the central yard, a cold Tokarev to the back of the head, a plaintive cry from the prisoner of 'Long Live Comrade Stalin!' and then oblivion. 'Sentenced without right of correspondence', as the secret policemen euphemistically called it. After the Stalin regime, things changed. Summary execution was out, mind-numbingly long interrogations of dissidents like Alexander Solzhenitsyn and the 'Refuseniks' including Natan Sharansky became the order of the day. Political prisoners from the Brezhnev years spoke of cells without beds, damp concrete floors, and trying to stop themselves going mad in a twilight world where they were never fully asleep or wide awake.

The KGB had termed Lefortovo an 'Investigative Isolator', and although it would be fair to say the regime had liberalized somewhat after the collapse of Soviet communism, even in 2004 its obsession with isolating the prisoners from one another held true.

Walking under escort to his cell, Skripal noticed the curious and obsessive rituals observed by the turnkeys, procedures that certainly went back to the Soviet years and perhaps even to the tsars. Approaching each security door, stairwell, or junction the guards would stop and click their fingers. If they heard clicks returned from around the corner or through the door, further wordless signals would follow. At intervals along each corridor there were cupboard-like boxes, and if a warder divined that he must give way to a colleague escorting another prisoner, the first would be walked into one of these odd cubicles and the door shut behind him. The other detainee would then pass, unseen, through the corridor, and once at a safe distance, signalled by more of the inevitable clicks, the first man would be brought out of the cupboard, and his journey resumed. These routines of signalling were so much a part of daily life in the jail that inmates of Lefortovo ended up scrutinizing the warders' hands. Some carried metal clickers. Why not? You might wear your fingers out otherwise with this crazy routine. Skripal soon grasped the purpose of it. The old KGB concept of 'investigative isolation' dictated that people accused of involvement in a conspiracy should never be able to see whether their co-accused were in there, let alone communicate with them. Control would then remain in the interrogators' hands, to use the 'your friend has told us everything' ploy, or engineer a dramatic face-to-face confrontation between a turned suspect and an unbroken one.

Reaching his cell, the retired colonel soon realized that he was not going to be held in solitary. The surprisingly spacious room had three beds, each bolted to the floor. He endured the first night, always the hardest, and began to get to know his cellmates and the Lefortovo routine.

There was Sasha, 'a real Moscow bandit, he'd killed three policemen and for this reason he was charged with terrorism rather than a simple crime'. He lived up to the popular image of a hardened criminal, '190cm high, broad too, and covered with tattoos'. There are elaborate jailhouse codes spelt out in the ink on a Russian convict's body. They can show the type of crimes he's been convicted of, his gang affiliation, even sexual preferences. But what the retired colonel noticed was that many of Sasha's tattoos seemed to have far-right, even Nazi, themes.

As for the other cellmate, let's call him *Oleg, Skripal liked the look of him even less. He was a smaller man, quieter too. So what was wrong with Oleg? Skripal objected to the tone of his remarks and he didn't trust him. Along with the tattoos and jail-house routines, every Russian has heard of the *stukatchi*, the prison informers who share a cell, trying to extract information from a target inmate. After a few nights, and a smart remark too many, Skripal handed Oleg a good beating. And with that pumping of fists into his cowering cellmate, maybe Colonel Sergei Skripal, one-time member of the GRU's 1st Commission, now reduced to the status of common prisoner, worked out some of the anger and confusion engendered by his fall from grace. Sasha, of course, didn't get involved. The following day Oleg was removed from the cell, and in the weeks and months that stretched out ahead, nobody replaced him. That was just fine by Sergei and Sasha, each had established that the other was not to be trifled with, and over time a sound rapport built between them.

The routines of Lefortovo came to dominate every hour of his life during the crushing, dark weeks of that first winter. The prison day ran from 6am to 10pm when 'lights out' was officially called. There were three square meals, and the menu was on a three-day cycle. Once a week they would be individually escorted for a shower – with the inevitable finger-clicking there and back to the cell. The sheets were changed once a week also. Smokers got given a packet of cigarettes every day.

After a few repetitions of the cycle, it was in January 2005, oh happy day, Liudmila was allowed her first visit. The inmates of Lefortovo were at least allowed certain privileges in the new Russia, as befits people who have not yet been convicted. They were permitted to wear their own clothes, and their visitors could bring other goods and comforts that, after suitable inspection, were allowed in their cell. Once a month they were allowed a parcel too, up to 10kg, usually made up of clothes and food. Liudmila made sure that a TV and small fridge got delivered, which made Sergei even more popular with his tattooed cellmate.

What touched Sergei most though was that during her monthly visits, lasting around forty minutes a time, she would bring him home-cooked food. Meatballs and gravy with kasha, cured fish, you name it. What an angel! And while he knew that he could rely on his fists to get him through some situations in there, Skripal understood from the outset that it was the love and support of his family alone that would sustain him through the daily interrogations.

These began soon after his arrival and went on, with only occasional breaks, for months. Out of the cell at 9am, up the corridors, clicking fingers, to the interrogation room in the FSB Investigations Department, back four hours later. He'd have some time off then back up for more. Sometimes two sessions a day, sometimes three.

Such is the formalism of the Lefortovo process, and the veneer of legality that surrounds it, that the interrogators observe their own protocols. Sessions cannot last longer than four hours, and his questioners kept to a shift pattern. Over the months he added them up – there had been seventeen different FSB officers asking the questions. The interrogation rooms have exterior windows, but in keeping with the old KGB 'isolator' principles, they had been covered with paper so that light could come through but there could be no looking across the courtyard or glimpses caught of other inmates.

At night, lying in his cell, Skripal would mull over the day's interrogation. Was he going to end up like Yuri Burlatov, murdered in prison? They still wanted to find things out from him, try to get him to the point where he would confess everything in return for some leniency. Maybe that would keep him alive for the time being.

As for the sessions themselves, they followed a certain format. 'Against me, they never used physical force,' Skripal recalled, 'they knew I could take pain, it would not work.' He had certain rights also – for example to plead Article 51 under the penal code in court, which allowed the suspect to avoid self-incrimination.

The questioning itself followed monotonous and repeated cycles; endless details of his identity, his service, his routines in Malta or Madrid, his contacts with foreign intelligence services. What was their game? Trying to catch him in lies? Or was it just the ponderous stumbling, day after day, of seventeen different interrogators who each felt they had to go through the motions, ticking off their own checklist?

Of course he could deduce a certain amount from their questions. He was asked again and again about the .22 pistol that Yuri had given him. Was it some kind of payback or honorary gift from the CIA? Ridiculous. Stupid questions like that give the suspect strength. And he was asked about his businesses and other contacts in Madrid.

He knew of course that Yuri had been through Lefortovo too, before his murder, and began to obsess on the idea that he had been broken in interrogation. But what did Yuri actually know about Sergei and his contacts with Richard Bagnall or Stephen Jones? Very little. It was Sergei who had spotted Yuri after all, not the other way around. But some of the information underlying the interrogators' questions about Madrid could have been underpinned by things Yuri had told them.

They knew something, his FSB interrogators, that was for sure. He'd happily talk about the pistol all day long. But there were other things that had been found in the Skripals' flat. Bank statements from Spain, and that souvenir given to him by Richard on the day he took Sergei's family to the flamenco club.

Little by little it became clear also that they had logged his trips abroad. They knew a lot about Izmir, and of course it dawned on Sergei that he'd been under surveillance, but somewhat less about his previous journey abroad, to Malta, early in 2004. Well of course that told him something about how long he'd been under close scrutiny. Had Yuri broken in interrogation or done a deal? Of course he couldn't be sure, but what did Yuri really know about his dealings with MI6 anyway?

Early in 2005, far away from the ongoing interrogations in Lefortovo, Stephen Jones checked into a hotel. It was a nice place, somewhere pleasant with good food and a few sights. But Stephen knew the drill. He would wait in his room, read a book perhaps, mark time until his asset turned up. But of course FORTHWITH did not arrive. He was engaged in altogether less convivial conversations in the KGB's infamous lock-up.

Stephen returned home. Skripal was a no-show. There were protocols to be followed at Vauxhall Cross. There could be no attempts to contact their agent or Liudmila – that could just make things worse for the prisoner. Discreet inquiries via the Russian authorities, ditto, they would just establish Skripal's guilt. The counter-intelligence people were all over it too. The arrest and murder of Captain Burlatov, well, that was one thing. He might have made an awful mistake, revealed himself by a slip in his communications or in a drunken moment of candour with a colleague. But two GRU penetrations lifted within six months of each other? No, there was something else going on here that called for a full-scale counter-intelligence investigation.

Over months in his Russian interrogation room, Skripal knew that nearly all of these FSB questions could be answered truthfully or by reference to cover stories. The souvenir? That was just something his friend the Gibraltarian businessman had given him. That gun? It was a present from a fellow Russian officer. Invisible ink? He had needed it to show his own agents how to communicate. And as for the questions about his last couple of trips abroad, well, if they'd actually spotted him talking to British spooks, why not confront him with the evidence? Skripal deduced that the surveillance in Izmir could not have followed him up to Stephen's room nor identified the MI6 man as he arrived or left the hotel.

Skripal understood what many Western counter-espionage professionals knew during the Cold War, that spying is not an easy crime to prosecute, particularly if those under suspicion had observed decent tradecraft and held their nerve during interrogation. As the questions came around one time after another, sessions after session, day by day, and as he noticed small variations in the interrogators' routine a conviction grew in him. He and Yuri had been dropped in the same shit because of a mole.

They had the gun, they had some of his secret writing things they'd found in his flat, well, yes, that was awkward. But he had an explanation for that too, of course, that a GRU officer naturally had these things, a leftover of his agent work overseas. Then they had evidence that his spending and lifestyle were inconsistent with someone living on a GRU colonel's pension. But they couldn't tie him to anyone specific in MI6, even on that last trip to Izmir, when they'd been following and filming him. They couldn't prove any intelligence had passed between him and them. And as for his money, he went over it again and again, he'd been doing business. So why was he sitting there? Like any trained, competent intelligence officer, the cycle of questions that whirred around his head started and finished with the possibility of a penetration.

And as the interrogations went on through 2005, his early inkling grew into certainty. These second-rate FSB guys had been given the task of preparing a court case against him. But the reason he was slammed up in Lefortovo was because someone had ratted him out, likely betrayed Yuri too, and that fact, that person, had to be protected at all costs. Somehow these FSB people would have to concoct something for the court that would prove his guilt but protect the source of their intelligence.

This mind game took months to reach its conclusion, and while he had no idea how long he would endure this tedious interrogation and walking up and down the corridors, he felt he could hold on, just as he had held on all those times in the ring. He had the love of his wife and kids, somehow everything would turn out OK.

In 2006 the day arrived for his trial to begin. It would be heard in a military court, almost all of it in camera. Sessions continued sporadically for months, culminating in the verdict in October, two years after he had been arrested. There had been some interesting evidence shown in court, surveillance footage of him leaving Sheremetyevo for Izmir for example. There were also some bank statements produced that had been recovered from his flat. They show an account opened early in 2004 (during the visit to Malaga when he had met Richard and Stephen), and in one it can be seen that he had received two payments in euro amounts equivalent to $3,000.

Some of the charges amused Skripal, for example, some allegations relating to Madrid late in 1992, several months before he had been posted there. He suspected that the prosecutors had made a crass mistake, copying and pasting elements of their indictment against Yuri Burlatov, who was serving in Madrid at that time, into his own file.

He had parried many of the accusations, shrugged off others, and when all else failed, relied on Article 51 to avoid self-incrimination. But of course this was not some battle of great forensic minds in which the most coherent case would triumph. This was a process designed to reach a particular conclusion, and he could never have doubted a guilty verdict, which came on 9 August 2006. He was sentenced to thirteen years in a labour camp.

The case produced headlines and a good deal of interest from the Russian media. The Chief Military Prosecutor, Sergei Fridinsky, interviewed on Russian TV that evening, said this about Skripal's spying:

> The damage cannot be measured in roubles or in terms of anything else. The fact is that the interests of the Russian Federation have been damaged by the dissemination of classified information. And as a result of this any consequences could have ensued regarding the activity that was the subject of this trade, because, of course, money was paid for this information.

Russian reporting contained a blend of truth – for example that he had been recruited in Spain or that Spanish bank statements had been found in his flat – exaggeration, and complete fiction. It was alleged in one Russian report that Skripal had been paid $50,000 a meeting, in another that he had got $100,000 in total for his spying, and elsewhere that he had been paid $3,000 per month.

In fact the payments, it seems, were per meeting, and from the moment that FORTHWITH provided his GRU organizational chart in that Madrid hotel there were something in the order of fifteen or sixteen meetings (including Liudmila's two 'book deliveries' to Richard). Sometimes there were bonuses for specific titbits. His reward was, then, probably in the $70–90,000 bracket, though of course MI6's commitment to house and look after him if he ever defected involved far larger sums.

The FSB cover story about why they had become interested in him emerged in its fullest form in a 2014 documentary, *A Mole in the Aquarium*, in which an FSB colonel, Andrei Sharov, was interviewed in silhouette. Sharov pointed to Skripal's post-retirement socializing with GRU friends, saying, 'I think he became of interest to counter-intelligence, because as a pensioner he became very interested in the affairs of his former colleagues, which naturally aroused suspicion.' As for the proof of Skripal's guilt Colonel Sharov added:

> Counter-intelligence officers became interested in the source of his income. In Spain it turned out he had an account into which three thousand dollars was flowing every month, and nobody knew where from. It was concrete proof that the man was linked to espionage.

By the time of his trial, Russian media was already taking its cues from FSB and other officials about blackening traitors' names. Many of these themes, such as the moral corruption, greed, or egocentricity of those who spied for the West were familiar from Soviet times. Russian reporting on the Skripal case tried to undermine him in other ways too with claims that were perhaps designed to damage MI6's faith in their own asset.

It was suggested for example that Skripal had cooperated fully with his interrogators, making a full written confession, and tried to plea-bargain a reduction in his sentence. A Russian website claimed that he had pleaded guilty to charges of treason and espionage. Since the actual proceedings of the court were in closed session, there is no definitive record. However, in his conversations with me, he was adamant that he had turned down a plea bargain and, as we will see, his refusal to admit to his guilt became a complicating factor in discussions years later about his possible release.

In Skripal's account of his interrogation the investigators had tried and failed to prove that he had communicated secrets during his trips abroad. Faced with the task of putting him on trial without proof, a confession or guilty plea would have turned the whole matter around for the FSB. He says they therefore offered him a sentence of five to six years if he confessed to that, a term that might reduce to two to three years with parole.

Western intelligence officers have offered me differing views about the extent to which Skripal did or did not confess. Those who support his version point out that in cases where those accused of espionage in Lefortovo had really broken and told all, there was often no trial. Or the convicted spy would be quietly released shortly after sentencing. There were many matters, also, relating to his career as an SIS asset that did not emerge at the time of his trial or in the various

Russian media hit pieces about him. These details, such as his method of communicating via secret writing in books, do not appear to have been discovered by his interrogators.

However, others I've spoken to do think it is quite possible that he gave up extensive details of his espionage during interrogation. From my perspective it is noteworthy that Russian media accounts, such as the 2014 documentary, seem to contain a blend of things that likely did come from Skripal's interrogations and others that are simply wrong and maybe reflect the journalists' or investigators' erroneous suppositions.

As Skripal's case concluded, Russian TV was given a short clip of the verdict being read out in the Moscow Military Court. A prosecutor dressed in a black legal robe announced he had been found guilty and the sentence was passed.

Skripal was shown in those reports wearing a tracksuit, caged in the dock, and chatting amiably enough to his lawyer. Whatever the superficial dignity with which he negotiated his trial, everything was about to change. Wearing your own clothes, getting frequent family visits and generous food parcels were features of being on remand in Lefortovo. He was now a convict entering the criminal netherworld, on his way to a harsh regime institution in the Gulag.

10

LITVINENKO

A few months after Skripal's sentencing, on 1 November 2006, a former FSB officer living in exile in London made his way to a smart hotel in London's Mayfair, the Millennium, for an afternoon meeting with an old associate, another former KGB man called Andrei Lugovoi, and someone else he'd dragged along, Dmitri Kovtun. The ex-FSB man, Alexander Litvinenko, had become a part of that world where corporate, personal, and espionage interests blend together. He was hoping to use Lugovoi, who, unlike him, could still travel freely to and from Moscow, as a discreet correspondent in the Russian capital, finding out about people and companies that were of interest to London-based commercial clients.

Upstairs, in the hotel's Pine Bar, Lugovoi and his associate were knocking back the drinks, consuming gin and tonics and a champagne cocktail, and a £15 cigar for good measure. They also ordered a pot of green tea for three, Lugovoi knowing that Litvinenko was not a great boozer. After a while Kovtun, who Litvinenko had only met once before and did not like the look of, complained of being hungover and left the bar, presumably heading up to his room. 'We're going to be leaving soon,' Lugovoi said to Litvinenko, 'if you want some tea, then there is some here, you can have some of this.'

Observing the social niceties, Litvinenko took a few sips. As things were drawing to a close, Lugovoi's wife and eight-year-old son appeared. He introduced the boy to the ex-FSB man and the party broke up.

At home in Muswell Hill that evening, Litvinenko and his wife enjoyed a quiet celebration. It was six years to the day since they had escaped Russia and arrived in the UK.

It was not long after going to bed, at about 11.10pm, that Litvinenko began to feel very ill. He went to the bathroom and vomited violently. And that was just the start of it. Every twenty or so minutes, racked by convulsions, he returned to the toilet. He retched and retched until only bile came out and he was frothing at the mouth. The next day passed in agony, despite attempted remedies, and by the early hours of 3 November his wife Marina was calling an ambulance to take him to their local hospital.

Litvinenko's condition gradually worsened: on 7 November Marina first shared with the doctors the possibility that he'd been poisoned; on the 11th his hair started to fall out in great clumps; and by the 14th doctors treating him were starting to look seriously at the possibility of poisoning. Two weeks after his first admission, Litvinenko was transferred to University College Hospital in central London, and the police were brought in.

Two detectives interviewed Litvinenko, who immediately made clear his suspicion that he had been poisoned. He also let them know, a little coyly, that he had a contact in MI6 who was then called by police. As for the possible motive of the poisoning:

I have no doubt whatsoever that this was done by the Russian Secret Services. Having knowledge of this system I know that the order about such a killing of a citizen of another country on its territory, especially if it is something to do with Great Britain, could have been given by only one person.

Litvinenko then explicitly blamed Putin – and his testimony to the two detectives was promptly classified. It did not become public for eight and a half years. Hours after giving his statement, Litvinenko was moved to intensive care and on 23 November he died. 'You may succeed in silencing one man,' his last statement read, 'but the howl of protest from around the world will reverberate, Mr Putin, in your ears for the rest of your life.'

Hours before his death, having scrapped their diagnosis of poisoning by thallium, scientists at the Atomic Weapons Establishment Aldermaston had finally identified the poison as a rare radioactive isotope, polonium 210. Investigations with Geiger counters had revealed nothing: they are designed to detect more common forms of radiation, gamma emitters, but polonium can only be found by looking for alpha traces.

Once they had cracked the riddle of the poison, detectives retraced Litvinenko's steps and those of the men he had met on 1 November. An alarming picture emerged.

In the weeks leading up to the Millennium meeting, Lugovoi had twice tried to poison his target. Both times, as he did after the successful attempt, he had flushed polonium down hotel sinks, leaving astronomical radiation readings in those three different places.

In the days before that fateful get-together, Kovtun had flown to Hamburg with another vial of polonium. Aeroplane seats also showed high levels of polonium. German police, following up Kovtun's part in it, had spoken to a friend of his in Hamburg. This witness alleged the Russian had told him, 'Litvinenko is a traitor! He has blood on his hands!' He spoke about giving the ex-spy a rare poison and when asked by his friend why they didn't just shoot him, Kovtun replied, 'It's meant to set an example.'

These investigations, percolating up the police, MI6, and government chain of command, soon set alarm bells ringing in Whitehall. If this was a state-sponsored murder the entire Anglo-Russian relationship could be jeopardized. For their part, the Russian government and commentators replied with a number of alternative narratives – MI6 had killed him, it was a Russian mafia feud, or the culprit was none other than his old patron, the exiled oligarch Boris Berezovsky, who had also been given asylum in London.

President Putin, asked in February 2007 at a press conference about a number of recent murders, said that it would be for a court to determine responsibility. As for Litvinenko, he 'was dismissed from the security services', noted Putin, 'there was no need to run anywhere, he did not have any secrets. Everything negative that he could say with respect to his service, he already said long ago'.

The implied notion, that a victim didn't merit murdering, echoed his response to the death in October 2006 of a prominent Russian journalist, Anna Politkovskaya. She had been a vociferous critic of Putin and the Chechen war, and many in Moscow believed she had been assassinated on Kremlin orders. Challenged on this while visiting Germany, Putin replied that Politkovskaya was indeed a government critic, but 'the degree of her influence over political life in Russia was extremely insignificant'.

The concept that murdering opponents was implausible because it wasn't worth the effort was made explicit by Russian Foreign Minister Sergei Lavrov. He responded to a question on the Litvinenko case: 'Why would the intelligence services spend millions in order to send to kingdom come a former rank-and-file agent, whose absurd allegations against them have long ceased to be taken seriously?'

They had found in this approach a way of ridiculing Western allegations while at the same time denying the victim or their loved ones any sympathy.

'As the Chekists have become entrenched in power,' Politkovskaya wrote in 2004, 'we have let them see our fear, and thereby have only intensified their urge to treat us like cattle. The KGB respects only the strong. The weak it devours. We of all people ought to know that.'

The many cases of political murder in Russia, including hers, had demonstrated a technique of political management. It was important for the authorities to allow certain investigations to go on, or at least appear to do so. These often ended up pointing the finger at the Russian mafia or hired assassins, but left unsolved the question of who was ultimately responsible. This approach was now deployed in the Litvinenko case, perhaps based on a Russian calculation that British politicians had no more interest in following it to its final conclusions than the Kremlin did.

British detectives were allowed, late in 2006, to visit Russia and question, albeit under restricted circumstances, Lugovoi and Kovtun. But when this process pointed clearly in the direction of Lugovoi's guilt, Scotland Yard charging him (in absentia) with murder in May 2007, the Kremlin shifted its ground.

Lugovoi was found a seat in the Duma, giving him immunity from prosecution or extradition, and the battle of wills between London and Moscow moved to the issue of possible trial in a third country, something that was never likely to happen but testified to Moscow's ostensible willingness to find a solution. Lugovoi took a lie-detector test also, which he passed.

In London, meanwhile, the murder posed its own problems. Although the Scotland Yard investigation had pointed clearly to a criminal conspiracy using a very rare substance obtained in a Russian state facility, Downing Street did not want to endorse in any way Litvinenko's dying accusation that it had all been done on Putin's orders. As long as there were plausible alternative theories – from rogue elements in the FSB to organized crime – why paint yourself into a diplomatic corner that could easily derail the entire national relationship with Russia?

People in Vauxhall Cross of course had their own view. Several officers in the P5s or Russia sections had known Litvinenko well and they were both shocked and angered by his demise. 'He was a completely irrepressible character', one MI6 man noted of Litvinenko, 'always talking, always fizzing with ideas and theories.'

Although he had not been an MI6 agent when he arrived in the UK in 2000, Alexander Litvinenko was by 2003 meeting officers of the agency regularly. They had limited insights into the FSB and its thinking and found him an excellent sounding board, so much so that from 2004 they were paying him £2,000 a month as a 'consultant'. In return, Litvinenko came in for meetings, provided background on leading FSB personalities, and was lent out to friendly services.

During 2006, he travelled on a few occasions to Spain, where prosecutors were preparing two trials of Russian mafia figures. Litvinenko knew much about the connections between organized crime and the FSB, and the emergence of this work informed one of the main explanations about the motive for the poisoning and its timing, for one of these trials got under way as he lay dying in hospital.

Litvinenko's work with MI6 and the Spanish authorities provided an explanation or even justification for some as to why he had been murdered. But if the Kremlin was responsible, Litvinenko had probably long sealed his fate by being an ally of Boris Berezovsky.

Having made a fortune after the Soviet collapse by dealing in cars, oil, and a variety of other enterprises, Berezovsky personified pretty much everything the FSB bosses hated. He had benefited enormously from the USSR's collapse, become a close ally of Yeltsin, was intimately involved with negotiating what the *siloviki* regarded as the humiliating end to the First Chechen War, and was Jewish to boot. When Putin campaigned in 2000 on his 'Dictatorship of Law' slogan, Berezovsky was exactly the type of target he had in mind.

Nearly three years before he arrived in Britain, Litvinenko, then a serving lieutenant colonel, went to Berezovsky with the extraordinary revelation that he had been ordered by his FSB boss to kill the tycoon. There followed a period of conflict with the authorities, a press conference by Litvinenko and other FSB dissenters, and finally time in jail before the intelligence officer fled the country.

Once in London, Litvinenko was initially very much Berezovsky's creature, taking money from him and co-authoring a book, *Blowing Up Russia*, that accused the FSB of carrying out the 1999 apartment bombings as false-flag operations that would create a pretext for a second Chechen War. Later their relationship became more distant. From a Russian perspective, it was London's willingness to give asylum to the tycoon and former FSB officer that did much to sour the post-9/11 spirit of cooperation. The Kremlin regarded the British playing host to people making such incendiary and hostile claims as a basic breach of good faith.

The relevance to the wider story of the Litvinenko affair is that it began to undermine those in Whitehall who felt the imperfections of Russian democracy should be overlooked in the interests of trade and close cooperation (for example through the United Nations Security Council) on a whole range of world problems. Litvinenko's murder and Russia's refusal to extradite the suspects were just too egregious to be ignored.

Of course all of this was meant to send a message within Russia. In consolidating his power Putin was dealing with an issue that had long bugged the *siloviki*, the removal in 1996 of the ultimate sanction for treachery. Shortly before the poisoning of Litvinenko, Russia's parliament, the Duma, had passed a new law allowing for the elimination of terrorists outside Russia's borders. This was intended principally as a means of providing legal cover for operations to kill Chechen militants who had gone into exile, however some also regarded it as providing a more general rubric for dispatching 'traitors' abroad. Whether dealing with rebels in the north Caucasus, corrupt businessmen, or those tempted to spy for the West, what Putin and the *siloviki* realized was that fear was very useful to them. The days of Article 64 and the firing squad might be gone, but there were other ways to stimulate that emotion. If someone felt they might be eliminated then they were far more likely to be obedient.

At MI6, where John Scarlett had become chief in 2004, Litvinenko's murder derailed the twin-track policy he had long favoured – of maintaining liaison relationships with the Russians while at the same time upping the espionage effort against them. Cooperation with the SVR had to be suspended as these events subtly strengthened the hand of those in his service and elsewhere who saw profound moral hazard in cosying up to Putin and his dubious friends.

And what of the importance of Litvinenko's tragedy to Sergei Skripal? The murder was instructive in many ways: in showing the willingness of elements within Russia to murder in the UK; in the use of a rare poison that was traced back to a state institution; and in establishing how the Kremlin would respond to the grave accusation of sponsoring assassination overseas. As we will see, the Litvinenko affair also – rightly or wrongly – defined the response of many in the British state to what happened in Salisbury in March 2018.

None of this was apparent of course in November 2006, as Litvinenko lay dying in University College Hospital. For at that time, following his sentence, Skripal was adjusting to the grim reality of his thirteen-year sentence, and to a life transported away from those he loved so deeply.

11

IK 5

The train to Pot'ma leaves from Moscow's Kazan Station and rattles 500 kilometres to the east, into the isolation of Mordovia. These days an express can do the journey in under eight hours. But the condemned travel at a more leisurely speed.

It is in Pot'ma that the convicted are inducted through a transit camp. Their clothes and valuables are taken from them and they are given a suit of dark grey or blue clothes in which to begin their journey into the misery of captivity. After processing they are ready for their trip north on a narrow-gauge railway built in the early years of Stalin's terror. Thousands of poor wretches who'd been sent to Mordovia had to carve a path through the forest of pine and birch, laying the tracks that would bring successive waves of raw material for the camps that sprang up along the iron way. And in patches marked by simple wooden markers along the route, many of them still lie where overwork, malnutrition, and the harsh prison regime brought them to an early end.

This corridor runs fifty kilometres to the other side of the green desert to Barashevo, where there's another mainline railway station. Along its length are more than a dozen camps that form a penal colony for more than ten thousand inmates known as the Dubrovlag. There were decades when the number of camps swelled to dozens, others when it shrank back to just a few. For the Dubrovlag and the communities it supported the 1940s were a boom time, the 1970s also, with its combination of dissidents and 'Refusenik' Jews who'd applied for visas to go to Israel. Then things got a little leaner, the Jews were sent to Perm instead by the Gulag management in Moscow, and then in the mid-1980s Mikhail Gorbachev arrived. He had actually pledged to get rid of political prisoners, long an important part of the Dubrovlag's trade, and for a few years he achieved his ambition.

Each penal colony or Izpravitelno Kolony has its number and its purpose. In the 1970s, the dissidents were sent to IK 1, IK 3, or IK 19. In IK 14 they put the female 'politicals'. There is one for foreigners, and a couple for known sex offenders. The people who run the Dubrovlag have learnt to keep certain types separate, in the interests of good order. Everybody heading into the Mordovian forest knows about convict law, with its hierarchies and vicious enforcement of cell-block discipline.

Skripal was sent to Izpravitelno Kolony 5, IK 5, where like so many before he endured the customary period of hospital 'quarantine' before being assigned to a block. The concept is a medical one, naturally, in which any infectious diseases will show themselves before the convict or *zek* mixes freely among the wider jail population. But it also serves a psychological purpose, as a time for adjustment, an airlock, between the outside world and the closed reality of the Dubrovlag. Even in quarantine the new man can learn what awaits from other *zeks* and guards. Skripal soon discovered that IK 5 'was a camp for people with epaulettes', as he put it wryly. Many of the convicts there were policemen, army officers, even the odd disgraced FSB type. Such prisoners had to be kept apart from gangsters, murderers, and politicals who might have a score to settle.

In time, as the new *zek* was assigned a block and detachment, he was able to get the lie of the land and reassure himself about his own physical safety. For Skripal soon gravitated towards a group of convicts who'd served in the VDV or airborne forces. His time in elite groups such as reconnaissance companies, his age, physical presence, and rank of colonel gave him a natural authority among them. VDV veterans 'formed my first circle of protection in the camp'. In every walk of life, Russians seek a 'roof' or 'circle' to guard against the vicissitudes of fate, and Skripal well understood that in IK 5 that would be more important than almost anywhere else. If some bully was looking for a prisoner to put the squeeze on, the arguments against picking on a guy within a gang of paratroopers were self-evident.

He got to know the warders, little by little, too. And they told him tales about how their fathers and grandfathers had come there decades before. This had a sobering effect on Skripal, Lord knows nobody could doubt his patriotism, but this was a sick place, somewhere being a camp guard had become a hereditary family occupation – like fishing or farming in the world beyond the watchtowers. There had been nothing there before the Dubrovlag. But with its founding, little townships had sprung up along the narrow-gauge line for those who ran and serviced the penal colony. And their sons or daughters had followed them into the trade of managing human misery. There was simply nothing else to do around there. In IK 5 there were some third-generation warders. Most pathetic of all were the ex-prisoners who had joined their one-time overlords in these little communities once their sentences were over. These broken spirits found they lacked the money and motivation to leave – family having died or deserted them during their years of penal servitude – and simply stayed in Mordovia, making a living doing menial jobs during their twilight years. Nobody who understood Sergei would imagine that would happen to him: he was a fighter of course and he knew from his time in Lefortovo that he could depend on the constancy, love, and devotion of Liudmila, Sasha, and Yulia.

Mordovia's brief summer gives way suddenly to autumn, and that season is also all too short-lived. Winter is king in those miserable forests. There is snow on the ground for four to five months and temperatures below –30C can be recorded. In the gloom of those short days, many succumb to despair. 'Grey faces, grey or blue jackets, grey barracks, and grey fences', wrote another Dubrovlag inmate, 'even the snow, powdered over with coal dust, had lost its whiteness.'

The layout of IK 5 divided its workshops from the accommodation blocks. It was part of the communist penal philosophy that people transported to these colonies should redeem themselves through labour. In Skripal's camp there was a shop for woodworking and one for making metal pylons, and a place where army and prison uniforms were sewn. It was in the last that the former colonel was employed. The dormitory blocks in IK 5 held something like twelve hundred *zeks*, making it one of the bigger places in the Mordovian complex.

Skripal would joke to other prisoners that IK 5 was more comfortable than some of the army billets he'd had. He set about boosting his spending power in the camp. There was an official system of pay, given in return for work, and usable in the commissary. But if he was going to make life bearable, he'd need some hard cash. His bank accounts, containing thousands of dollars he'd made in his private business dealings, had been emptied by the FSB. Confiscation came with conviction for espionage as a matter of course. The money MI6 had been paying into his Spanish account was safely secreted abroad, but of course he could not draw on it, for there could be no clearer confession of guilt. What to do?

The Skripals sold some family possessions, Liudmila scrimped and saved, and a couple of Sergei's old friends came through. One was an old pal from the VDV, another who ran a Russian car dealership in Spain was a much more recent acquaintance. His brother Valery's family helped also. They gave Skripal more spending power in the camp and that could be used to bribe people; 'for me life there was no problem because I paid money to the administration'.

Things started to happen in the dormitory block where he and around a hundred fellow prisoners lived. New showers and toilets were installed. And if he wanted to absent himself from the IK 5 workshop where inmates made prison and army uniforms, nobody seemed to mind. Instead he tried to keep his edge – physically and mentally. He would push weights for hours, proud he could still bench-press 120kg, he would skip, shadow-box, working frustrations out and appetite up. There were TV and books too.

As for food the camp stuff was rubbish, and many inmates of the Dubrovlag soon became skeletal. He couldn't have that – not least if he wanted to maintain his fitness regimen. So Liudmila made sure the 20kg parcel he was allowed monthly was usually full of ingredients, there being a cooking area in Sergei's hut. He meanwhile realized that there were many less fortunate prisoners who had nobody to send them parcels, so offering them a cut, he used their monthly allowance to get more and more food sent in.

Skripal's camp regime had its rigours but also its small pleasures. A well-cooked dish, a satisfying workout, or a classic movie on the TV all helped to lift his spirits. He found solace also in sipping a hot cup of *cheffir*, tea stewed so long and so heavily sugared that it had the consistency of soup. 'For 99 per cent of people it's terrible,' he joked, 'but I liked it.'

At home in Moscow life was far from easy. While some of their friends came through, others made themselves scarce. The shame of treachery, instilled in Soviet times, was still alive and well in 'democratic Russia', especially among the older generation. Things were particularly difficult at the flat. Because so many GRU officers lived in the building, Liudmila faced frequent insults as she came and went. This climate of disapproval was hard to bear – all the more so as her own health began to suffer and a little support from the neighbours might have gone a long way. For it was while Sergei was in Mordovia that she first developed cancer, having to face this trial without her husband by her side.

The question of what Liudmila knew occurs again. Sergei told me with some pride that during his years of imprisonment she had not used an emergency phone number that he had given her, presumably belonging to the team handling him at MI6. How had he explained this number exactly? Was it just 'friends who might help in an emergency?' Whatever minimal explanation he might have given, she knew better than to ask more. And following his conviction why do something to confirm the accusations made against him, given the atmosphere of shame they had to contend with?

And it hung about the family as a whole. Skripal's mother Yelena had gone to live with Valery in the city of Yaroslavl, east of Moscow. Valery's daughter Viktoria felt conflicted after Sergei's conviction; 'as a citizen I have to accept that there was a court verdict and he was convicted. But as a relative, I can't accept it.' Yelena and Valery tried to do their bit, supporting Sergei in IK 5 with food parcels and letters. Viktoria though saw her cousin Sasha sink into despair during his father's prison years.

Talking to those around Skripal, it is clear that the emergence of Sasha's drink problem was a source of great sorrow during this time. As Viktoria explains it, Sasha, who idolized his father, was hit hard by the conviction and its accompanying social ostracism. However, others point to a complex of reasons for his problems. Sasha's marriage broke down at this time, without producing the kids he had wanted so dearly. Physical exercise, something he had always thrived on, also became much harder due to a back injury. Having gone from being a highly ranked handball player, Sasha was dealing with a great deal of pain. There were lots of reasons then why he hit the bottle.

As for Sergei's daughter, she also had to deal with fellow students' comments at university. Her college years came and went while her father was in Lefortovo and IK 5. It seems that at one point, fed up with the jibes, she even tried to change her surname. But if that marked a nadir, Yulia managed to keep going, staying true to her father's 'life is what you make of it' philosophy. College friends say that Yulia closed down the subject of her father's conviction, 'she simply wouldn't talk about it at all'.

Yulia graduated and began working while her father was inside. Her priority became finding a decent job, not least to help her mother financially. The parcels and visits to Mordovia were all well and good, in terms of keeping her dad going, but it all cost money.

Month followed month, 2006 became 2007 and slowly he started to scale the mountain that was his thirteen-year sentence. He was getting things in IK 5 sorted out, life was becoming a little more comfortable. Or a little less shit. But it was still a labour camp, and apart from quarterly visits he had been wrenched from his family. He was missing so much, not least the pride of seeing his daughter graduate from Moscow's Humanities University.

Even so, he managed to entertain some hope about the years stretching ahead. 'I knew I would not be in a prison camp for thirteen years,' he told me. Instead he looked at the very least towards the distant prospect of parole, which he would be eligible for after eight years, including the pre-trial years in Lefortovo. His dream of the future involved walking out of the gates and then leaving Russia, making a new life abroad.

In fact the answer to the questions he found himself ruminating on time and time again in IK 5, who had betrayed him and when would he get out, would be resolved in what might be called the manner that is central to the whole business of spying: betrayal. And the resolution of these issues would take not just one episode of treachery, but three – as we will see.

The snow lies in the shadows and hollows of Mordovia until June. Spring often comes on with a riotous energy, for a few weeks there is colour and a new warmth, and then it gets uncomfortably hot. And during that longed-for spring a few flowers delight the prisoners and hordes of forest insects come out to devour them.

As for the people who had run FORTHWITH – and indeed the other agents that the FSB was scooping up – they knew there was simply nothing to be done. 'You think about them every single day, and my God it's hard to live with,' a Western case officer says, 'but you know that any move you make could just make things worse for them.'

The post-9/11 honeymoon between Western leaders and Russia was all very well, but from the Kremlin's perspective, the cooperative atmosphere had been abused. As for the State Department or Foreign Office advocates of continued good relations with Russia, their challenge was about to get a whole lot harder.

12

HITMEN

In June 2007, Ruslan Atlangeriev flew from Moscow to London. To any casual observer he looked like just one more Russian businessman taking advantage of the opportunities to combine some work and pleasure in a great world city. He'd even taken his son along for the trip, and because he wasn't short of money, he had checked in to the London Hilton on Park Lane. That was handy for the sights, the designer shops in Knightsbridge or on Bond Street, and of course for the business meeting he was expecting to have a stone's throw from the hotel.

MI5 knew that Atlangeriev was coming. They knew which flight he'd be on, and what day. More importantly they knew why he was coming. He was coming to London to kill somebody.

The intelligence, passed to the Security Service by MI6, was explicit and stark. As a result, from the moment the visitor picked up his bags from the carousel at Heathrow he was being tailed by watchers from A4, MI5's surveillance section. For the watchers it made a nice change from the counter-terrorism work that had taken over their lives since the jihadist London bombings of 2005.

Those who've seen A4 in action can be evangelical about their prowess. They sometimes deploy dozens of watchers against a single target, all kinds of people from middle-aged ladies to hipsters. Mobile surveillance can switch slickly in minutes between a builder's van, a motorbike, and a London cab. Targets conditioned by spy or cop movies to expect two thirty-something men sitting in the front of a Ford or Toyota saloon will never spot A4.

So they mounted surveillance on Atlangeriev. Like most intelligence-led operations MI5 had some pieces of the puzzle but not all. They knew why Atlangeriev was in London, and they knew who his target was, but they didn't know how exactly he planned to strike. His room at the Hilton was checked for weapons and they found none. Because of the unknowns, and concern that there might be more than one hitman, the decision was taken to move the target out of harm's way.

Officers, people who identified themselves as police in any case, approached the target, the exiled tycoon Boris Berezovsky, and told him of a grave threat to his life. So not long after Atlangeriev arrived in London, Berezovsky was leaving, ever so discreetly, on a private jet to Israel.

After a couple of days watching their suspect, officers from Scotland Yard detained Atlangeriev and he was deported on a flight back to Russia.

On 16 July 2007 the UK announced the expulsion of four Russian intelligence officers. This was framed as a response to Russia's refusal to hand over Andrei Lugovoi, the prime suspect in the fatal Litvinenko poisoning. Two months earlier, British police had charged Lugovoi (in his absence) with murder and it was becoming clear that the Kremlin had no intention of handing him over.

Although the expulsion of the four Russians was not linked (publicly at least) to the attempt on Berezovsky, news of it broke soon afterwards. Both the government and the tycoon himself (who had been fighting a battle with the Home Office about his right to asylum) had a motive in bringing the affair to light. For the authorities, already nettled by the Litvinenko affair, a threat to Berezovsky compounded the crisis with Russia.

Atlangeriev was not named in the 2007 reporting of the story and many details were unclear. Some papers suggested the would-be hitman had tried to buy a gun in London, others that he had been watched attempting to break into Berezovsky's office one night. Since Berezovsky had made so many enemies in his business and political dealings the list of potential sponsors of a hit was, to put it mildly, extensive.

With Berezovsky, as with Litvinenko, there was talk of a possible Kremlin motive (both were ardent critics of Putin), but also of 'rogue elements' in the Russian intelligence services, criminality, or Chechen vendettas. Both men had had extensive dealings with the opposition in Russia's war-torn southern region and when some journalists learned that the man allegedly sent to London to kill the businessman was a Chechen, it compounded an idea for some people that 'it could have been anyone'.

In 1990s Russia it had become almost a cliché that 'mafia' from the restive region were the assassins of choice for those with any number of grievances. But of course the Russian state also had a motive to kill Berezovsky.

In an interview Nikolai Patrushev, the FSB boss, had castigated Britain for leading the charge in spying on Russia.

'The special services of the NATO states continue to be extremely active with respect to Russia,' he said, 'in this category one should specially single out Britain, whose special organs not only conduct intelligence in all areas but also seek to influence the development of the domestic political situation in our country.' He pointed the finger at Berezovsky and Litvinenko, having noted, 'in order to achieve certain political objectives, the British have recently gambled on people accused of committing crimes who are hiding abroad from Russian justice'. People like the exiled oligarch were using the UK as a base for sedition that sat ill with the usual rules for political asylum.

Patrushev's interview was published just a few weeks after MI5 frustrated the attempt on Berezovsky's life. In it the FSB boss had blended the threat to Russia from conventional espionage (mentioning Skripal among others convicted) with political subversion and some new details of MI6 technical innovations being used in support of its spying in Russia. The 2006 revelation of the 'spy rock', a device used by SIS officers in Moscow as a sort of Bluetooth dead-letter box for agents, had been followed by leaks to the Russian press exposing several people described as MI6 officers operating against Russia. Undoubtedly he was venting about what he regarded as a series of unacceptable escalations by the UK. Particular hatred though, among his Kremlin bosses, was reserved for the oligarch stirring up opposition from Mayfair.

And indeed Berezovsky hardly held back from incitement in his critique of the president and his cronies. In 2006 he had told an interviewer, 'President Putin violates the constitution and any violent action against him would be justified . . . the last year and a half we have been preparing to take power in Russia by force.' These comments outraged the Kremlin –

but they also nettled the UK immigration authorities, who warned the exiled tycoon that such remarks could jeopardize his continued asylum in the country. Berezovsky moderated his language a little after this, but was evidently a self-declared enemy of Russia's leader.

Even in the Litvinenko case, where two prime suspects had clearly emerged from the investigation (Andrei Lugovoi and Dmitri Kovtun), the UK government held back from directly accusing Putin or the Russian state of ordering the assassination. Litvinenko's death-bed interview with detectives in which he had explicitly blamed Putin for ordering the hit was kept secret for many years.

This was regarded by many in Whitehall as a way of limiting the damage caused by the polonium poisoning, and reserving one final escalatory option. There were also hopes, as so often in the post-Cold War Russian relationship, of a 're-set', as Vladimir Putin's second term was nearing its end, and under the constitution he could not run for a third.

Months later, in May 2008, several dozen invited 'influencers' made their way to the Mandarin Oriental Hotel overlooking Hyde Park for a power breakfast. The guests of Atlantic Partnership, an advocacy group, included politicians, bankers, captains of industry, and a handful of journalists. They consumed one of London's pricier and most delicious cooked breakfasts as they took their places in the hotel's banqueting suite. There was an atmosphere of anticipation in the room brought on by the prospect of a rare public talk by the Director General of the Security Service, Jonathan Evans.

A new Russian president, Dmitri Medvedev, was nearly a fortnight into the job. The new man eschewed Putin's tough-guy photo-ops and appeared to take a more moderate tone. Western advocates of a re-set were optimistic that a page could be turned, though Putin remained on the scene as Medvedev's prime minister.

At the Mandarin Oriental that morning, guests devoured their bacon and eggs and prepared for the main event. The DG was a tough, bullet-headed operator who had reached the top of the service via G and T Branches, countering Irish and international terrorism. Many in the audience were expecting him to major on the threat from jihadists since his service had been so heavily committed operationally since the 2005 London atrocities. In his prepared remarks Evans did indeed start with counter-terrorism when signalling his three greatest concerns of the moment. But when he described the few months preceding this breakfast as 'relatively quiet' on the counter-terrorism front some listeners were surprised.

Number two on his list of worries was Iran and proliferation, though he didn't spend too much time talking about it. It was when he got to his third that many paid closer attention. Russia, he believed, had 'increased as a source of concern'. There was a growing assertiveness, he argued, and not only had Alexander Litvinenko been murdered, the anger in his voice becoming noticeable, that was 'not the last attempt the Russians made to kill someone in London'. As for the withdrawal of cooperation on counter-terrorism announced by the Kremlin in the wake of the expulsions of ten months earlier, he noted scathingly, 'We haven't noticed because there wasn't any going on anyway.'

When the besuited listeners got their chance for questions, the topic reverted to counter-terrorism, possible legislation, and the importance of the home-grown militant threat. But when he was asked about Russia and his apparent confidence that Russia had been behind the Litvinenko hit, Evans resumed an uncompromising tone, saying there were 'very strong indications that it was a state action'. It was MI5's strong 'assessment' – and that word has important meaning in the Whitehall intelligence game – that elements of the Russian state were behind the Litvinenko operation.

Of course that was unsurprising to many listeners who had assumed for months that the Kremlin was behind the murder, but given the government's careful avoidance of this type of blame, that MI5's DG made the case so forcefully, and that Russia had tried another assassination, it set me thinking.

It didn't take long to find the reporting on the Berezovsky affair of the previous summer. Was this the further attempt that Evans was referring to? I asked an official. Yes. Could I have a briefing on it? We'll get back to you.

A few weeks later, I was directed to the empty upstairs bar of a restaurant in Mayfair for a mid-morning rendezvous. There I met a 'Whitehall official' who briefed me on the intelligence underpinning Jonathan Evans's public, or at least semi-public, remarks at the Mandarin Oriental. Russian espionage numbers had built back up, close to Cold War levels, despite the flourishing of business and cultural ties during the preceding years; about thirty people accredited as diplomats, half of Russia's official representation in London, were thought to be spies. Recently though there had been a change, they 'are now looking to target regime opponents', and as for the Litvinenko and Berezovsky operations, he argued, 'our assessment is very clear that this was Russian state activity'. But while the embassy people belonged to the two traditional arms of foreign espionage – the SVR or successor agency to the overseas arm of the KGB, and the GRU – these more aggressive operations had been set up by the FSB.

That the FSB was taking care of business on its SVR and GRU overseas rivals' turf in the UK would have been entirely unsurprising to someone like Skripal, serving his time in Mordovia. He was all too familiar with the agency power struggles in Moscow. But for the British spooks this was new and deeply unwelcome. Indeed the official said that state-sponsored assassination would mess up the Anglo-Russian relationship 'big time'.

Litvinenko's murder had been set up as 'the perfect crime', and it was only because he had taken just a few sips of the poisoned tea offered him at London's Millennium Hotel rather than a full mouthful that he had taken so long to die, giving doctors time to isolate the cause of death as polonium poisoning. If he had perished faster, it would never have been known. In both cases the FSB had opted to use someone known to the victim in order to get close to them. Litvinenko was inherently suspicious, and Berezovsky had hired a formidable Israeli bodyguard team to protect himself. Interestingly, although some reporting suggested the Chechen was planning to use a gun in London, there were people I spoke to whose hypothesis was that, like Lugovoi and Kovtun, Atlangeriev would have used the proximity of a 'business meeting' to administer a poison.

Several more days passed and we started to film a story on the attempted murder of Berezovsky, adding lines from the Evans event (which could not be directly attributed to him) and the subsequent briefing. Berezovsky himself gave me the name of Atlangeriev, and of another suspect who had travelled over from Russia at about the same time, as well as many other details of what had happened. The Russian businessman described the urgency of warnings by Scotland Yard and what happened next:

They commanded me to leave the country, I said I don't have so many opportunities . . . Russia had a red flag on Interpol to arrest me. I said I'm not able to move anywhere, just to Israel, and I said maybe Scotland? They said no, you move to another country. OK, I said, I'll try but how urgently? Better today or maximum tomorrow . . . next day I left the country, I remember it well, it was 16th June.

Berezovsky had met Atlangeriev before, when he had come over, seeking funding for a new political party. The exiled businessman told us the Chechen had asked for a meeting, at which he would carry out the murder, accepting that his arrest and trial were highly likely to lead to a long sentence but that the Russian authorities had promised to compensate his family for it.

Officials confirmed that Atlangeriev was indeed the man deported in June 2007 and we were in business.

The story then was that despite official coyness by UK diplomats or Downing Street in the Berezovsky and Litvinenko cases, MI5 was quite clear that these were acts planned and carried out by the Russian state in the form of the FSB. As for whether Putin had personally ordered these hits, those I spoke to were candid enough to say they didn't know one way or another.

When, early in July, I rang the Whitehall official who had organized my briefing, to discuss the quotes that we would use (this process was a condition of the meeting), he put heavy pressure on me to tone our story down. The suggested changes would essentially have rendered it meaningless so I conceded a point or two and held firm on the others, despite threats to penalize the BBC as a whole if we put out our report.

What he could see – and lamentably I could not until the day of transmission because I had journalistic tunnel vision – was that it would run on the day that Prime Minister Gordon Brown had his first meeting with President Medvedev at a summit in Japan. Our *Newsnight* piece made world news but not in the way I had anticipated.

Medvedev's adviser Sergei Prikhodko briefed the press in Japan that our report showed 'not everyone in the UK has a constructive approach', and that its timing was 'not coincidental'. It had been designed to prevent Brown and his president from turning the page on the conflicts of the past, for example over Litvinenko. Downing Street told reporters that it had not authorized any briefings to the BBC by the intelligence people. Having had a key meeting in a deserted restaurant, Number 10's denial hardly came as a great surprise to me.

The initial impetus for the story and several of the best quotes had of course come from the MI5 boss's event at the Mandarin Oriental where there had been close to a hundred people. That had been nearly seven weeks before the Japan summit. It had taken time to get the necessary corroboration, interview Berezovsky and all the rest. While Evans, and the official who subsequently briefed me, had been clear that they did not think the coming of Medvedev would change things for the better, the idea that they thought they could sabotage the summit seemed tenuous at best.

The roasting I got from Whitehall people immediately before and after our transmission indeed rather suggested that our timing was almost as horrifying to them as it was to Mr Prikhodko. Our timetable had, until the actual day of transmission, been entirely coincidental. There were other personal repercussions, including that I was never invited to another Atlantic Partnership power breakfast, and formal briefings from the intelligence services, dwindling during those years in any case, effectively came to an end for me.

The issue of how far Russia was to be trusted, let alone embraced for every pound UK PLC could make, was the subject of intense disagreement within Whitehall. Whatever the ambiguity that British leaders had been using in their pronouncements about the Litvinenko affair, people in the Security Service, and MI6 for that matter, were quite sure that these were FSB assassination plots.

As for Berezovsky, he had alleged a couple of previous murder attempts and all manner of threats from the Russian government. Although he did tone down his anti-Kremlin campaigning he became fatalistic about his life and how it might end. Asked by another journalist about his security detail, the businessman replied with mordant wit, 'He's not a bodyguard, he's a witness.'

It took years of struggle by Sasha's widow, Marina Litvinenko, to force a proper inquiry into his case. It finally reported in 2016, a decade after his assassination, that it had been an act of the Russian government 'probably' approved by the FSB head and President Putin.

However, even at that long-awaited inquiry, the Foreign Secretary had issued a Public Interest Immunity Certificate to prevent the release of certain intelligence service documents. These included details of Litvinenko's work for MI6, but also those key intelligence agency judgements that his murder and the 2007 attempt on Berezovsky's life had been acts of the Russian state. Even eight years after our *Newsnight* story about MI5's assessment to this effect, the government still regarded the view of its own experts as being too hot to handle.

In the case of Berezovsky it became clear that the British had picked up Atlangeriev's trail at Heathrow on the basis of secret intelligence. Whether that was an agent in Russia or intercepted communications, who knows? In Berezovsky's case there was less of a lasting impact because, of course, the plot was unsuccessful. But both of these examples showed up an official nervousness about calling out the Kremlin or the FSB, its favoured security agency, for plotting murder on British soil. Because once such an accusation is made, and there is a refusal on Russia's part to acknowledge what has happened, let alone cooperate, the consequences would plague the Anglo-Russian relationship for years.

In the years since that attempt a number of people connected with Russia have died in suspicious circumstances in the UK, leading investigative journalists at Buzzfeed to compile a list of fourteen cases worthy of further examination. Among these were Berezovsky's death in March 2013 in the bathroom of his home. An inquest returned an open verdict, though the likeliest explanation is that Berezovsky took his own life, having talked of suicide after being ruined financially by a disastrous legal fight with fellow oligarch Roman Abramovich.

Interestingly, while the Kremlin might assume that ardent critics would take any chance they could to make mischief against Russia, my own contacts have not claimed to have any particular evidence in the fourteen cases compiled by Buzzfeed. Rather they go back to the Litvinenko case and the June 2007 attempt on Berezovsky's life when asked about Russian state assassination plots in this country. And what that second planned act shows most clearly is that even after the diplomatic damage done by Litvinenko's poisoning, the FSB was ready to try another assassination in Britain.

At the time of these events Skripal himself was languishing in a Russian labour camp, of course. An attempt to appeal against his thirteen-year sentence had failed and he had been consigned to the forested oblivion of Mordovia. He had plenty of time to reflect there on his choices, especially that one he had made to take Richard Bagnall's offer in 1996 in Madrid. He is not a man given to too much introspection or regret. But Skripal, ever the professional intelligence officer, did entertain a good deal of curiosity about the way he was caught. He had learned from his interrogation and trial that the FSB took quite a while to build the case against him. But how had it started, what was the impetus? It was years into his sentence, and back in Madrid, that some answers finally emerged.

13

THE FATEFUL LETTER

On a chilly January morning, the Guardia Civil prison bus dropped its passengers outside the Audiencia Provincial. Just two men descended, walking up towards the shiny modern office block that serves as one of Madrid's main courts. One of them was a compact, tough-looking character, shaven-headed, suited, and handcuffed, the other one his uniformed guard. The defendant was arriving for a case so secret that he had been held incommunicado for years while on remand, and the court documents used a codename, Teofilo.

In the court room itself were the defendant's lawyer, a couple of prosecutors, the three magistrates who would sit in judgement (it was not a jury trial), and some other guards. Cameras were briefly allowed to take a shot of 'Teofilo' sitting next to his attorney – they captured rows of empty seats where the press, public, and relatives would normally sit but would not be allowed in this exceptional case. Lawyers love to break new ground, to explore areas of untried jurisprudence, and that morning in 2010 they would get their chance. It would be the first, and so far only, trial for treason since the restoration of Spanish democracy in 1978. As soon as the media people were shooed out, proceedings could start. 'It was like the players were on the pitch for a Premier League match,' one participant would observe, 'but with nobody in the stands.'

Over the five days of this hearing, the charges were laid out: that the defendant had accumulated a hugely damaging trove of documents during his work for the Spanish national intelligence service; that these materials had been found during a search of his flat following his arrest in 2007; and that he had communicated state secrets to a foreign power. Teofilo, alias Roberto Florez, had served Spain's secret state between1991 and 2004. Both his own former service and MI6 believed he was the man responsible for giving away Sergei Skripal and Yuri Burlatov. In terms of the three betrayals that would be needed to resolve the questions Sergei asked himself, that of Florez appears to be the first. But as so often in counter-espionage cases, the question was whether they could prove it to the satisfaction of a court.

Florez, a native of the northern region of Asturias who was forty-four at the time of his trial, joined the Spanish intelligence (then called CESID but subsequently known by the acronym CNI) from the Guardia Civil or paramilitary police. He served undercover bravely and effectively for years in the north of the country, countering Basque extremists. People who know him told me how smart Florez is, and how good with people too.

Late in 1999 he was posted to Lima, in Peru, where he was given the task of political information-gathering, while working undercover at the Spanish embassy. His cover was blown by a newspaper, and the allegation that Spanish spooks were trying to influence Peruvian elections resulted in his speedy recall to Madrid two years into his posting.

Back in Spain, his bosses decided that since he had been comprehensively blown, with his name and photo appearing across the media, his days as a field agent were over. Florez, who had relished the challenges of being an undercover operator, found it hard to accept that from now on he could only be a desk man. So a grievance emerged between employee and bosses, normal enough in any workplace but always potentially hazardous in an intelligence agency. That was particularly so when the desk that the disgruntled spy would eventually get to was in the Counter-Intelligence Division. In the meantime Florez busied himself with a number of projects, including a paper on techniques for recruiting human sources.

Being back at headquarters, Florez was able to access and copy all manner of secret documents.

Given the study he was engaged in, he would have been well aware of the activities of one of Russia's most successful penetrations ever, FBI agent Robert Hanssen, since he was arrested early in 2001. Hanssen's long spying career, going back to the mid-1980s, depended for most of its length on never meeting the Russians face to face. The Russians were too heavily penetrated for him to want to do it any other way. Hanssen provided classified information (leading to the death of several Russians working for the Americans), and the Russians in return left him large amounts of cash in dead drops.

The Hanssen affair may well have shaped the Spaniard's ideas about how the perfect spy should operate. But he knew from this and other examples that the Russians might be very wary of someone offering information anonymously. There had been all too many cases of KGB or SVR officers being expelled, having nibbled the bait in anonymous messages that were being offered by writers who were not traitors at all, but Western intelligence people who had opened communications for the very purpose of entrapping the Russians. In order to convince them, you needed to offer a hefty up-front disclosure of classified information, something really convincing. That's what Hanssen had done.

The collection built up by Florez (and eventually seized in his flat) would be listed at his trial, including: 'complete document titled "document and classified material security plan"'; 'complete document titled "Counterintelligence Division"'; 'Alphabetical personnel list', this being the entire agency staff; and a complete 'organigram' or organizational chart of the CNI. In the context of our story, though, the most interesting paper was one he purloined, which was described in court as an eighteen-page document called 'Double Agents in the GRU and SVR stations in Spain'.

Central to the prosecution case was 'Card 1', a document drafted on a computer, but – it was argued by the state – printed out and sent with an accompanying package of documents to establish Florez's bona fides with the Russians, then posted to an address where it would find its way to the SVR *rezident* or station chief in Madrid, one Pyotr Melnikov. In this card, Florez wrote:

> I am an operative of CESID who is interested in communicating his readiness to collaborate with the service and country you represent. As proof that I belong to the Centre I would simply point out the documents and information attached to this card, on the assumption that your service is interested in this collaboration, I inform you that in order to make this relationship work the precondition is, in exchange for this first delivery

of documents, the amount of two hundred thousand American dollars in cash.

He provided details, kept secret from the court, about how this money should be paid to him. In the body of the message Florez said he was offering Melnikov 'information on the working procedures the Centre uses against your country (in Spain as well as in the Russian Federation and third countries) . . . as well as the operations, sources, and procedures used by the [CNI] to achieve its global role'.

The issue of whether Florez had betrayed his country – and by extension been the author of all of Sergei Skripal or Yuri Burlatov's misfortunes – would now be tried in court.

For people in Vauxhall Cross or Langley a view had been reached about the Spanish intelligence operative years before, following his arrest and the seizure of so much compromising documentation. Nothing though had happened quickly in this case. The arrest had taken place in July 2007, and the counter-intelligence types had been trying to figure out what had happened ever since 2004 and the arrest of Skripal and Burlatov.

For their part, the Spanish had launched their first serious mole-hunt in July 2005, four and a half years before the trial. The CNI gave evidence in court that it noticed distinct changes in the operating procedures of the Madrid GRU and SVR stations from December 2002 onwards. These had allowed the Russians to nullify certain surveillance programmes that they were subject to. Although the likely compromise of these operations triggered concerns at the CNI it would seem from the dates that it was the arrest of

Burlatov and Skripal that gave the more serious impetus to their efforts – Skripal having failed to turn up for his last meet with Stephen Jones a few months before the full CNI leak inquiry started. At MI6 the lights were flashing about a possible penetration and it was apparent from the outset that there was a Spanish connection with these two compromised Russian assets.

The business of hunting moles though is one where only fools rush to judgement. How certain could SIS be that it wasn't one of their own people who'd betrayed the two agents? Or maybe it was someone in a third country who had been indoctrinated in their intelligence? People at Vauxhall Cross grew confident their own people weren't the source of the leak, but best make certain inquiries, examine who had access to what, before pointing a finger at the Spanish. This took time, and indeed the initial Spanish searches proved fruitless. Florez had left the CNI in the spring of 2004 and perhaps there was an element of him being out of mind once he was out of sight.

Assessing the whole matter afresh, there were other questions for the Russian espionage team in MI6: why had Burlatov been murdered in prison and not Skripal? The agency's Russia people came to a conclusion that Burlatov had made a fatal mistake during his interrogation at Lefortovo in 2004. They believed that he tried to bargain with his knowledge of the corrupt goings on in the Madrid GRU *rezidentura*, notably the diversion of the funds assigned for Moscow's technological shopping spree. Burlatov's 'roof' or protector was a certain senior officer at GRU headquarters, General *Volkov. He had taken his cut, allowing the field man in Spain to keep siphoning off funds without fear of an investigation. 'Between these people,' Skripal told me, 'money decided everything.'

However, General Volkov must also have had his own fears about discovery so he had paid off someone himself. The trail led ultimately to the top of the FSB and its director, General Nikolai Patrushev. Once Burlatov revealed the corrupt goings on to officers interrogating him (members of Patrushev's organization), the decision had been taken that he had to be disposed of. And the FSB didn't want its fingerprints on the deed either: it couldn't happen in Lefortovo. So Burlatov had been transferred to the military psychiatric ward for an evaluation and murdered there by GRU people. Volkov had thus contained the scandal, and insulated high-ups in the FSB from ultimate blame.

Skripal had played things rather more wisely during his interrogation. What knowledge he had about the diversion of official funds in Madrid, and it is clear that he not only knew about it but had shared his suspicions with his MI6 handler, he kept to himself in Lefortovo. It may well have saved his life.

How did the investigative net finally close on Florez? One Spanish newspaper suggested that the Americans had relayed a lead from one of their Russian penetrations. It would be entirely unsurprising if this cycle of betrayal from Skripal, to Florez, and then back to an unknown Russian agent did indeed provide the critical starting point. I have not asked further questions on this theory, not least because of the danger that anyone who had provided the Florez lead would be in. But comments made to me by interviewees imply there was indeed intelligence that a Spaniard had communicated with Russian intelligence. This 'CI Lead' from a mole, presumably in Russia, was then the second of the three betrayals needed to answer Skripal's questions in prison camp because it compounded the suspicions circling by early 2007 around the Spanish suspect, who at that time was living in Tenerife, in the Canary Islands, with his girlfriend. It would emerge that for some time before his arrest, the CNI had been intercepting Florez's phone calls and had covertly entered his apartment, finding his stash of classified material.

The discovery of 'Card 1' and the other documents in the Tenerife flat caused many uncomfortable questions to be asked at Vauxhall Cross. If Florez had indeed communicated with the SVR and in particular provided them with the stolen document 'Double Agents in the GRU and SVR stations in Spain', had Skripal been blown soon after that message was written in December 2001? And if the Russians had figured out what he was up to had they been feeding useless or misleading information to their man for much of the four-year period after FORTHWITH left the GRU and before his arrest?

In the 2014 Russian documentary *A Mole in the Aquarium* there was evidence of some official briefing, presumably from the FSB. The film suggested that the Russian counterintelligence people did indeed disrupt Skripal's activities. 'The former GRU colleagues with whom he so persistently wanted to meet were always unavailable due to a clash of appointments,' said the film commentary, 'some were on a sudden business trip, some were ill. But when they were eventually able to meet, the conversations stubbornly evaded the topics which interested Skripal.'

The conclusions that the Western damage assessment reached were not quite so simple. Intelligence people have told me that the internal CNI inquiries suggested that Florez was never in possession of Skripal's name, rather he had passed on to the SVR that there was an asset who was 'a senior GRU officer who often visited Spain'. This was enough to guide the FSB to quite a short list of potential suspects.

So if the Russians got Card 1 late in 2001, presumably spent a little time verifying it was genuine information, and then a little longer narrowing their search for possible moles onto Skripal, it might be supposed that he was indeed being prevented from gathering information of real value from around mid-2002 until his arrest just over two years later. 'We have to assume that was the case,' one of those party to the Western investigation told me.

One thing is clear though, which is that the discovery of Burlatov, Skripal, and perhaps other GRU penetrations who we do not yet even know of at last empowered Putin and Patrushev to bring the military intelligence organization to heel, something they had wanted to do for years. A newly created mandarin of the secret world, the Deputy Director for Counter-intelligence was appointed to the Glass House, GRU HQ, and of course it was someone with an FSB background. The *chekists* now had one of their people at the GRU's top table.

All of these events, followed through multiple reporting lines in Western agencies, were collated in Vauxhall Cross during the years that Skripal was in jail. They had reached their own view about Florez and what he had or hadn't betrayed. But of course, as any intelligence professional knows, the divide between their type of information and the kind that passes muster as evidence in court can often be fundamental. So the CNI and the Spanish prosecutor had much to prove against the man who had gone on trial at the start of 2010.

•

The proceedings in the Audiencia Provincial lasted five days. They were marked by considerable secrecy, not least in what was disclosed to or withheld from Florez's lawyer, a pugnacious human-rights advocate named Manuel Ollé. So while the prosecutor had listed the type of documents secreted in the Tenerife flat, Ollé was able to discover little about their content. By contrast, the three magistrates sitting in judgement were allowed to read all the classified material.

Although Florez and Ollé were not allowed to learn the full extent of the case against him, they did their best to construct a defence: the phone taps and other surveillance had not produced any evidence that the Spaniard had ever met any representative of Russian intelligence; and there was no proof that he had ever received any money from them, let alone $200,000.

The critical element of Florez's defence was his denial that he had ever actually initiated contact with the Russians. Although CNI people gave evidence about the compromise of their operations against the Russian intelligence stations in Madrid they did not present a damage assessment as such to the three magistrates. The betrayal of Sergei Skripal was therefore not mentioned in that Madrid courtroom. It simply wasn't possible to make such an allegation not least because, at that moment, Skripal was still sitting in IK 5 in Mordovia and any airing of his case in Spain might have been seen by the Russians as confirmation of his service as an MI6 asset, making matters even worse for him.

It was therefore only later that Florez specifically addressed the betrayal of Skripal. 'Amongst the information in my possession,' the Spaniard said, 'there wasn't a single date, note, diary, tip, paper record, memorandum, [or] document in which the name or circumstances of Sergei Skripal were stated.'

How on earth did Florez explain that fateful letter, Card 1, at his trial? He claimed that it was part of his study on recruiting human sources, a fictional document, almost like a role play, in which he had set out how a Western intelligence officer might offer their services to the Russians.

The magistrates knew though, from another document found on Florez's computer, called Card 2 in court, that there was some evidence he had initiated contact with the Russians. This second message to the SVR *rezident* in Madrid was written in March 2002, around four months after the first. Florez began, 'I understand that the proposition that I sent needs time for consideration'. The prosecutor pointed to this as proof that the first had been sent, and no reply received by that point. Card 2 also underlined the CNI agent's determination to avoid face-to-face meetings with the Russians, noting: 'the high number of defections that have happened in recent years oblige me to be cautious'. Interestingly, he deleted Card 2 from his computer, but investigators were able to recover it.

As with Skripal's trial in Moscow, and the irony could scarcely be more bitter, there were aspects of the CNI's unmasking of Florez that could not be aired in court. If indeed they had been led to him by an American source still in place in Russia, that was obviously a secret that had to be guarded. The prosecution claimed to have evidence that Card 1 had been sent to the Russians, proof that went beyond the statement in Card 2 that it had been posted but no reply received. This added evidence was never spelt out to the defendant and his lawyer.

When the verdict was announced on 11 February 2010, the court found Florez guilty of illegally removing classified documents, of keeping them at his home, and of treason in the sense that he planned to give these secrets to a foreign state. Manuel Ollé took some comfort from the fact that they did not find him guilty of being an agent of another power. Florez was sentenced to twelve years in jail, though it was appealed and reduced to nine years. With time served and parole, he was already free by the time of the Salisbury poisoning in 2018.

One only has to believe that Florez sent Card 1 and that first packet of thirty-nine intelligence documents to Melnikov, as indeed the prosecution alleged, for the rest to be explained. Florez's assertion that nothing in his possession revealed Skripal's name or 'specific circumstances' is not that different to the conclusion that the CNI and MI6 reached. And it is quite likely that Melnikov did not reply to that initial dump of information, fearing entrapment. Card 2 underlined that the Russians did not take the bait. The fact that Florez left CNI in 2004 just weeks after being posted to the Counter-Intelligence Division would also suggest that there was no ongoing relationship with the SVR because clearly they would have very much valued him in such a post. So it's quite possible, likely even, that there was no 'relationship' with the SVR in the sense of communication going in two directions and that Florez never received a cent, let alone $200,000 from them.

That said, it would only have taken eyes other than Melnikov's months or even years later to re-examine Card 1 and its enclosed documents and to proceed on the assumption that it was a genuine attempt at treason for all the other pieces to fall into place. The simple reference to penetrations in the SVR and GRU, even without further detail, would have been enough to trigger mole-hunts in Moscow. Knowing from the other papers that the source was Spanish, and the time window in which the information had been learned, the Russians would then quickly have homed in on people with a Spanish connection such as Burlatov and Skripal. Surveillance of them would have started and their fate would have been sealed.

Those involved in the Skripal damage assessment held Florez responsible for his betrayal and did not look for any other leak once the Spaniard had been detained. Things are rarely 100 per cent certain in the world of counter-intelligence but they felt confident they had discovered who was responsible for their man being in the Gulag.

A wheel of fortune had turned for the Spaniard, as he was led away to start his sentence in Estremera prison, not far from Madrid. In terms of the three betrayals I have mentioned, those necessary to resolve the questions that bedevilled Skripal, as the months of his sentence crept by, the Spanish case represents two of them: Skripal's identification as an MI6 asset, and the information that in turn helped convince the Spanish authorities of Florez's guilt. But what of the third betrayal? Before the wheel could turn again, and Skripal be freed, another layer of treachery, espionage, and deceit would have to be exposed, this time across the Atlantic.

14

OPERATION GHOST STORIES

It is mid-afternoon in Manhattan and a Russian agent named Anna Chapman is meeting her contact, *Roman. He has contacted her by phone and requested the meeting. Chapman, who has been in America for several months, has been making her reports back to the Centre via a laptop. Each Wednesday she has sent her material by a simple expedient almost undetectable in a modern city. She has gone to a cafe or restaurant and established a connection with another computer, one belonging to Russian intelligence people sitting nearby. Her file, encrypted, naturally, has been copied across to their machine by private wireless network without the operatives ever speaking or even necessarily seeing one another.

But there have been some problems with the transfers and Roman is sitting face to face with her. They discuss whether she should take the laptop back to Moscow with her – she's due to make a trip in a fortnight – or whether he should take it to be checked out. Roman also tells her there's another reason he has asked for the meeting. 'There is a person here who is just like you, OK?' he explains. 'But, unlike you, this person is not here under her real name . . . I have documents for you to give her tomorrow morning.'

He produces a fake passport and gives it to Chapman. 'This is not her real name, but you can call her this name if you wish.' Roman describes the procedure for meeting the other agent, complete with holding a magazine so she can recognize Chapman as the courier. The woman who is coming to collect the passport will ask, 'Excuse me, but haven't we met in California last summer?' Chapman's reply was to be, 'No, I think it was the Hamptons.'

There are certain indications that Chapman is a little suspicious of Roman, and she is right to be. On the indictment covering these events he is described as UC-1, short for undercover 1. UC-1 is an FBI agent.

Two and a half hours later, on the same day, 26 June 2010, and in a different city, another Federal agent, UC-2, is playing the role of a Russian handler too. His conversations involve Mikhail Semenko, a bright young Russian professional holding down a job in the Washington DC area. This encounter has also been engineered by the FBI, starting with a meeting on the street in which UC-2 asked Semenko whether they had met in Beijing. Like the New York conversation, these two started by discussing recent covert communications before the FBI man moved on to ask the Russian to do something for him.

Passing an envelope with $5,000 in it, UC-2 asked Semenko to take it the following morning to a hiding place under a bridge in a park in Arlington, Virginia. Another Russian agent would then collect it. Surveillance cameras record him leaving the money in the place described.

These encounters with Chapman and Semenko marked a closing chapter in one of the longest and most elaborate counter-intelligence operations ever mounted. The FBI code-named these interrelated investigations Operation Ghost Stories, and on 26 June 2010 a carefully choreographed drama was playing itself out.

By that day, after more than a decade of watching, caution was being thrown to the winds. The FBI was taking big risks in a final play. Using details of previous meetings between Chapman, Semenko, and their controllers that they had gleaned from surveillance, they engineered the rendezvouses of 26 June in such a way as to get the two spies, step by step, to incriminate themselves. The FBI was demonstrating that these two had regular contact with Russian handlers from the SVR foreign intelligence service, and that they were ready to take active steps to support deep-cover spies, or illegals, who had taken years to embed themselves in American society.

The trigger for this climatic phase of Operation Ghost Stories was the news that Colonel Alexander Poteyev, a senior SVR officer working for the Americans, had reached Minsk in Byelorussia the previous day. From there he was taken by the CIA into Ukraine and then to the US. This exfiltration had been full of tension, because when he requested a passport to travel overseas, Poteyev had been refused. He had only been able to make the train from Moscow to Minsk by using a fake travel document. And if his rescue didn't make things complex, and tense enough, there was another major moving part to this operation's final stage.

Just as the CIA asset was escaping Moscow, Russia's president, Dmitri Medvedev, was being feted in Washington by President Barack Obama. Protocol required some acting of a high order from Obama. Two weeks before Medvedev's arrival in America, the US president had received a detailed briefing about the Ghost Stories investigation. At this and a subsequent National Security Council meeting the principals had agreed the phased approach for bringing the whole matter to a head, but at the same time avoiding the presentational car crash of arresting a Russian agent network while that country's leader was in the US.

POTUS took his honoured guest out for some proper American food at Ray's Hell Burger, a crowded lunch stop over the river in Arlington. There they each had a cheeseburger, shared the fries, and Obama urged his visitor to watch out he didn't get the juices on his tie. Making their way back to the White House, the two men made all of the diplomatic noises you'd expect.

'It's a pleasure to be here with my friend and partner,' Obama began, then pledged, 'The United States wants to be Russia's partner as [Medvedev] pursues his vision of modernization and innovation in Russia.' Economic summits followed, more talk of cooperation naturally at the G8, then they flew up to Toronto for the G20 meeting. The FBI had been given its signal, once the Russian leader was out of US airspace, to up the tempo in their operation to dismantle an SVR espionage operation that had taken years of effort and millions to construct.

The actual takedown had to wait until Medvedev was on his plane home from Canada. Craig Fair, one of the senior officers in CD1, the FBI counter-intelligence section running Ghost Stories, later explained, 'We wanted to wait until he was out of this hemisphere to effect the arrests because it would not be proper to have that done during an international economic event.'

Poteyev, it is clear, had been an extraordinary agent. At the subsequent 'in absentia' trial held in Moscow, it was claimed that he was recruited in 1999. Western intelligence people suggest that was about right. The Russian had spent his career in Department S (sometimes called Line S), which ran the 'illegal' deep-cover operations considered the most sensitive and prestigious part of the former KGB's work. Poteyev's decision to spy for the Americans was the third and final of the betrayals I have alluded to in previous chapters because not only did it spawn this enormous, long-lasting Federal investigation, but it would also produce Skripal's opportunity for freedom.

The 'illegal' agents were spies operating in a Western country, with a false life or 'legend', pretending in this case to be regular suburban Americans. Naturally for each SVR officer engaged in this deep-cover work there were several others needed to support them. This might involve delivering money or communications kit to dead drops or preparing the false identities that illegals used. In addition to their working legend, each of these prized operatives could return to Russia (usually every three years), for a few weeks' leave and to see their families. These journeys usually involved going via two or three other places, changing identity on each leg of the journey, another administrative headache for the officers assisting them. These 'enablers' were usually posted under diplomatic cover, serving Line S sections within a *rezidentura*. Other officers in the station collected political or technical intelligence, each operating in their own silo, knowing nothing about the illegals.

Poteyev was working under cover at the Russian mission in New York when he offered his services as a walk-in to the FBI. At the time, he had been tasked to support some illegals in South and Central America, but returning to the US on a subsequent tour, in a more senior post, he had oversight of Department S operations in the Americas as a whole.

When he went back to Moscow, Poteyev was promoted to Deputy Head of Department S, giving him detailed knowledge of SVR illegal operations globally. From the FBI and CIA's point of view, he proved to be a quite astounding long-term asset.

The network revealed, bit by bit, to the Americans consisted of four couples. By June 2010 they were located in New York, Boston, and Washington DC.

The oldest of the illegals, *Juan Lazaro, had begun his work overseas thirty-four years earlier in Peru. He relocated with his Peruvian wife to New York in 1984. By the time arrests were drawing close, Lazaro had been living a double life for so long that, Western intelligence officers told me, he had actually succeeded in retiring from the SVR, who were content for him to stay put in the US. Many in Department S, indeed, regarded this as a perfect career for an illegal; to blend in so completely that you never left, so neighbours or colleagues never asked awkward questions.

Another of the couples watched by the FBI for at least six years prior to their arrest had arrived in the US after ten years of building up their legend, living in Canada and France.

These agents were the product of a remarkable investment by the KGB then SVR. Their training in Russia – both spycraft and attempts to perfect a foreign language to near-native proficiency – could take five to ten years. Add to that periods spent in third countries building up their false identities and you could have someone who had devoted fifteen to twenty years to becoming an operational illegal. Naturally, in this drawn-out process, there were quite a few failures or people who simply quit, adding further to the expense of the whole Department S operation.

Even in 2010, though, this type of spying still held a

special place in Russian intelligence history and culture. Some of the greatest heroes of the KGB and GRU, like those who'd gained the secrets of the atom bomb or warned of Hitler's plan to invade Russia, were illegals. During the Cold War such agents were regarded within the KGB as the most ideologically sound, since they were living lives of plenty in the West, something that many Soviet citizens might have dreamed of, but never forgot their true loyalty.

Many years after he became leader, it emerged that Vladimir Putin's 1980s KGB work in East Germany had been as a Department S officer, supporting illegals.

'I know what kind of people these are,' recalled Putin, 'these are special people, people of special qualities, of special conviction, with a special character. To give up their life, their nearest and dearest and leave the country for many years, and to dedicate one's life to the Fatherland, not everyone is capable of doing that.'

After the Cold War, it amazed many Western intelligence people that Russia still bothered with such deep-cover operations. After all, increasing amounts of information were obtainable over the internet, an invention which also made it far harder to invent a past life for your operatives. And while 1930s Russia had access to revolutionaries from all over the place, people who actually were native speakers of other languages, the characters sent to the US in the 1990s and 2000s were Russians who, in a few cases, never quite lost their accents.

The illegal network, like the GRU's caches of weapons for saboteurs, was evidence of the unreformed nature of Russia's agencies. These were after all preparations for war, one part of Department S's role being to provide an alternative presence to the officers in embassies if these were forced to leave in time of conflict.

Instructions to this spy ring intercepted by the Americans indicated its main mission, deriving from the Centre's preoccupation with infiltrating what they termed the country's 'ruling circles', the concept itself being a Marxist holdover. They thus gravitated towards academia, think tanks, or the financial world. In this way, it was hoped, they would be able to mix with State Department, CIA people, or bankers, even if their own false identities were never well enough established to join the Federal government themselves.

What did they achieve? The Russian press would later claim exotic recruitments on their behalf, but the Americans suggest that whenever the undercover Russians got close to anyone in possession of real secrets, they acted to disrupt any actual recruitment. FBI agents would have a discreet word, and the American would quietly break contact. All of this was possible, of course, because Poteyev's intelligence had allowed them to stay one step ahead of the undercover SVR officers, keeping them under surveillance for years.

Many times during this long investigation the officers in the CD1 section at the FBI, the agents masterminding it, had to ask whether the time had come to reel in the Russians. They had to consider not just the diplomatic ramifications but also, steeped in the Bureau's law-enforcement traditions as they were, what kind of case they might actually bring to court. A senior FBI agent told me:

> They're hard cases to make. Just because you're able to charge someone doesn't make it a winnable case. With the Russians we were trying to improve the relationship

and you know there'll be consequences. Thinking beyond
a conviction was really tough on that case.

Add to this the fact that their disruption of the Russians'
activities had prevented any actual disclosure of secrets (or so
the FBI always insisted) and the problem of building something that would stand up in court became harder still. With
matters moving to a head in 2010, they added Chapman
and Semenko to the file. These two, who had not been long
in the US, were not actually illegals at all but 'Nocs', the
term American intelligence types use for those under Non-
Official Cover. While they had been successfully entrapped
on 26 June, the same was not true of the illegals, where the
FBI cases depended more on their use of fake documents,
money-laundering statutes, other bureaucratic violations,
and a US law against being an 'unregistered agent' of a foreign
country.

There was another factor also underlying the timing of
any arrest, which was that it could not happen while Poteyev
was still in Russia. During the years of Ghost Stories surveillance, his safety was an absolute priority. As for what brought
matters to a head, early in June 2010, it is not completely
clear. It may be that Poteyev felt he was under suspicion and
triggered his own extraction or that for reasons we do not
yet know the CIA advised him to leave. However, if officials
are to be believed, it was a simple professional judgement
within CD1 that might finally have tipped the balance of the
decision. The operation had gone on for over a decade and
consumed considerable resources, after all. It was known
that both Chapman and one of the illegals were planning
imminent trips back to Russia and the FBI didn't want to lose
them. Furthermore, intelligence had reached the CIA that

*Christopher Metsos, a Department S officer who had run missions into the US a few years before to support illegals, happened to be in Cyprus. If they could get him too, then the evidence linking the others arrested to the SVR would be stronger as surveillance had shown Metsos delivering money to them in America during 2001 and 2002.

Having taken the decision to proceed much more aggressively, the FBI moved against Chapman and Semenko, in a bid to entrap them, so matters moved to their crisis. Sensing something wrong, Chapman had rung her father, a former KGB general, who advised her to go to the New York police and hand in the fake passport given to her by Roman. It could be an American 'provocation' designed to compromise her, so best play a double bluff. The next day she turned up at the NYPD's 1st Precinct to do just that. By then the word had been given by Bureau headquarters to arrest the whole network.

On the afternoon of 27 June, *Donald Heathfield and his wife *Tracey Foley were relaxing at their home in Cambridge just outside Boston. It was a Sunday and they'd been out for lunch at an Indian restaurant to celebrate their son Tim's twentieth birthday. He and his brother were upstairs when there was a knock on the front door.

Moments later teams of FBI agents poured into the house. Hearing the commotion Tim stepped onto the landing to see his parents being cuffed and walked out to waiting cars. An agent told him they had been arrested for being 'unlawful agents of a foreign government'.

The events in Boston were just one part of a coordinated global operation. In New York and Washington DC the other arrests were going down. Metsos was picked up in Cyprus also.

The following day, 28 June, an MI6 officer confronted a man on a street in Madrid. He had been living in Spain for the best part of twenty years under the legend of *Harry Frith. The Spanish government, it seems, did not want to arrest and try Frith, but they were willing to allow an attempted pitch by the British. A transcript of the MI6 man's offer was subsequently passed to a journalist.

'If we do not talk now then I'm afraid there's going to be a big problem for you here in Spain,' the SIS officer explained, 'I work for a Western special service and you work for Russian special services. I know this is a shock and I'm sorry that I have to do this on the street but it was the only way I could get to talk to you securely.'

Frith denied everything, telling the Briton that he was mistaken. But the next morning he fled Spain, never to return. Perhaps, once he was over the initial fright of the encounter on the street, he had rationalized that if the Spanish were willing to arrest him that's what would have happened already. Metsos too managed to slip the net, disappearing after a bail hearing in Cyprus.

But in the United States, the FBI had ten people in custody: seven deep-cover Russian agents, Lazaro's Peruvian wife, and the two Nocs, Chapman and Semenko. The interrogations began. Derek Pieper, an FBI man who'd spent years watching the *Murphys, a couple based in New Jersey, attempted to make headway with the wife, *Cynthia:

> I tried to talk to her about the kids, make sure she knew that we were taking care of the kids, that we were setting them up with friends. She wouldn't budge, she was cold, she gave me the 'I understand what you're doing, I understand your job, but I think I'm going to talk to an attorney'. Cold. That was it.

At Yasenovo, the SVR headquarters outside Moscow, these dread bits of news came in one after another during the final days of June and first ones of July: Colonel Poteyev of Department S had disappeared, presumed defected; their American spy ring was in the bag, complete; Metsos had just got away in Cyprus, Frith had managed to flee Spain. A few other illegals remained in place (in Germany and Canada for example) but they had to assume that the entire network had been compromised. It was about as big a disaster as any of them could imagine.

Then, on 4 July, the director of the SVR got a call. It was Leon Panetta, Director of the CIA.

'I got on the phone with my Russian counterpart, Mikhail Fradkov, who was right out of central casting for a Russian spy,' Panetta explained in a later CNN interview, 'and I put him on speakerphone and I said, "Mikhail, I want you to know that we're aware that they're your people." I looked around the room and you know, our people were waiting for what Fradkov would say because there was this silence. And then Fradkov said, "Yes they are our people." And you could see all these jaws drop in the room at the fact that he was acknowledging that they were Russian spies. I said, "Look, we would like to work out an exchange," and he agreed to those next steps.'

It was game on. The question for the CIA was: if there was going to be a swap, who did they want in return? The aftershocks of this sudden reversal for Russian intelligence were felt in many places. They even reached IK 5, that labour camp in Mordovia, where a GRU colonel was barely halfway through his sentence.

15

DELIVERANCE

Two days after Panetta's call with Fradkov, one of the guards went into Skripal's dorm in camp IK 5. It was not long after lunch, and the prisoner was resting on his bed. The summer is brief but intense in Mordovia. Its afternoon torpor had made Skripal a little sleepy.

'Please get all your stuff ready and be at the HQ block in ten minutes,' came the order.

'What's happening?' Skripal replied, raising himself on the bed.

'Maybe you're going to another camp.'

He started to move quickly, packing things away and summoning his mates. If he was really being transferred there was precious little he could take with him. He wanted his paratrooper friends to have all the stuff he wouldn't be allowed – food and other goodies, his clothes. He called them his prison 'family'. That's what you did for family. So after packing a small bag and bidding them farewell, he made his way over to the HQ block where he stood around outside the camp offices. Nothing happened.

After an hour, a warrant officer appeared. He told Skripal

he was being taken to Moscow. More time passed and two black FSB cars arrived. Well, this is professional, he thought, having a back-up vehicle in case one breaks down. He was directed into one of the vehicles and their journey began.

Skripal peered out of the window, watching the Mordovian forest flickering by. They drove for more than six hours without anyone saying a word to him. But of course as they got nearer to Moscow, he could read the road signs and his spirits climbed. The cars, the roadside clutter, the babushkas idling as they sped past, everything grew more dense as he escaped the endless forest, and neared Russia's capital. Definitely not another camp.

A little later they got to Lefortovo prison. It was nearly four years since he'd left it, following his conviction. He settled down for 'a nice meal, and a sleep'.

While Skripal slumbered, officials in Washington worked away, putting the finishing touches to their deal. From their side there was a presumption that the Russians they had in custody would want to take their children with them. But some of them were not minors and would be able to make a free choice. Juan Lazaro's son, for example, decided to stay in New York.

Ever since the Panetta–Fradkov phone conversation on 4 July, the question had been debated at Langley as to who they should ask for in return. They quickly agreed on Alexander Zaporozhsky – the high-value SVR asset who had been conned into coming home to Russia in 2001 and promptly jailed. Finding a second name wasn't actually that easy. Despite the FSB's claims to have jailed dozens of Russians spying for the West (Patrushev had given a figure of thirty-five caught between 2000 and 2004) there weren't actually that many genuine US or indeed UK assets in Russian prisons.

Eventually Langley came up with Gennady Vasilenko. His was a long and involved story, going back to a Cold War spy game in which an American officer and Vasilenko each tried to recruit the other. The Russians had prosecuted Vasilenko in 2006 on a charge of keeping an unlicensed weapon – there being no credible evidence of actual espionage.

As the British had been junior partners in the global Ghost Stories takedown, acting in Madrid and a couple of other places, it was decided to ask them if they had people they wanted released in the impending swap. Skripal's name, like Zaporozhsky's, was easily arrived at. FORTHWITH had after all been a high-value asset, giving excellent insight into the GRU, prior to his arrest. But as for others, that wasn't simple.

They would like to have freed Valery Ojamae, an SVR officer who had been convicted in 2001 of spying for the UK, but he was known to have died while serving his sentence. Yuri Burlatov, although primarily a Spanish asset, had of course also perished, believed murdered, in 2004 while in custody. However there was another name they were interested in, Igor Sutyagin. He had been imprisoned for espionage in 2004 after three trials, having become something of a cause célèbre for the Russian human-rights movement. Michael McFaul, President Obama's Russian-policy staffer, had already put his name into the mix.

The case against Sutyagin was hardly a compelling one. Having been arrested in 1999 he had been charged with spying for the West simply because, as a member of a Russian academic think tank, he had agreed to write a paper for a foreign consultancy. The FSB had claimed it was passing secrets, Sutyagin that it contained nothing more than open-source data and his own analysis. Many saw the charges as another of the FSB's attempts to clamp down on NGOs, academic exchanges, and contact with Westerners in general. Sutyagin had endured a nightmare journey through the Russian criminal justice system, undergoing repeated trials and languishing for years in a succession of labour camps.

MI6's decision to put Sutyagin on their list did not however result simply from a desire to right a particularly egregious injustice. It came, rather, from their guilty conscience because in this unusual case, the FSB's paranoia happened to be justified. I discovered while researching this book that Alternative Futures, the consultancy that the Russian had written a paper for, was indeed a British intelligence operation. It had been set up at that time in the late 1990s when Russia operations were being ramped up again and, even in an agency known for its sometimes ruthless behaviour, Sutyagin's arrest had caused recriminations. Revealing that this operation had flouted safeguards about making an agent aware that he was providing information to the British government, an MI6 man comments, 'his arrest and imprisonment raised some difficult ethical questions for the Service'. Another Western official puts things a little more starkly saying, 'Sutyagin had got screwed big time – they [MI6] should have been ashamed.'

It was time, then, for MI6 to do something for the man they had caused such hideous difficulties. His name was given to the Russians, and he had been brought from the penal colony where he was serving to Lefortovo.

Having had his night's rest, Skripal was taken on the morning of 7 July to an upstairs office. In this airless room he found two Russians and three Americans: Daniel Hoffman, the CIA Moscow Station Chief, and two others. Hoffman had been the agency's point man in bringing together the prisoners for the swap, as well as making sure there was a formal agreement with the Russians on the terms of their release. The CIA man was one of those formidable characters hardened by the agency's missions of the previous decade: ex-military, he had run Russian agents in Moscow in the late 1990s before serving in Pakistan and Iraq after 9/11.

It was Hoffman who broke the sweet news to Skripal that an exchange had been arranged. Skripal had seen a newspaper report about the illegals being arrested in the US so he already understood the background. Hoffman told the prisoner that under the agreement with the Russians he could soon leave the country but that the choice was his.

Skripal asked how the swap was going to work and the CIA man told him that he would first have to read and sign a document. It was a request for a presidential pardon from Dmitri Medvedev. A sense of unease was growing in the prisoner. Eventually, Skripal told them he wouldn't sign because the paper amounted to an admission of guilt. Even after nearly six years in jail, he was determined not to give those FSB bastards the satisfaction.

Skripal was not the only prisoner to object to this paper. Igor Sutyagin, considering himself entirely innocent, felt the whole thing was very suspect.

It was Hoffman's turn to be anxious. Knowing Russian officialdom, he understood that these bureaucrats would not simply turn a man free, let alone allow him to fly out of the country, without paperwork setting the whole thing on a proper legal footing. The Russians had insisted that the prisoners do this because their detained officers in the US were being asked to acknowledge that they were foreign agents operating illegally in the US. The FSB wanted reciprocal admissions from the convicts in Lefortovo.

At this stage there were plenty of people in Washington

and London who thought the deal might miscarry. And of course in that cramped office in Lefortovo the prisoners whose signatures the agency people now sought had enough bitter experience of the FSB mindset not to take anything at face value.

First gently, then in a more direct tone, Hoffman explained that he had not set these conditions but that they were non-negotiable. If Skripal wanted to leave the country he would have to sign.

The Russian asked for time to think it over and, later, saw the CIA station chief again, putting pen to paper. The CIA man allowed his two companions to take the pictures and deal with the forms needed to issue Skripal's travel documents.

Returning to his cell, Skripal realized that he was a free man, or soon would be. He had rights, including to phone calls. So he tried to contact Liudmila but was disappointed to discover that she was out of Moscow, on a trip to Kaliningrad. His son, Sasha, who was in town, hastened over to Lefortovo in her place and was allowed in to visit. They discussed what might happen next. Skripal was anxious above all that his family be able to join him, wherever he might end up.

The following morning, Skripal was taken down to the courtyard outside the Lefortovo administration building. He was put in a van where he met the other three: Zaporozhsky, Sutyagin, and Vasilenko. Skripal was disturbed to see that the two men on the American list appeared to have been beaten. It seemed some angry *chekists* wanted to have the last say with those two, but parked as they were inside the prison precincts, it was not a time for questions. None of them knew what was going to happen next. They were taken to the airport where a Tupolev jet belonging to the Ministry for Emergency Situations was running through its pre-flight checks.

Inside, the aircraft was laid out as a transport for senior officers. In place of the usual rows of seating it was arranged more like a train compartment, with seats facing each other across tables. Picking one of these, Sutyagin and Skripal sat on one side, Zaporozhsky and Vasilenko on the other.

With palpable tension, and just before the doors were closed, Hoffman and some other Americans came aboard and went to the cabin's forward section. For Skripal and the other three, having spent years in the Russian prison system, they were only too used to the raising and dashing of hopes. But slowly the Tupolev taxied, and then, with a roar of its engines, took to the sky. There were others on board, an uneasy mixture of FSB, SVR, and CIA people, all there to make sure things happened as they were supposed to. Not long after take-off, Hoffman unbuckled and came back to the four released prisoners. He explained that they were flying to Vienna where the exchange would take place. From there, two of them would go to the US, and two to the UK.

Things were happening very quickly to these men who had spent years languishing in the Gulag. They had no luggage, they were sitting there in dark grey prison clothes, and they had little idea what would become of them. Hoffman presented them each with a bag though he urged them not to open them until they got to Vienna. There were so many questions. Skripal knew what had happened with some previous defections – how the KGB had kept families apart for years. He was anxious about that.

'What about my wife? When will she be able to join me?' Skripal asked. 'Don't worry,' Hoffman answered, 'it's all been agreed with the Russian authorities.' That came as some comfort, at least.

After touching down just outside the Austrian capital, the four Russian prisoners were taken by bus across to a Boeing belonging to the suitably obscure Vision Airlines, taking their goody bags up the stairway. They were greeted there by Rick DesLauriers, the FBI agent who had masterminded Operation Ghost Stories.

The Russian illegals had arrived from the US on the same jet, but had already been taken across to a private terminal. Skripal and the others did not, therefore, see them. However, having got his released prisoners onto the American jet, Hoffman doubled back to the Tupolev, after the Russian party had boarded, to make sure everything had been done to plan.

Once Hoffman was on board the Boeing, the relief became palpable. The Russians were invited to open the bags they'd been given, each one containing a tracksuit, some underwear, toiletries, and a soft drink.

'Keep looking,' Hoffman told them, as the men, rooting around, discovered one by one that he had put a small bottle of Scotch in each bag also. It was time to toast freedom. Skripal and the other two former intelligence officers knocked back the amber nectar with relish. Sutyagin, apparently, abstained.

The Boeing took off, its pilots having filed a flight plan for RAF Brize Norton and from there to the eastern seaboard of the US.

On board the climbing Tupolev meanwhile, there was Juan Lazaro, actually Mikhail Vasenkov, who had been living undercover for so long that he just wanted to go back to his retirement in the US. Donald Heathfield and Tracey Foley, or rather Andrei Bezrukov and Yelena Vavilova, were Siberians who had joined the SVR many years before as a real-life couple. They had their sons on board also, two boys who had grown up believing themselves to be Canadians. The illegals were heading back to Moscow, where they would be feted as the ardent *chekists* and master spies their government and media wanted them to be.

The Boeing made a short stop at Brize Norton. Some people from MI6 came abroad, greeted their two Russians, and bade the rest of the party a safe flight to America. Making their way across the pan, the freed men were accompanied by the senior SIS officer to an RAF helicopter. It flew them southwards, across the rolling hills and hedge-lined fields of Wiltshire and Hampshire, down towards the south coast, or to be more precise, the Solent.

Arriving at the Fort, they were shown their rooms before being ushered by their MI6 host into another. 'It was full of clothes, very good clothes, and shoes,' Skripal explained, 'and he told us to take what we wanted. Really, there was no limit. It was all for us.'

Burdened by his goodies, Skripal went back to his room and decided to take a shower. Suddenly he caught sight of himself in the mirror: although he was in southern England he was still wearing the rough prison uniform from IK 5. He had come all the way from Mordovia to this place without having the chance to change. 'For days,' he explained to me, 'I didn't believe it was real.'

There was elation, but the weeks that followed were also tinged with disquiet for Skripal. His days were taken up with debriefing. Gordievsky's debrief in the same place had lasted months. It would be quicker for Skripal. They went over many matters with him, and of course he learned certain things from them, like the arrest and imprisonment of Roberto Florez in Spain. It was a time when the spies sat talking for hours, each trying to reach their own forms of closure. How much had Skripal told his interrogators about Bagnall, Jones, and their meetings? These were delicate questions.

In conversations years later, Sergei and I discussed Florez. Certainly he held the Spaniard responsible for his arrest. He knew Florez hadn't provided his name, but simply alluding to penetrations in the GRU's operations in that country would have been enough to start the mole-hunt. Skripal did not express anger towards Florez, rather he seemed to accept that spying had its risks, and he had always been aware of them.

Since Sergei had just spent years in a camp, he had a right to know about his betrayal and that of Burlatov and to get some sense of how the leak had been detected.

There was a host of practical things also. The SIS people quickly spruced their two guests up, and took photos for their new passports. That was important psychologically, in under-lining their new identity. And they asked Skripal where he wanted to live, did he want to stay in England or go to Spain? They knew from their clandestine meetings with him that Sergei had sometimes talked about a future in the Spanish sun. No, on reflection, he would prefer Britain. They would get people looking for some possible homes – within the Ser-vice's budget, of course. Where would he prefer? Winchester, Chichester, or Salisbury? He would have to think it over.

While business went on in the Fort, back in Russia Prime Min-ister Vladimir Putin went to a party to celebrate the return of the SVR's illegals. As he left, a group of journalists asked him questions. Was it true he'd been singing karaoke with them?

Not quite, they had sung a song together called 'Where Does the Motherland Begin' and some similar numbers. This tune first featured in a 1968 series called *The Sword and the Shield*, which extolled the heroism of the Soviet secret police.

Putin then quoted President Medvedev, saying that the compromise of this agent network was the result of treachery, adding, 'and traitors always come to no good, they end up in a ditch either drunk or on drugs. The other day one such traitor kicked the bucket, exactly like that, abroad.' One of the reporters, almost egging on the former FSB chief, asked whether these traitors living abroad wouldn't be punished. 'I think it's an improper question,' Putin answered, 'and such decisions are not made at a press conference. Intelligence agencies have their own code, and all their staff follow it.'

No doubt there was something uniquely infuriating to Putin, a one-time Department S man, about Poteyev's betrayal of the deep-cover network. The resources involved were so enormous in creating it, and the personal sacrifices made by the Russian officers serving as illegals could hardly be imagined.

A few months later, when asked again about treachery at an end-of-year press conference, he returned to the theme of treason, but in a more general way, making a statement that clearly went beyond Poteyev and the American spy ring. While denying that Russia still has assassination squads, he still predicted a grim end for those who'd betrayed the Motherland: 'With regard to traitors they will kick the bucket on their own, I assure you,' Putin seemed to promise, noting, 'Whatever thirty pieces of silver those people may have gotten, they will stick in their throat.'

Back in southern England, at the MI6 training base, there were procedures for these debriefs, honed over the years, among them that the newcomers were kept in a rather British form of 'quarantine'. It was more comfortable than the Gulag version, for sure. They could get outside and walk (escorted) along the coastline and enjoy a well-cooked meal and few drinks of an evening. But what Skripal couldn't do was make a phone call to Moscow, not from the Fort at least, and that made him anxious. He needed to talk to Liudmila and his mum.

After one month, the formal debrief was near its end. Skripal was taken somewhere where he could call his loved ones, and 'after I spoke to them, I became calmer'.

It had been so hard talking to his mother. He knew the deal with Liudmila was that she could come over to Britain. But although his mother was allowed under the US–Russian agreement to join him she showed little sign of wanting to uproot herself. He must have doubted whether he would see his poor old mother, and embrace her, ever again. He had tried to comfort her with some hopeful words. Maybe one day he would be allowed to come back, they would be united again. 'Don't even think about coming back to Russia,' she told him firmly, 'you would never be safe.'

The women in Sergei's life had always been so central to it, anchoring him through all the ups and downs he had come through from the army, to the GRU, and prison. Now there would be a subtle realignment within this constellation. His mother would be further away, beyond his reach, and Yulia's gravitational pull would grow. When he was arrested she had just been a girl in his eyes, a university student. Now she had matured into a confident young woman who, with her gift for languages, after graduating, had quickly got a job in Moscow with Nike.

It was Yulia's turn to lead the way for those left behind in

Russia. She flew to Britain while her father's debrief was wrapping up at the Fort. She took the house-hunting upon herself, touring around the three towns that had been discussed with her father. She did not take long to reach her conclusion. With the money that the British government would give them they would be able to have a house too, not a flat, a proper Englishman's castle. The place she had fallen for was Salisbury.

16

CHRISTIE MILLER ROAD

Driving down to Salisbury one morning in June 2017, I was heading for Sergei Skripal's home. Approaching from London you pass the city's main cemetery, and head around the town centre on the ring road before branching off uphill, towards the area where he lived. The houses are newish, well kept, and in many ways undistinguished.

It was almost as if he and Yulia had set out to choose an anonymous location, an archetype of middle England. The British intelligence people guiding her house-hunting may also have liked Christie Miller Road because the dwellings there were built as houses for the police. Although the Wiltshire force disposed of them, among residents of this cul de sac there are apparently still quite a few retired officers.

While they had not ended up in Sergei's archetypal tumbledown English country cottage, the cathedral city certainly gave them a rich sense of history. In its centre medieval buildings nestle alongside the proud Regency stucco and the boxier form of more recent constructions. There are any number of restaurants and bars to relax in, many of them lining the River Avon running through the middle of Salisbury. On the plain above this well-incised valley there are pleasing walks, like the one up to the fort at Old Sarum which offers a fine view of the cathedral.

Sergei and I had already met somewhere else and had a long talk about his life. We had spoken subsequently by phone and he had agreed I should come to his home for a proper working session of half a day, with notebook, to drill down into his experiences. So I was in a state of some excitement when I reached Christie Miller Road. Driving up towards the end of the cul de sac, scanning the houses for numbers, I couldn't spot his, 47. My momentary confusion ended when he emerged from his front door, directing me with military-style hand signals to park right outside the entrance. He welcomed me, and noticing the lucky horseshoe over the entrance, I followed him in.

Turning left from the front door we entered his sitting room. It was cosy, well worn, and certainly not affluent. Things were tidy, as you might expect from an old military man, but not fastidiously so. What caught my eye immediately were the signs of someone who had grown used to killing time. There was a stack of jigsaw puzzles for grown-ups – not quite two-thousand-piece ones of a summer sky, but you get the idea. I also saw an Airfix scale model of HMS Victory. Sergei had put Nelson's flagship together, including rigging the masts with cotton, a fiddly task requiring considerable patience. I read later that he also spent a great deal of time playing online tank games, though I didn't spot his computer on that occasion.

He showed me some items that had been brought from their old flat in Moscow by Liudmila and his kids. It was a way of making things more homely. There was a picture on the wall and some ornaments on a bookcase. It was with particular pride that he picked up the resin model of an English country cottage, the one that had been given to him twenty-one years before in Madrid by Richard Bagnall as part of his cultivation. To me the small resin casting didn't look like much, it was a typical souvenir. But it set me thinking about the cottage's meaning to Skripal. He had, after all, taken it from Spain back to Moscow and made sure, after all those years in prison, that it was brought over to his new place in Salisbury.

My reason for visiting Sergei that day was that I was intending to write a book about East–West espionage and how it had carried on despite the end of the Cold War. That's a big and amorphous subject, so my intention was to focus the story on a handful of people, using their stories, and the moment these narratives intersected at Vienna airport, during the swap of 2010, as the key to its structure. Skripal was to be one of the central half-dozen or so stories in this book. That said, I was doing this in my own time – there was no contract. The only sense in which this was a 'book' in June 2017 was in my own imagination.

Skripal said he would be happy to help. I could use everything he told me, but as for direct quotation, we would need to talk further. When he offered me a hot drink, we stepped into his kitchen. Tea or coffee? Sergei is an inveterate tea drinker. I asked for coffee, and as he reached for an ageing jar of instant, thought to myself, 'wrong call'.

'I'm sorry, you know,' he said as he was spooning the Nescafé into my cup. He wanted to explain his nervousness about being directly quoted. 'It's because of Putin,' he said. We talked a little about how his kids were essentially based in Russia, they wanted to be able to come and go freely from there, and he added, 'You see, we are afraid of Putin.'

Later, during our conversations, I said to him that he was talking to me so freely, giving so much detail, that it would be obvious that he had spoken to me, however we dealt with the issue of quotation. 'You can use everything,' he reiterated.

As we sat down, getting to business, I opened my notebook. He asked whether I was going to record it. I said no, because these were research interviews. I didn't want to record on my iPhone, the only suitable device I had on me at the time, it might get hacked. Then the FSB, GRU, whoever, would have incontrovertible proof. He agreed. It was a decision I would come to regret enormously later, but at the time I took it as a good sign; he was comfortable enough talking to me not to mind being recorded.

The house in Christie Miller Road had been bought for Skripal, in his own name, in 2011 for £260,000. The MI6 investment in bricks and mortar thus dwarfed what he had earned in his career as an agent. Welcome to Britain. The FSB had emptied his bank accounts at the time of his arrest but he may have had a little cash squirrelled away in Spain. The Skripals sold their dacha also to help with the costs of a new life in Britain. The UK government would also be paying him money from time to time.

Ross Cassidy and his wife Mo soon made friends with their new neighbours. Cassidy, who was in his early fifties at the time, was a road-haulage contractor and former Royal Navy submariner. Although he and Sergei became firm friends and drinking buddies, they never discussed his espionage career during the years that followed. Cassidy quickly drew his own conclusions about the new family in the street, and of course you could always google 'Skripal', but as a former member of the Silent Service, he knew better than most not to pry.

Ross and Mo sometimes discussed whether Liudmila was happy in her new life in Britain. He thought her a fish out of water, but Mo believed that maybe it was simply Liudmila's limited grasp of English that held her back. Yulia at that time was clearly ahead of the rest of the family in mastering the language.

For some months after Liudmila joined him in Salisbury they had lived very happily. During his latter years in IK 5 she had been suffering from the effects of uterine cancer. She had been treated for this in Russia, though it has been suggested that she eschewed surgery while Sergei was in prison, saying that she would deal with the problem upon his release. But symptoms emerged again in Salisbury, and then came the dread news that it had spread. She underwent further treatment, both in the UK and Russia, but it was to no avail. In the summer of 2012 she died, aged fifty-nine.

The loss of Liudmila was undoubtedly a hammer blow to Sergei. 'She was a formidable woman,' notes a friend, 'he simultaneously admired, adored, and feared her.' She was buried at Salisbury's London Road cemetery, and he frequently visited her grave, often more than once a week.

With her passing, Sergei's focus inevitably shifted to his daughter and son. Yulia spent a good deal of time in England as he established a new life, and once again with her language skills and positive attitude had no difficulty finding employment. Among other jobs, she worked in the conference and events team at the Holiday Inn, Eastleigh, near Southampton.

Yulia though, it is clear, at that time saw her future in Russia, and by 2014 was looking once more for a job there.

She would continue visiting her dad, of course, but she wanted to get on in life, not least in finding a soulmate.

With Sasha matters were more complicated. I met him on a couple of my visits to Salisbury. He was polite, shy, and a little diffident. His grasp of English didn't seem to match his father's. One time, as Sergei and I sat deep in conversation in their front room, Sasha returned from the shops with a big bag of straw. We greeted one another and he soon disappeared. The straw, his father explained, was for the guinea pigs they kept in a hutch out the back. Superficially one might have thought that this was a happy cohabitation of a lad and dad. But there was much pain and awkwardness in the relationship.

Sasha after all was forty-three by this time, with a failed marriage and a good deal of alcohol abuse already behind him. However, he had found a new girlfriend (in Russia) and this was a cause of some hope. But in company Skripal used tough love, saying quite unambiguously, 'My son cannot drink, he is an alcoholic.' On the occasion that Sasha disappeared with the straw, Sergei leant forward, lowering his voice slightly: 'He has been told that if he drinks again it will kill him. But I know he drinks secretly sometimes. He thinks he can hide it from me,' he shook his head slightly, 'but he can't fool his father.'

A few weeks later, Sasha flew back to Moscow, planning a trip to St Petersburg with his girlfriend. According to his cousin, Viktoria, Sasha was already drunk when Yulia picked him up at the airport. Sasha collapsed on board the train to St Petersburg and was taken to hospital where a few days later, on 18 July, he died of liver failure. Viktoria commented to one of my BBC colleagues, 'You make your own fate in life – that's what Sergei used to say about it.' While she would later become a controversial figure, this remark of Viktoria's was indeed quite in keeping with Sergei's views.

A few weeks after it happened, I rang Sergei to offer my condolences. Frankly, after everything Sasha had been told, his father said, his decision to hit the bottle again 'was a kind of suicide'. You say what you can, but of course I was not an old friend and feared I could not rise above platitudes in this dreadful situation. 'Yes,' Sergei summed up at the end of our conversation, 'life will not be so easy for me now.'

Skripal, it is clear, did not regard his son's death as suspicious. Rather he saw it as the culmination of many wrong turns or missed opportunities. But if anyone had been tempted to run checks on his corpse it would not have been possible, because he was swiftly cremated in Russia. British diplomats assisted with bringing the urn containing his ashes to Britain, where it was placed close to the entrance of the London Road cemetery.

Even before this tragedy the people who took an interest in Sergei's life had been trying to keep him busy and engaged with the world. Although he was on friendly terms with the neighbours, particularly Ross and Mo Cassidy, I got the impression that the ones he was closest to were 'Team', said without the article, those from the intelligence agencies looking after his welfare. He was evidently in regular contact with them, and had a special mobile phone that went direct to their duty officer.

There is a special section within MI6, Agent Resettlement, or AR, that looks after the service's old Joes. MI5 are also involved with the protective security aspects of this, it's a joint operation. The agencies' bosses have learned over the years that looking after old assets is vital to the credibility of their operations – and indeed an important element of getting new people to spy for them.

Sergei spoke about 'Team' with a good deal of affection, mentioning recent visits, and using a few of their first names. He implied that he had made them aware of my visit and this was no more than common sense, given that allowing some-one alone into his home carried an element of risk. Skripal harboured concerns, no doubt about it, but expressed them in terms of his kids and their ability to travel to and from Russia. But of course he had also some awareness about pro-tecting his own security. It wasn't an obsession, because after all he had received a presidential pardon, as well as serving a good deal of his sentence. There was every reason to believe that if he didn't make political statements or give lots of interviews, life would continue in its sedate, if sometimes mournful, fashion.

For Sergei the latter Salisbury years presented a series of sorrows. His brother, Valery, passed away in 2016. And Yelena, his mother, fell and broke her hip in 2017, leaving her increasingly frail as she entered her nineties. Sergei and I did not discuss her health during our meetings but I have learned that he was deeply perturbed at not being able to care for her in person. 'Team', his Whitehall minders, apparently even offered to bring Yelena over to the UK and buy Skripal a bigger house so that they could live together.

At the end of 2010, a few months after he arrived in Britain, the Skripals had seen in the New Year together via Skype; Sergei and Liudmila in Salisbury, Yelena, Valery, and his daughter in Yaroslavl. It brought them comfort as they adapted to life apart. Sergei kept up the regular phone calls to his mother but did not, following her accident, use the video feature of Skype. Watching her in this predicament, fading away, when he could do nothing practical to help was too much for him, perhaps.

Although Sergei must have found this separation from family, and the inability to attend his brother and son's funerals, to be a great sorrow, he did not see an alternative. When I asked him whether he thought he might ever return to Russia, he was quite sure he wouldn't, and quoted his mother to me from 2010 telling him he should never come back because it would not be safe.

It is possible that Sergei had some sort of crisis after Liudmila's death in 2012, maybe he had even thought of returning to Russia. Perhaps that's why Team had made its very generous offers to bring his mother over and install them in a larger house. But if there was such a moment, it seemed well behind him by the time we met.

Some years after he settled in Salisbury, and very much to Sergei's delight, Richard Bagnall had got in touch. Richard had taken his old agent to the Army v. Navy rugby match at Twickenham, and they met up several times after that. He was not part of Team, and indeed had retired from the service by this point. It seems quite possible that under the old maxim that intelligence officers never quite leave, Richard had gone along with a general effort to gee Sergei up. Certainly the former GRU colonel regarded their relationship as a social one, a measure of the former MI6 man's diligence about pastoral care in a relationship that had, after all, lasted decades.

Of the theories that would later emerge that Sergei was involved in active intelligence work or had contributed to the notorious Donald Trump dossier compiled by former SIS officer Christopher Steele, there was no indication. Rather Sergei appeared to be a homebody and creature of habit, a man well into his sixties whose cravings for wealth and adventure had faded. He visited Liudmila's grave regularly, and the corner shop, where he would buy scratch cards a couple of times a week. In the months after Sasha's death he signed up for membership at Salisbury's Railway Social Club and became a regular there. His former neighbour and friend Ross Cassidy proposed his membership at the club.

Skripal did sometimes travel up to London for the day and occasionally MI6 made use of his services. The office had given him a similar package to previous defectors like Oleg Gordievsky, Vladimir Kuzichkin, and Vladimir Rezun. In return for a service payment they would sometimes sing for their supper. Gordievsky, an old MI6 hand once told me, had been 'produced as one of the after-dinner entertainments'. This might take the form of speaking to a training course or conference because after all, in Skripal's case how many former GRU colonels had many of these people ever met?

As far as I could establish, Skripal's work had involved talking to some military audiences, possibly to new trainees at the Fort, and to a few friendly intelligence services. In this sense he acted as a consultant about how the GRU might approach a problem or gave insights into its historical operations, say in another European country. But he did not have the energy or time to engage as energetically as Alexander Litvinenko did with the Spanish authorities in the year before his death.

Nevertheless, the use of Skripal as an authority on the GRU, giving occasional assistance to friendly agencies, might have been seen in Moscow as a sort of re-entry into the world of espionage, something that sat ill with his pardon of 2010.

Sergei did not seem to want much out of life at this time. He would make trips about Britain, often connected with military history, cook for himself, enjoy a quiet drink, and talk to his mum when he was missing her.

As in the camp or Lefortovo he would also watch a good deal of television, devoting many hours to Pervy Kanal – Russia's First Channel. There are entertainment and cultural programmes on it, of course, but the First Channel is also known for following the Putin line closely in its news coverage. Indeed, in its messages about the West's Russophobia or the imperative need for a strong Russia it might even be regarded as being to the right of the Kremlin in ideological matters. During Skripal's years in Britain, Putin had of course returned to the job of president, consolidating his power and flexing Russia's muscle. Military actions in Ukraine as well as interference in elections had people in Western intelligence agencies in quite a state.

Sergei and I discussed the world scene, including the crises in North Korea and Ukraine. He is, or was at least when we were talking in 2017, an unashamed Russian nationalist, enthusiastically adopting the Kremlin line in many matters, even while sitting in his MI6-purchased house. He was adamant, for example, that Putin had not surreptitiously introduced Russian troops into east Ukraine, as much of the Western press reported. If regular units had gone in, he insisted, they would have been sitting in Kiev very soon. Our Ukraine discussion produced an exchange which (from memory) went something like this:

> *Sergei:* The problem with the Ukrainians is that they are incapable of leadership. They need Russia for that. The Ukrainians are simply sheep who need a good shepherd.

Me: Um . . . Sergei . . . I feel I should tell you, my father
    was from Ukraine.
Sergei (unfazed): That's OK. Don't worry about it.

I smile whenever I think about that exchange.

There are volumes written about the torment of the
Russian exile, lost in a haze of drink and regret. And no
doubt it wasn't easy for Skripal. Equally, he would not allow
himself the luxury of self-pity, even if he remained true to
his country in general, and in particular to the version of it,
the USSR, that disappeared in 1991. By the time I met him
he was carrying a few more pounds than when he'd arrived
in Britain and his hair had thinned a good deal, but it would
have been a great mistake to have underestimated his mental
or indeed physical toughness. Life may have lobbed him some
gross misfortunes but he still intended to live every day of it
to the full.

There were however people who would wish him harm,
who were actively plotting it, in fact. Just as he was being
watched in the airport and Izmir back in 2004, so there were
eyes on him as he made his way around Salisbury. Sergei
didn't have a regular job or commute but at the same time
he wasn't always at home either. Those who would target the
old spy needed to establish his 'pattern of life'. And as that
summer, with all its sorrows, ended, time was running out for
his carefree existence in Salisbury.

PART THREE

TARGET

17

SUNDAY 4 MARCH

It is mid-winter in Salisbury. There are patches of snow in the city centre following heavy falls a few days earlier. A man in his sixties is walking from Zizzi's restaurant towards the Maltings. It's a short journey, around the corner and, briefly, through an arcade to the open area beside the Avon where on sunny summer days people come to loll by the waterside. It takes about one minute, even moving slowly.

Alongside him walks another person. She's wrapped up against the cold but you can see it's a young woman. Maybe she is having some concerns. He had become irate in the restaurant, raising his voice at the staff, complaining loudly as the time came to pay the bill. They make their way to a bench. It is not the kind of day when you would normally sit and watch the waterfowl gliding by, it's far too cold for one thing. But anyhow, they've brought some bread to feed the ducks.

As she sits beside him, for anything up to twenty minutes he complains of feeling worse and worse, her concerns are mounting.

He is sweating profusely, he cannot see properly, his world

is darkening as his pupils become tiny. The man looks sky-ward, trying to see the light. Now she is feeling terrible also.

Passers-by gaze at them. Probably junkies. An odd couple, old man and young woman, but you sometimes see these unlikely pairings when they're pooling funds, searching for a hit. Someone walking by can't help but giggle as she sees him almost clawing at the sky with his hand. What are they like, these druggies?!

Moments later, she has keeled over, her head coming to rest on his lap. He is still upright on the bench, but losing consciousness. There are other passers-by now, and they are more worried. Maybe they've overdosed? Someone decides to call an ambulance.

Among the first to approach them, checking they are OK, is an army nurse. Another woman comes over, a local doctor. Being professionals they are deferred to by the rest of the little group that has gathered beside the bench, and they are immediately concerned by what they see.

Both of the people on the bench are sweating heavily, and have lost control of their bodily functions. It's hard to find a pulse because they're so weak. They are becoming pale, life is draining away because they're not breathing. It's just a matter of minutes now until hypoxia, brain damage due to lack of oxygen, starts. It may already have begun.

Minutes, luckily, is all it takes the first ambulance crew to arrive, hot-foot from the Odstock Road station on the southern outskirts of Salisbury. As they hit the road, sirens blaring, a couple of police officers have arrived at the bench. It's only four minutes after the call to the emergency services. Moments later the paramedics are there also, and get to work, quickly joining the medical passers-by in giving breathing assistance to the two junkies on the bench.

They've seen it before, the emergency services, drug users who bed down under the car park just a short walk from the Maltings, scoring there and getting it wrong. Maybe they've just bought some bad stuff, maybe taken too much. But these two are in a desperate way. A second ambulance is called, while the crew of the first on scene go through the drills for overdose with an opioid, maybe fentanyl. Pinpoint pupils? Yes. Respiratory arrest? Check. Low blood pressure? Clearly.

The paramedics set about administering some standard treatments for an opioid overdose, they know they need to get these two to hospital as soon as possible. But the police are suspicious, these people aren't right for junkies. They're too clean, too well turned out, for rough sleepers, and the age difference is odd too. Someone is looking through the two patients' pockets for identification. A couple of CID officers, plainclothes people, have come over to the bench, having been nearby on an investigation of local businesses using illegal labour.

It doesn't take them long to find ID: they are Sergei and Yulia Skripal. The Ops room radios back to the officer on the scene: Sergei Skripal has a 'Don't Stop' flag on the Police National Computer. On screen there is a note beside his listing and a number to ring. It's a rare thing, that Don't Stop, and the few officers on duty in Salisbury that afternoon, seven or eight of them, all take notice when they hear it over the radio.

The ambulances meanwhile have loaded up their patients and are racing towards Salisbury District Hospital, turning onto Odstock Road, passing their station, and ploughing up the hill. The vehicles drive up the ramp, execute a 180-degree turn, and disgorge their critically ill patients into the Emergency Department, where they are taken straight to the Resuscitation bay.

One level up, on Radnor Ward, Sister Sarah Clark gets the call: two patients are on their way; they're critical and need ventilation. She's been at the hospital since 1984, working most of that time in intensive care – there's not much she hasn't seen. But these cases will prove quite unlike any they've treated before. The unit is already full, they have to shuffle a couple of people into other wards.

Everything that needs to be done is done swiftly on Radnor Ward, and soon Sergei and Yulia are coming up in the lift. Their journey through the Emergency Department has been very fast, around half an hour, and during that time Sister Clark has learned a little more, their names and that they are father and daughter. The patients arrive, and are connected to ventilators and the host of lines that will be needed if they are to have a chance of survival. 'Our role was supportive,' Sister Clark told me in a BBC interview, 'to make sure they are getting enough oxygen in their system and that they had a stable blood pressure.'

The Skripals had been hooked up to the full battery of life-support systems within an hour of the call to the emergency services operator coming – and of course had medical help for most of that time, the so-called 'golden hour'. They had been given a chance of survival. As a member of the hospital team said to me, 'Imagine if the timings had been a little different and they'd fallen ill at home, the odds are they would have died very quickly.'

The wires had been buzzing at Wiltshire Police. They had called the number in the police computer and found out that Sergei Skripal was a former Russian spy who had been reset-tled in Britain. More officers were summoned to Salisbury. The police sent somebody up to the hospital to see what more they could learn. Could the two people have been poisoned? Clearly, that was a possibility.

The two CID officers meanwhile went to Skripal's house on Christie Miller Road. Approaching the front door, Detective Sergeant Nick Bailey extended a gloved hand to grasp the front door handle – always worth a try. It wouldn't open so he went around to the back of the property, where he managed to gain entry. What was he looking for? Signs that their house had been searched, perhaps, or maybe even the presence of a would-be assassin. Everything seemed to be in order.

That night passed swiftly at the hospital, and at 6am the senior person on duty, one of the directors of the hospital trust, began calling fellow members of the board to tell them what was going on. There was some information about the Skripals' condition but also that Sergei was a former Russian spy and that poisoning was suspected.

One of the directors wanted more information, so he called Dr Duncan Murray, the senior intensive-care specialist, who in turn rang the ward. 'I spoke to the nurse who had been on that night,' recalled Murray, an enormously experienced South African-born anaesthetist, 'and it was this conversation I could never have imagined in my wildest imagination as having with anyone.'

The Chief Executive, meeting with the rest of her board at the hospital that morning, Monday 5 March, put the necessary measures in place to declare a Major Incident at 10am. This allowed them to mobilize all the people and resources needed to handle the crisis. It also allowed for an attempt at decontamination of the place where the Skripals were brought in. It was done with hoses and scrubbing brushes, since they still thought they were dealing with an opioid. Of course having made this announcement, and briefly closed the Emergency Department, there was bound to be press interest in this poisoning.

News of what was happening was percolating through London also. People at MI5 and MI6, jointly responsible for the team looking after Sergei, had known since the police phone call of the previous evening. They were aware, presumably from Sergei, about Yulia's impending visit, and immediately started to wonder whether, somehow, inadvertently, she had led assassins to her father's door or even brought something with her from Moscow that might be poisoned. It was time to alert ministers and the like. For many of those hearing the news, assessing each new fact, trying to understand it all, there was a sort of default setting; the Litvinenko affair.

At the BBC, Home Affairs Correspondent Tom Symonds got on to the story that morning. It didn't take him and his producer long to extract Sergei Skripal's name from someone in Salisbury. They recorded a report for the *Six O'Clock News* that evening, and circulated an article on the BBC computer system that began, 'A man and a woman are critically ill after apparently being poisoned by an unknown substance in Salisbury'. This copy was shared with others in New Broadcasting House, including staff on my programme, about one hour before that news bulletin, but under an embargo until 6pm.

'What do you make of this?' I was asked by two of our senior editors on *Newsnight* within minutes of one another. I filled them in with a good deal of background about Skripal, after which one of them asked, 'But how do you know all of this?' Taking them into my confidence, I explained about my meetings with Sergei, but also that it had been for a book project, he hadn't anticipated it being used on the BBC, and that I would prefer not to compound his difficulties in his hour of crisis by talking publicly about our conversations.

That night, Monday 5th, we led *Newsnight* with a brief report and interview about the poisoning. Although I was not going to state explicitly that I had interviewed Sergei, I loaded a great deal of detail into this live 'two way': about the circumstances of his recruitment, his role in the GRU, and the type of intelligence he had been able to pass on to MI6. Much of this was not in the public domain. Many colleagues, I think, shared that 'How does he know all this?' feeling that my editors had voiced earlier that evening.

Watching the news that evening at home not far from Salisbury, Ross Cassidy was horrified. Having got to know the Skripals soon after they moved into Christie Miller Road, Cassidy, his wife, and Sergei had travelled up to Heathrow just a couple of days earlier (on Saturday 3rd) to collect Yulia. Sergei had been worried about the snow, and Ross owned an Isuzu D-Max pick-up, so they had decided to make an outing of it. After dropping the Skripals at their home around 5.30 that evening, the Cassidys had arranged to see them later in Yulia's stay. Now this. Cassidy called the police, who later that same night conducted the first of what would be many interviews.

The following morning, Tuesday, things became even more fraught. Detective Sergeant Nick Bailey had been admitted to the hospital having fallen ill during the night. After entering the Skripals' home on Sunday, Bailey had gone back to the Bourne Hill police station to type up a report on the day's events. Taking off his gloves before he did so, he had become contaminated with a small amount of poison.

It took another twenty-four hours before he began to come down with the symptoms. Although DS Bailey was also dealing with sweating, heart, and vision problems he did not need ventilation. He was never classed as 'critical', presumably due to having absorbed a much smaller dosage. Those though are the judgements of hindsight: on 6 March his condition caused alarm at the hospital. With the poisoning becoming big news, some people who had been out in town on Sunday afternoon also started turning up, reporting odd symptoms.

'There was a real concern about how big this could get,' Lorna Wilkinson, Director of Nursing, told me later, recalling thinking on 6 March, 'Have we just gone from two index patients to having something that actually could become all-consuming and involve many casualties?' The decision was taken to move to 'barrier nursing', the type of additional precautions taken when people have infectious diseases or compromised immune systems. The nurses working directly with the Skripals used visors, aprons, gloves, and so on. However they never donned army-style protective suits or used full isolation techniques.

By Tuesday afternoon, results were also coming back on some toxicology tests that had been carried out for the hospital several miles away, at the Porton Down laboratories of Public Health England. The civilian facility, supporting the health service in matters of rare diseases, radiological, or chemical contamination, nestles close by the military research establishment. Initially, they had been asked to look at all kinds of indicators since the Skripals might have been hit by anything from opioids to shellfish or snake toxins. One thing came back clearly from the lab: the Skripals had levels of a key enzyme, acetylcholinesterase, that were so low that they were barely measurable.

This substance regulates the body's nervous system,

effectively switching off the impulses transmitted by its biological opposite in activating nerves, acetylcholine. Without acetylcholinesterase certain functions, like sweating or urinating, remain 'switched on'. Critically, respiration can speed up, as the diaphragm is overloaded with messages, to the point where the muscles give out and the person stops breathing. Furthermore, if the patient remains in this state for any length of time, the brain can become flooded with acetylcholine, which acts as a neurotransmitter, effectively short-circuiting the central nervous system with the potential for lasting damage. The patients were evidently in a dire way because of this bodily emergency, something experts call a cholinergic crisis.

There's a considerable body of medical knowledge about cholinergic crises, much of it stemming back to the period when people on farms became accidentally contaminated with large amounts of (now banned) organophosphate insecticide. It was the development of these substances, designed to kill insects by blocking the release of acetylcholinesterase, in the 1930s into something much more potent, becoming chemical weapons that could wipe out people in large numbers, that created the first nerve agents. There are plenty of staff in Salisbury District Hospital who know about these substances, some of them ex-military with training in chemical warfare, as well as some who worked with scientists at Porton Down. Just a few weeks earlier the hospital had been put through a major-incident exercise dealing with chemical, biological, radiological, or nuclear weapons, so the indicators of nerve-agent poisoning were fresh in many people's minds.

By the end of the working day on Tuesday, a diagnosis was firming up: the Skripals had been poisoned with a nerve agent. It was a time for rapid consultations among doctors.

Dr Stephen Jukes, one of the intensive-care consultants who became part of the team caring for the Skripals several days after their admission, had been poring over anything he could find in the way of medical literature. He and the others exchanged ideas frequently using a consultants' WhatsApp group.

As he made his way up to the Radnor Ward, there were immediate signs that the usual atmosphere of the place had been upset. Armed officers from the Metropolitan Police had taken station outside the doors of the rooms off the central intensive-care bays where the Skripals lay. These guardians would remain there for weeks, along with detectives who were anxious to question them as soon as they regained consciousness. If they ever did. Dr Jukes recalled:

> When we first were aware this was a nerve agent we were expecting them not to survive. We would try all our therapies. We would ensure the best clinical care. But all the evidence was there that they would not survive.

This then was the depressing panorama that greeted the doctors. While they fought their desperate battle, the machinery of national incident control and crisis management was swinging into action.

A major incident-control room, the Strategic Coordinating Group, was established at the police headquarters in Devizes, with Paul Mills, the Deputy Chief Constable of Wiltshire, as Gold Command, leading the response. His boss, Chief Constable Keir Pritchard, had only taken over in post the previous day. Although emergency service senior management regularly exercise for terrorist incidents or major accidents, they were in uncharted territory. 'There isn't a plan on the shelf for nerve-agent attacks in a small city such as

Salisbury,' Mr Pritchard said later, 'this was brand new, and it was brand new for many of us across the country.'

Things were done in the first few days, before the nerve-agent diagnosis firmed up, that left many of those in the Devizes operations room with a whole new set of worries. The fire brigade had done ad hoc decontamination in one or two places simply using hoses – which led to discussions in the coordinating group about whether the nerve agent might have been washed into the Avon, and everyone should be told to look for dead fish or wildfowl. Would it end up in the water supply? The questions multiplied apace during those early days. There were uncertainties about the public health advice also – would it be enough just to wash your clothes if you'd been in Zizzi's?

For members of the Coordinating Group meeting in Devizes almost every morning for the first month, this crisis required an unprecedented response. In all more than 1,200 police and 300 members of the military were brought in to deal with it. Much of this, put in place under the codename Operation Fairline, was about securing various sites while evidence was gathered and they were made safe. But of course it was also quite natural that the police would want to catch those responsible if they possibly could.

On 6 March the Metropolitan Police Counter-Terrorist Command had taken control of the investigation. An official from Public Health England had been dispatched from Porton that evening in order to report the nerve-agent diagnosis to the Cabinet emergency committee in Whitehall first thing on Wednesday 7th.

Outside the hospital, meanwhile, the world's press was descending. Reporters from CNN or Al Jazeera stood there round the clock, doing their live shots to TV newsrooms around the globe. Journalists fanned out across the little city, seeking eyewitnesses, with some contacting the doctors and nurses directly. The hospital reminded everybody of their duties of confidentiality towards their desperately ill patients. Coming in and out each day, often to shouted questions from the press, the staff jokingly christened their hospital 'Fortress Salisbury'.

Sergei and Yulia were of course entirely oblivious to all of this activity. They were lying on Level 4 of the hospital deep in what the newspapers call 'a medically induced coma'. The doctors don't like that term, preferring instead 'deep sedation' or similar phrases. Whatever the argument about terminology, the reality of Sergei's fight was plain enough. He was clinging to life by the slenderest of threads.

18

THE FIGHT FOR SURVIVAL

The morning of Wednesday 7 March saw the medics at Salisbury District Hospital with three patients, each presenting a different clinical picture. The best of them was Detective Sergeant Nick Bailey. He had suffered from a relatively modest contamination, and was classified as 'serious' rather than critical. He was conscious though hardly able to speak.

Yulia Skripal and her father on the other hand were both 'critical', and receiving what is termed Level 3 care – ventilation, deep sedation, and the full battery of support available in Radnor Ward. There were differences between them. Even though Yulia had not been breathing when found on the bench in the Maltings the paramedics had clearly done something for her because she was fleetingly responsive as she came through the Emergency Department and before the doctors put her under deep sedation.

Sergei was in a worse way. He had shown almost no sign of life and although experts cautioned us at the time against expecting age to make a difference when a substance this deadly was having its effect, his diabetes, his lifestyle, and the extra pounds he was carrying cannot have counted in his favour. That evening, speaking to someone who was 'in the loop' before going on air, I was told he was not expected to survive the night.

These three patients had each been found a room just off the main or open-plan part of Radnor. There was an armed guard in place outside each one, but apart from this presence the relatives of those who lay just yards away, locked in their own fights for life, continued to come and go. For Sergei and Yulia though there was nobody to offer prayer by their bed-side or stroke their heads, urging them on. Their weeks in intensive care passed without family – except for one another and the tight-knit team caring for them.

With the diagnosis of nerve-agent poisoning the military side of Porton Down became more involved. Their judge-ments defined much of what happened during those early days, and not just in the hospital. Everything from public health advice for those who'd been in the Maltings and were worried to the language used in Parliament or pointers given to detectives about how long before their collapse the Skri-pals had been poisoned was conditioned by what the scientists said about the type of agent used, and how and when it could have entered the body.

Initially the supposition was that it might be an agent such as VX, a military chemical weapon produced in large quantities by both the US and Soviet Union during the Cold War. This was the type of agent used to assassinate the North Korean leader's half-brother Kim Jong-nam in Kuala Lumpur airport in February 2017, killing him swiftly. However this theory was soon questioned.

An Incident Response Team from Porton that had gone to the key sites in Salisbury with a chemical-agent monitor (hand-held detection equipment) had not found any traces of

VX. What's more, it had not turned up any of the other well-known nerve agents such as soman or sarin either. The word coming out of the research establishment was that it was 'something very exotic'. But for as long as the agent remained a mystery, key questions were left hanging; from treatment options, to how it entered the Skripals' bodies, when that might have happened, and therefore how far back detectives should be looking at their movements as well as harvesting CCTV images from around the city. Everything therefore rested with a handful of scientists trying to find a testable sample.

For a fleeting moment, early in the investigation, there were hopes that they might be able to trace any residues to a specific facility. This remarkable science had been used on samples from Halabja, where Saddam Hussein used sarin against Kurdish civilians. Essentially it involved finding the molecular signature of the agent and its constituent chemicals, unique identifiers resulting from the water and other environmental factors at the production site. With the Halabja samples a precursor chemical had been traced to a German factory. But as we will see, the Salisbury poison was to prove altogether more obscure, and therefore the chances of being able to match it to known samples from particular factories fell.

The Porton experts knew that if the basic detection equipment couldn't produce results, they would have to send items or swabs back to their labs several miles to the north. There they could be subjected to the dual process of gas chromatography/mass spectrometry (often shortened to GC/MS by the chemical warfare experts), using large lab machines that can't be shifted to the locations being investigated. The first stage of this analysis involves burning a sample and studying the flame produced, and the second weighing the atoms of the residue. Each test took time and there was a small number of testing rigs: that produced a major bottleneck as samples started coming in from all over the city. The GC/MS at Porton Down did though begin pointing the scientists towards an answer, and it was Novichok. That word, unknown to almost everyone outside the chemical-weapons community, was soon to be on people's lips the world over.

Many different compounds had been researched and tested during the dying days of the USSR's chemical-weapons research programme – in fact the dissident scientist who wrote about them in the mid-1990s suggested that there were actually up to a hundred different Novichok formulas, and to confuse matters further some Russian scientists referred to them by different names. However, the picture was not as complicated as it at first seemed. Only three of these compounds had been developed to the point where they could be weaponized – used to fill bombs or shells.

There was A230, which was designed for use in very cold climates and specifically requested by the Soviet Army because its existing agents solidified in such conditions, rendering them ineffective. Then there was A232, which one might term the main Novichok agent. Designed as a VX replacement, it could be made from precursor chemicals that were not on the list of substances regulated by the Chemical Weapons Convention. This offered Russia a ready-made solution should the day come when it wanted to break out of the disarmament treaties. It was a way of retaining a dormant capability that the Russian state had pledged to give up.

Designed to fall from an exploding munition in a fine mist of droplets that could be inhaled or absorbed through the skin, A232 was created with a chemical signature that is almost impossible to detect with standard NATO equipment. The successful German intelligence operation had by 1998 however brought some A232 to the West, so Porton Down had examined actual samples and retained all the reference data. Alas, it was not the substance coming back from Salisbury. This left one more 'production' standard Novichok, A234.

This last formula had the advantage that it could be produced as a solid, then ground into powder. In some situations that could be used, for example via ventilation systems, to get A234 inhaled by the victim, in others it might be produced as a very viscose liquid. If this suggested some obvious possibilities as a poison for assassinations, that hypothesis fitted neatly with intelligence MI6 had received in the late 2000s, suggesting Russia had retained some small stocks of this agent for precisely this purpose.

It isn't entirely clear whether scientists at Porton Down had ever synthesized their own A234, an activity that would have been allowed (in very small quantities) under the Chemical Weapons Convention, for example for the purpose of developing new filters for gas masks. Although they knew the chemical formulas for A234, some people have suggested to me that they may have refrained from making it for many reasons, not least cost, and therefore have never been able to carry out detailed studies on its properties. Others have implied that it was studied at Porton, though whether they made it or obtained some Russian A234 by clandestine means would be highly classified.

Whatever the truth, this was the substance that was coming up in their GC/MS testing. It had been found at the bench, and at Zizzi's. Tests on blood and tissue from the Skripals now revealed the presence of A234 within their bodies too. The scientists also formed the view that it was a substance of great purity, something only a handful of labs in the world could have produced.

So if the experts were fixing on that obscure nerve agent, what did that mean for the patients in Salisbury Hospital? Asked this question, Dr Duncan Murray, the senior intensive-care consultant there, told me: 'You don't know the what I'll term the kinetics of the agent: how long it takes to reach its peak effect; how long it's going to last for; when things might start to improve . . . any metabolites of the drug that might have any long-lasting effects; and probably more the longer-term outcomes.'

The 'metabolites' he referred to are by-products of the body's attempt to clear the poison. With some nerve agents these are well understood, sarin for example producing a complex acid so distinctive that it can be used as a marker for contamination with that agent. With Novichok A234 there was simply no idea what might happen as the body metabolized it, and whether this by-product might destroy the kidneys, brain, or some other vital organ.

Indeed even when I talked to the hospital's Medical Director, Dr Christine Blanshard, in May 2018 about possible lasting effects she noted, 'I think the honest answer is that we don't know. And we have a total world experience of treating three patients for the effects of Novichok poisoning, and I think it's safe to say that we're still learning.'

Late on in that first week though, as the identification of A234 firmed up on the Wednesday and Thursday, these were not questions uppermost in the minds of the clinical team. They were struggling to keep the Skripals alive. To begin with this meant the Level 3 array of intensive care plus large doses of the standard three drugs used to treat this type of crisis: atropine, pralidoxime chloride, and diazepam.

The most important of these drugs, when dealing with nerve-agent patients, is atropine. It shields the body's nervous system by limiting damage to acetylcholinesterase production. However, in order to do this, it is best administered quickly. Atropine has some other uses too, for crises rather more common than nerve-agent poisoning.

The paramedics who treated the Skripals on 4 March had, by serendipity, given them small doses of atropine. Suspecting an opioid overdose they had noted the pair had very weak heartbeats – and atropine is carried in many ambulances for use in such scenarios. So they administered what may have been life-saving medication to the Skripals based on a false premise of what had made them ill. 'The doses given at the scene were small but significant,' one medic told me, 'after the nerve-agent diagnosis we flooded them with atropine.'

Another unknown was how much damage hypoxia, oxygen starvation, might have done to the brain. Doctors did not initially have a precise idea how long the Skripals had stopped breathing before the medics had arrived. Brain damage can occur within several minutes of such a crisis. Through scans of brain activity they became surer that the paramedics had performed a remarkable duty in this regard also, reaching the scene as well as supporting the Skripals' breathing with great speed.

Other tests on the ward, such as those for kidney and liver functions, also showed some kind of normal activity. So as the patients entered their second week on Radnor Ward confidence started to rise, just a little. They were becoming, in the words of one of their consultants, 'stably sick'. Every day survived was another day in the fight and Nick Bailey was showing that recovery was possible. He was sitting up, receiving visitors, and rallying even if some reported him a little confused and 'not his usual self'. By 22 March he was well enough to be discharged.

Having got through the first couple of weeks with all their patients alive, the doctors began to think ahead to stage two of the fight. The medical literature had led them to believe that the 'survival phase' might last up to one month – that was the upper limit given for the active effects of the agent VX on the body, for example. But once that initial battle was over, and tests on Yulia's organ functions were starting to give them confidence in that respect, a whole new stage began.

Production of acetylcholinesterase, the nervous system's 'off switch', might take months to re-establish itself. Preparing for this eventuality they shifted ventilation from the mouth to the trachea (the windpipe, at the base of the neck below the voice box), which is less intrusive as well as allowing the patients to speak once the time comes to dial down their sedation, bringing them back into the world of the living.

This process was starting for Yulia at around the time that Nick Bailey was discharged. Having established that key organs appeared to be working, they looked for signs that the patient might be able to breathe with less help from the ventilator. They had begun scaling back her support in that regard just eight or nine days after the poisoning. And with the evidence that she could support her own breathing for a time, the medics started adjusting the drugs, as consultant Stephen Jukes explained: 'We would begin to reduce the amount, literally taper the amount of the medications that [we] are using to a point where it's no longer necessary and constantly review [the] response. If we worried that actually the response is damaging in some way or has potential to be damaging, we pause and perhaps backtrack. If things look stable, then we can slowly take away that support.'

Her father meanwhile remained deeply sedated. The tests being given to him suggested his kidneys, liver, and other organs were having a hard time getting back to normal. Sergei was still far behind his daughter, and therefore that much closer to death.

With Yulia beginning her journey out of deep sedation there were hopes she might be able to talk to police. Outside the intense, insular world of Radnor Ward there was an international crisis playing out.

19

'HIGHLY LIKELY' RUSSIA

Early on Wednesday 7 March, a group of senior ministers and officials made their way to the Cabinet Office on Whitehall. They processed through the high-security entry system, juggling cups of coffee, passes, and briefing papers, and down to the basement and Cobra. The government's emergency committee is one at the same time a group, a place, and an acronym: Cabinet Office Briefing Room 'A'. In its modern form it is a windowless place, electronically swept to prevent bugging, and plugged into a wide range of communications equipment including secure phones and video-teleconferencing facilities.

Around thirty people arrived that morning to find Amber Rudd, the Home Secretary, and a couple of officials waiting. Tall, precise in manner, and already well briefed, she would be chairing the session. Among the others filing in were Boris Johnson, the Foreign Secretary, Gavin Williamson, the Defence Secretary, and two dozen other ministers and officials.

None of them harboured any doubt that Russia was responsible for what had happened in Salisbury. But in appointing Rudd to chair the meeting, the Prime Minister was concerned firstly to deal with urgent practical questions arising from the poisoning and secondly not to rush into publicly blaming Russia. But one figure at the Cobra table on the 7th had already come very close to doing that.

The meeting followed remarks in the House of Commons the previous day by Boris Johnson. He and the Home Secretary, entrenched on opposite sides of the Brexit debate, were also quite different political animals: Rudd the more deliberate and measured, Johnson given to rhetorical flourishes and shooting from the hip.

'It is too early to speculate as to the precise nature of the crime or attempted crime that has taken place in Salisbury,' Johnson told MPs, 'but I know members will have their suspicions. If those suspicions prove to be well founded then this government will take whatever measures it deems necessary to protect the lives of the people in this country.'

Having urged parliamentarians and the watching world to avoid jumping to conclusions, Johnson had then himself spoken of the 'echoes' of the Litvinenko case, and the 'malign' influence of Russia in recent world events. His insinuations were undoubtedly informed by an initial briefing from the intelligence people. These remarks nettled Downing Street, which, used to finding him a force of nature who would often stray off script, decided to sideline him in the response to Salisbury.

In the Cobra room, Rudd had the advantage that she had already received detailed police and intelligence briefings. It was the format of Cobra that she relayed this information to her colleagues, who then came up with a common response to the challenges identified. Crucially from No. 10's point of view, it was the Home Secretary who would lead in the public presentation of what was going on – from visiting Salisbury to giving TV interviews.

That morning Cobra heard the Public Health England determination that the Skripals had been poisoned with a nerve agent, the latest on the police investigation, and a résumé of the intelligence (circumstantial as it was) about Russian responsibility and motive. I have talked to people at various levels about the response to Salisbury, and all can remember questions that were discussed with great urgency and seriousness at the time but proved in hindsight to be not worth worrying about.

In that first Cobra meeting, the possibility that the poisoners might still be in the UK, with additional nerve agent to use against other targets, apparently gave rise to a good deal of debate. It might have seemed alarmist, but nobody at that stage wanted to be complacent or to underplay the seriousness of what had happened.

Reporting to Parliament on 8 March, Rudd's statement reflected both the early take of Whitehall officialdom and her desire to strike a more measured tone than Johnson's. 'If we are to be rigorous in this investigation, we must avoid speculation and allow the police to carry on their investigation.' She avoided even using the word 'Russia' on this occasion, let alone reciting a list of Vladimir Putin's recent misdemeanours.

The other noteworthy thing about Rudd's initial message is that it reflected some optimism on the part of the police that they could soon find suspects. She spoke of 'a fast-paced criminal investigation', and while asking for time for investigators to do their thing, promised, 'The investigation is moving at pace, and this government will act without hesitation as the facts become clearer.'

It is evident that the counter-terrorist police who were briefing her were guardedly optimistic based on their recent experiences of quickly unravelling jihadist plots, and the early scientific advice they were hearing from chemical-weapons experts. This emphasized the possibility that the Skripals had breathed or ingested poison, so that its effects would therefore have come on in minutes. The investigation focused on who was about in the Maltings and Zizzi's restaurant in the hope it might quickly yield suspects. As we will see, things would go very differently.

There were a number of reasons why her initial readout was more cautious in attributing blame than the Foreign Secretary. She wanted to put clear blue water between herself and Boris Johnson, evidently. But she and those briefing her were also conditioned by the investigators' desire to bring people to trial for Salisbury, and to avoid saying anything that, by pointing a finger before the evidence was clear, might prejudice the process. In this way the early reactions of the Home and Foreign Secretaries reflected the classic division between evidence and intelligence. The latter would be available much sooner than the former, and would not have to pass the same standards of proof.

Among those briefing key decision-makers during these days following the poisoning was Harry Murdoch, who nearly two decades earlier ran the Operations section of P5, galvanizing MI6's Russia agent recruitment, but who by 2018 was serving in a more senior role. Murdoch may have felt a sense of personal affront about the Skripal affair, having had the GRU man operating as an active case during his years working the Russia target. He and other senior intelligence officials set in train a series of assessments that looked at the question of Russian responsibility and were presented to ministers during the first ten days of the crisis. This work soon found its focus in the re-examination of previous material in two key areas: CX or agent-reporting about Russia's continued possession of chemical weapons; and traces, mainly electronic, showing that the Skripals had been kept under surveillance by Russia.

His erstwhile colleagues across the river in Vauxhall Cross were in a state of shock during the early days after the poisoning. One insider characterized the mood as 'bewildered'. He might have added 'angry', because the Salisbury poisoning was threatening to the agency on many levels: by showing it could not protect someone like Skripal it might deter anyone tempted to spy for Britain, threatening MI6's core business; the exposure of security around him as inadequate simultaneously demonstrated the agency's underestimation of the threat; and although they would be able to deliver intelligence relevant to the incident, none of their sources was able to give detailed insight into how the operation had been mounted, still less to warn it was about to happen.

During those days the questions asked of the Secret Intelligence Service, and indeed of the other intelligence agencies in the UK and worldwide, ranged across three broad areas: motive; timing; and how exactly the operation was carried out.

When it came to motive, many people, from the officers on duty in Wiltshire Police control room to the Foreign Secretary, had quickly pointed to the similarities with Alexander Litvinenko's poisoning in 2006. But how was Skripal comparable?

Litvinenko had been an outspoken public opponent of Putin, accusing him of all manner of crimes, not least blowing up apartment buildings (killing hundreds of Russians) to frame Chechen separatists. The murder of Litvinenko was also part of an acute period of confrontation between the Kremlin and Britain, in which an upsurge in espionage activity as well as sedition by Litvinenko and his paymaster Berezovsky were all seen as part of a pattern of unacceptable activity by Putin and the *siloviki*. The FSB boss Nikolai Patrushev had indeed even publicly voiced their suspicions of an extensive anti-Kremlin British plot, an implicit explanation of why a message had been sent, by means of polonium.

Skripal by contrast had never gone public or campaigned in this way. Nor was there a Berezovsky figure in the picture either, actively calling for the overthrow of Putin and doing so with the help of the onetime GRU man. Was there anything Skripal had done to make the Kremlin or even his former employers angry enough to kill him?

The security people examining the case soon focused on Skripal's relationships with foreign intelligence agencies. Could there be something here that would have provided a trigger for an assassination plot – particularly, they reasoned, if there was a Russian agent in one of them who had reported back to Moscow about the help Skripal was giving?

Piecing Skripal's travels together I found out that he went to the US in 2011 and the Czech Republic in 2012, and there were a couple of visits to Estonia. In the summer of 2017 our interviews had been interrupted by a week-long trip that he had made to Switzerland to talk to their federal intelligence services. That last one might seem innocuous but it will be recalled that Litvinenko had been helping investigators in Spain shortly before his murder, and there were a number of investigations of corruption linked to Russian officials ongoing in Switzerland.

I have heard it said also that Skripal had been talking to

the Ukrainian security service, the SBU, though not apparently in Ukraine itself. The GRU had played a key role in channelling Moscow's support to Putin's proxies in the east of their country. Might Sergei have given the SBU some advice on his former organization's methods? I find this idea ironic, given the disdain Sergei showed for Ukrainians when we met. And certainly when we chatted he made no mention of having helped them as a consultant. But if he had played the role of 'good shepherd', that could easily have nettled people in Moscow.

These rumours are, I've been told, untrue but it is a measure of interest and intrigue generated by the Skripal case that some people have spread them. Some of his travels though, particularly to places that were formerly in the Soviet bloc, might be seen as re-entering the game, particularly if the person reporting it to Moscow exaggerated Skripal's role. In such a scenario the 2010 presidential pardon might be seen as null and void. Had I been able to question Sergei after the poisoning, queries about these foreign trips would have been near the top of my list. But despite many attempts by me to restart our conversations he chose not speak to me after he and Yulia were struck down with Novichok.

A further idea that gained some traction on social media was that Skripal had been linked to the notorious 'Trump dossier' put together by former MI6 man Christopher Steele and his company Orbis in 2016. The 'Steele Connection' appealed to some people, who thought the Americans might want to kill Skripal for helping in the embarrassment of Trump, and others, who were convinced that the document had given Russian agencies a motive to assassinate him. My own checks could not produce any hard fact to support this theory (though proving a negative is never possible). Orbis denied any connection with Skripal either singly or through an alleged British 'former handler'. It's very hard to imagine Sergei having much to contribute to Steele, given he'd been away from Moscow for many years, and from the intelligence business for even longer. Rather this story, given some weight by pro-Kremlin voices in the old and new media, gained some wider currency among those who found the British government narrative hard to believe.

Another theory that received some attention among Western agencies was the idea that Skripal may have been some sort of victim of a fight between the GRU and FSB or SVR. This might, as in the case of Yuri Burlatov's murder in Moscow, have been a matter in which corruption was part of the picture also. If the key message being sent was that of targeting a former GRU man overseas, well, there was a pretty limited supply of those. A couple were in the US but quite well hidden there, and in the UK there was also Vladimir Rezun – but having defected in 1978 he really was ancient history. That might have left Sergei as the obvious choice.

Even so this idea of an inter-agency feud did not find much purchase among those in the secret world. One former Western spy boss that I put it to found the notion contemptible, adopting the role of Putin in his reply to my question: 'I would cut off the heads of those GRU and FSB chiefs if they created an incident like this because of their own infighting.'

If there was some scepticism about an internecine fight between Russian agencies, there was a stronger sense among analysts that Skripal was a traitor who worked for certain intelligence agencies and that might have been enough to make him a 'legitimate target'. In this context it might have fallen to the GRU, as it had years earlier with Burlatov, to 'take care of business' with Skripal, for the sake of its reputation in the Kremlin. And the Putin calculus had changed in the years since Litvinenko, after all. In his quest to assert Russia's power there had been a good deal more risk-taking, from Ukraine to Syria. Some of the consequences, for example shooting down the Malaysian Airlines flight MH17 over rebel-occupied east Ukraine with 298 people on board, had been enormous both in terms of loss of life and impact on Russia's reputation.

The reaction to MH17 or events in Syria though had shown the Kremlin that the hue and cry after a major event was limited. Condemnation, sanctions even, could be weathered, and had the useful side effect of contributing to Putin's messages about Western hostility to Russia and its people. Many of the counter-theories about the poisoning, ranging from a false-flag operation (i.e., one by someone other than Russia) to wreck the World Cup to 'why would Putin do it in the run-up to the election?', ignore this simple truth: the events of the previous few years had shown it was a reasonable bet that an assassination could be carried out without any really serious effect on Russia's relations with the wider world.

Maybe the main difference between 2006 and 2018 was simply that the Kremlin's kill threshold had lowered, the murder of its foes having become so commonplace.

For some, using an exotic method of assassination – polonium with Litvinenko and Novichok with the Skripal attempt – was axiomatic to Putin's purpose. It was a deliberate signal, aimed both at people within his own intelligence agencies and to the wider public, that treachery would never be forgiven, and a way of making a statement of Russian power and impunity. Dan Hoffman, in 2010 the CIA Moscow station chief who had assisted with Skripal's journey to the West, told me in a BBC interview:

> It's not a new strategy for Russia, for the breadcrumbs, so to speak, to lead back to the Kremlin. Part of this is revenge, but the bigger part of this is about delivering a message to Russians inside Russia, to Putin's own electorate in advance of the elections, and to his security services who are enabling him to remain in power.

In sending a message, who was more deserving, more despised in Putin's Russia, than a traitor? Here too we see a traditional *chekist* imperative, of liquidating one who had betrayed the Motherland, a tactic that had faded away during the years after the fall of communism but come back with a vengeance under Putin and arguably intensified still further since Litvinenko's murder. For those taking the 'trail of breadcrumbs' interpretation, the choice of the Novichok A234 agent as poison was intended as a deliberate Russian fingerprint. And here, while acknowledging the many differences from Litvinenko's murder, one can see a point of similarity: if the aim is to send a message the choice of a very rare poison such as polonium or A234 is a useful way of doing it.

Those who wanted to dispatch traitors to send political signals needed to find victims, though. In this matter, the Western analysts knew, there was evidence that Putin's agencies were keeping tabs on people who were suitable targets overseas, trying to fix their whereabouts and pattern of life, while a vigorous public-information campaign kept their names alive, but despised, for the Russian public.

There can be little doubt that Alexander Poteyev, the SVR colonel who betrayed Russia's illegal network in America, would be near the top of any Kremlin list of targets – the damage arising from his disclosures was surely greater than Skripal's. His work for the Americans had moved Putin to public fury in 2010 with his 'traitors will kick the bucket' remarks. But since his exfiltration, Poteyev had been carefully looked after in the US by the FBI. How to track him down?

'According to certain information', Interfax news agency reported from Moscow on 7 July 2016, 'Poteyev died in the USA. At the moment, the information is being verified.' The news of his death was quickly picked up by Western newspapers and the story travelled around the world. If the Russians wanted to kill Poteyev, who was sixty-four by this time, it would appear to have been too late.

Except Poteyev wasn't dead, and I was told while writing this book that he is still very much with us. What's more, the Americans believed that the Interfax story was planted as part of a plot. Russian intelligence would monitor the communications of his friends and family in the hope that their reactions to the news story revealed something about the defector's whereabouts. If they really hit the jackpot, Poteyev might even send a message himself of the 'I am still very much alive' variety and provide a way of finding him.

A few weeks after I learnt about the Poteyev 'fake death' plot, the Ukrainian SBU used the same ploy, albeit more elaborately, with Russian exile journalist Arkady Babchenko. Here too, we learned, the aim was to intercept online chatter that might be triggered by the 'fake news'.

What the Poteyev case shows was not just the ongoing Russian effort to pinpoint traitors but also why, when faced with difficulties in going after their top targets, they might have moved down the list a little to someone that was easier to find. Sergei had never hidden himself. He was on the Salisbury electoral roll – unlike Litvinenko and Gordievsky, who used British aliases provided by the UK agent-resettlement people. And there was another thing that made him easier to find: his communications with Yulia and Sasha when they were back in Russia.

One of the important discoveries made by UK agencies as they investigated the Salisbury affair was one, presumably by the electronic eavesdropping agency GCHQ, that the Russians had hacked into Yulia's email account in 2013. They traced it forensically back to a server linked to Russian intelligence. If they already knew the 'where', Skripal's home in Christie Miller Road, reading emails might have suggested a 'when' in the targeting plan. Yulia's email hack was one of several signs British intelligence had discovered that the Russian services were tracking the Skripals – other details remain classified but were evidently part of the case that Cabinet ministers and allies had found convincing several days after the attack. There were other curious, circumstantial signs.

Making the 2014 *Mole in the Aquarium* documentary, thirty-seven minutes no less, relied on FSB assistance, with two of its officers interviewed in the piece. And in February 2018, weeks before the attack, a nationalist Russian YouTube channel that often featured espionage themes uploaded two videos about Skripal's treason. No point dispatching someone the Russian public had forgotten about.

If the motive in attacking Skripal was therefore a combination of sending a message, the continuing campaign against traitors, and simple opportunism in that he was an easier target than some others, what about its timing? The use of a nerve agent on British streets just a few weeks before presidential elections was claimed to be significant by both believers and sceptics. Putin has suggested that such timing, just before he was voted in for a third term, would be illogically reckless. His enemies in the West, though, argue, much like Hoffman's 'trail of breadcrumbs' concept, that the idea was to demonstrate the president's power and impunity, perhaps even deliberately stimulating Western reactions that could be framed as Russophobia at a time when Putin's political machine feared electoral apathy.

The view in Vauxhall Cross seems to have been that the timing was conditioned by tactical factors rather than strategic ones. One former officer told me laconically, 'I don't find the timing at all odd – they do not operate according to British civil service priorities.'

From the outset, they regarded Yulia's flight from Moscow to London on 3 March as key. Those planning the operation could have learned of her intention to travel some time in advance by intercepting her communications with her father. If they'd gained a few weeks' warning, this could have prompted them to put other elements of the plan into place – critically, obtaining the poison and getting it into the UK. Once she was in Salisbury they could use her phone to locate her father swiftly and precisely. In this scheme the timing, and indeed the whole plan, is entirely about operational factors, a view that fits with the chilling view of Russian actions expressed to me by a senior Whitehall figure: 'You kill traitors like you brush your teeth. It wasn't a political matter, it was an operational matter.'

In this interpretation, political murder has become such a well-established tactic in the Russia of 2018 that there is considerable autonomy given to the FSB or GRU to conduct it in the way they see fit. This view fits also with the British 2007–2008 intelligence assessments that the Litvinenko and Berezovsky operations were actions of the Russian state but that Putin could not necessarily be connected personally

with a directive to carry them out. These analyses acknowledged that there was no intelligence, no smoking gun,
linking Putin with any of these plots, and indeed that such
proof would be near-impossible to gather. It also, cynically,
might be argued to mean that Britain could still make the
case for diplomatic engagement with the Kremlin, avoiding
complete rupture.

The arguments rehearsed here about motive, timing, and
operational responsibility were those briefed to Boris Johnson, Amber Rudd, and indeed Prime Minister Theresa May
during the weeks after the Salisbury attack.

Johnson remained an ultra, continuing to attack Russia
in ways that sometimes caused alarm among his officials. In
an interview with a German broadcaster he implied that the
Salisbury Novichok had been traced back to a Russian factory
by Porton Down, a statement for which there was no evidence, not publicly anyway. In the same interview he found a
way to blame Putin personally while implicitly acknowledging that his intelligence briefings didn't go that far:

> I'm afraid he's in charge of the clattering train, as we say
> in the UK. Somebody has to be responsible, and we in
> the UK think that the evidence, the culpability points
> to the Russian state, as it did in the case of Alexander
> Litvinenko. You remember that the trail of polonium
> led back very clearly to the Russian state. In the end,
> Mr Putin is in charge, and I'm afraid he cannot escape
> responsibility and culpability.

All the key decision-makers in the British set-up met in
the Cabinet Office on the morning of 12 March, sitting as the
National Security Council (NSC), to formulate a strategy. It
was in this forum that the intelligence agency heads joined

the Prime Minister and those Cabinet ministers involved in the earlier Cobra sessions. Mark Sedwill, another alumnus of MI6, runs the NSC and was to prove a key figure in galvanizing Britain's allies to join in joint action against Russia.

Two key developments relative to attribution had happened between the first Cobra meeting on 7 March and this NSC meeting five days later. First, Porton Down moved on from its generic 'nerve agent' determination to a specific identification of Novichok A234, a substance it assessed had been developed and produced – historically – at the Shikhany facility in southern Russia. The second, more sensitive, resulted from British assessments about the efforts that the Russian intelligence services had made to keep tabs on Sergei and Yulia Skripal, as well as to intercept their communications. Armed with this new information Theresa May was confident enough to escalate the international blame game.

It was following this meeting that the Prime Minister made her statement to the House of Commons, quoted at the start of this book, in which she said it was 'highly likely' that Russia was responsible for the attack.

The approach agreed in the NSC then mapped out in the Commons aimed to snare the Russians in a series of bear traps: giving them the choice of taking responsibility for the attack or admitting that the nerve agent had been stolen, simultaneously trying to place them in violation of the Chemical Weapons Convention, and implying that Putin was responsible in an overall sense for what had happened even if the specific proof that he'd ordered it was lacking.

Russia, as we will see, had its own strategy, answering these allegations in a way that would retain the Kremlin's political freedom of manoeuvre. A full-blown information-warfare battle had been joined. It took a few days for the

Russians to find their feet in this – a delay that may be attributed to awaiting instructions from Putin or perhaps wanting to wait and see just what kind of evidence the British might produce.

Sergei Lavrov, Russia's veteran Foreign Minister, bit back hard when asked by a BBC reporter about the Skripal affair on 9 March during a visit to Africa:

> We have not heard any concrete fact, we only watch your colleagues on TV with serious faces pompously saying that if it is Russia, then such a response will come that Russia will remember for ever. This is not serious. This is pure propaganda. This is just whipping up hysteria.

As for the Kremlin, it was slower off the mark. Even one week after the attack Dmitry Peskov, the Kremlin spokesman, declined to comment, noting Skripal 'worked for one of the British intelligence services, the incident occurred in Great Britain'. On the same day that Theresa May challenged his government (12 March), Putin, who was campaigning in southern Russia, gave his first reaction to BBC correspondent Steve Rosenberg. Asked whether Russia was behind the poisoning, the president replied, 'Get to the bottom of things there and then we'll discuss it.'

Other voices were far less cautious. Vyacheslav Volodin, Speaker of the Duma, was one of the first to suggest the assassination plot was a false-flag operation, claiming Theresa May was 'inappropriately attempting to shift suspicion away from Britain'. In this conspiracy, the British themselves wanted to kill Skripal as a pretext for further demonization of Russia. Sergei Stepashin, who briefly ran Russian security after the dissolution of the KGB, asked rhetorically, 'What kind of idiot in Russia would decide to do this? Where is the logic? . . . The

English just hate us because the World Cup will be taking place in our country.' This type of statement simply seemed to confirm the possibility that attacking Skripal was connected with Putin's long-term messages about Russia being besieged by hostile powers.

On 14 March, having had no answer from the Russians to her ultimatum, Theresa May reappeared in the Commons to set out her retaliation. There would be twenty-three Russian diplomats expelled, and a host of other measures relating to Russians visiting the UK and keeping their money in the country. And that wasn't the end of it. The Foreign Office had been busy, urging allies around the world to take coordinated action.

While some Tory politicians briefed journalists that the British response should include everything from arranging a boycott of the football World Cup to deporting oligarchs, the approach taken by the diplomats and intelligence professionals was rather more restrained. The view of one retired intelligence officer shortly before Britain's expulsion announcement was, 'There should be another clear out, leaving only a single acknowledged security officer through whom the necessary counter-terrorism intelligence could be exchanged, and a minimally staffed defence attaché group.'

This indeed was how the Foreign Office calibrated their action. The list of twenty-three heading home actually left a couple of Russian intelligence officers in post in London. In this way, the British spooks' desire to keep a minimal channel open, even in the midst of this grave international crisis, was gratified. In consultations with allies, Foreign Office diplomats were pleased to find that they were pushing at an open door – the number of countries that regarded the Skripal affair as a welcome opportunity to strike back against Russian spies grew. As will be clear, for example from the period Skripal spent in training before his first posting in Malta, Russia devotes years preparing its people for work in embassies overseas, so the disruption caused by throwing them out can be considerable.

During the days that followed, more than a hundred and fifty Russians were expelled: sixty from America; the twenty-three from Britain; thirteen from Ukraine; four each from Canada, France, Germany, and Poland; and so on. Notwithstanding that Russia threw out more than a hundred and sixty from these countries in response, the Foreign Office considered it a famous victory. They had assumed there would be retaliatory expulsions but had succeeded in orchestrating a global action larger than any Cold War move against Soviet or Russian espionage networks. By way of comparison, the tally following Litvinenko's murder was just four expulsions carried out by the UK alone, without similar gestures elsewhere.

That differential in the tally – more than a hundred and fifty in 2018 versus four in 2007 – tells us how far an international consensus had solidified about Russia's rule-breaking. Those who questioned the quality of proof Britain had shown its allies over Salisbury were only emphasizing that point in a way: many countries were itching to make examples of Russian spies for all sorts of reasons, and Putin's paradigm of a Russophobic West had, to an extent, become a self-fulfilling prophecy. 'I was surprised by the speed of reaction, the degree of hatred of the Russians,' one senior British figure told me, 'for many Salisbury was a tipping point because of what was going on internationally more broadly.'

In seeking the diplomatic high ground, the UK then invited experts from the Organisation for the Prohibition of

Chemical Weapons (or OPCW), the United Nations-backed international watchdog, to come to Salisbury to verify the UK's claim of Novichok poisoning. Russia tried but failed to thwart this, calling unsuccessfully instead for a joint UK–Russia investigation.

The OPCW team sent its first members to Salisbury a fortnight after the poisoning and concluded its work a few days later. Most of its eventual report is classified but the published summary noted that having taken samples from various places and the three people involved, the OPCW team 'confirm the findings of the United Kingdom relating to the identity of the toxic chemical that was used in Salisbury'. It added, 'the toxic chemical was of high purity', having an 'almost complete absence of impurities'.

Many people focused on the confirmation of the UK's Novichok claim but the line about purity was arguably more important, particularly to chemical weapons nerds. It was a hat tip to the people who made it, suggesting both chemistry and labs operating at a very high level. You could forget terrorists or the Mafia, the implication was that this was a substance that could only have been made in one or two places in the world.

Although the UK had secured a considerable diplomatic advantage in the second half of March, it was a long way from having an unimpeachable international argument. In its information war, the Kremlin took the Prime Minister's phrase 'highly likely Russia' and used it as a hashtag, a taunt, suggesting a case that was light on fact.

Of course there were weaknesses in the UK position: it was not claimed that the agent A234, although identified, could be forensically tracked to Russia's labs; if it had specific intelligence about how the Skripal operation was mounted, the UK was not releasing it; and of course there were no police photos of suspects seen boarding planes to Russia or other points east shortly after the poisoning, let alone a Lugovoi-style named suspect.

If the British government was to maintain its diplomatic momentum it needed a break. Perhaps Yulia or Sergei would come round sufficiently to give some new information. What was really needed was some kind of breakthrough in the police investigation, but that proved a forlorn hope.

20

THE INVESTIGATION FALTERS

On 23 March, just as doctors were starting to lighten Yulia Skripal's sedation, the Metropolitan Police issued an update on its Salisbury investigation. Early statements were given in person outside the New Scotland Yard headquarters but this was released in a low-key way, and it reflected a vanishing of any early optimism on the part of investigators. It was an exercise in expectation management.

'The investigation is highly likely to take many months and, where it is operationally possible, updates will be issued to the media,' said the police, adding, 'Locally, updates are being provided to the community of Salisbury by Wiltshire Police. Searches are ongoing in the Salisbury area and at this stage it is not possible to put a timescale on how long these may take to conclude.'

So how had two hundred and fifty officers experienced in complex counter-terrorism investigations achieved so little, nineteen days after the poisoning? Like almost everyone else responding to the event of 4 March they had been hampered by the time taken to identify the poison, and of course by the skills of those who had planned Skripal's assassination. And although many initially saw the similarities to the Litvinenko affair, there was a glaring difference: in 2006 that victim had been able to give a statement to detectives on his deathbed pointing the finger at Andrei Lugovoi as his principal poisoner.

The Salisbury investigation had started with just two people: Nick Bailey and the other detective who went to Christie Miller Road soon after Skripal was taken ill. There were only six or so Wiltshire Police on duty in the city at the time. Within days this mushroomed to a force of hundreds mobilized from across the south of England; the uniformed officers had a growing number of places to cordon off and guard, the detectives all manner of leads to follow up.

Like doctors, ministers, or diplomats, the police had to respond to each new discovery from the Porton Down people and during that first week important changes came almost daily. With the shift in analysis from opioid, to unnamed nerve agent, undetectable 'exotic' agent, Novichok, and finally A234 the police were forced to change tack. People were pouring in, trying to find desk space, clear orders from someone in authority, and find something constructive to do.

An officer who experienced the goings-on at Salisbury's Bourne Hill police station during that first week told me, 'It was absolute mayhem. There were people from [plainclothes] squads coming in giving orders, absolutely crazy orders, like "evacuate that street", or "seal off this place", without any real reason. Nobody had a clue what they were doing.'

Events took a surreal turn when parts of Bourne Hill station itself were sealed off. Contamination was found on computer keyboards used by Nick Bailey after his 4 March visit to the Skripals' home. Results coming back from Porton also suggested Novichok traces in his locker (presumably because he'd put his gloves or other equipment in there) and the station's evidence store where some items recovered on 4 March had been placed.

Meanwhile the number of sites cordoned off by uniformed officers multiplied to include Bailey's car; Skripal's vehicle; the tow truck that had removed it from the centre; two ambulances and a police car at the hospital; the bench in the Maltings; Zizzi's; the Bishop's Mill pub; Liudmila's and Sasha's plots in the cemetery; and of course the house in Christie Miller Road.

It did not take long for Gold Command at Police HQ in Devizes to realize that the police might be able to manage the cordons but they couldn't do all the sample-gathering and removal of vehicles. By 9 March therefore the military had been called in to help.

Those charged with decontamination found it slow work. They lacked basic things, like containers the right size to fit chairs or tables that had to be removed. The slowness of the lab-based GC/MS testing procedure at Porton Down also tried people's patience, working in 'the hot zone', as contaminated sites like Skripal's house or Bourne Hill police station became known. During this deliberate surveying and decontamination at 47 Christie Miller Road it was discovered that the Skripals' guinea pigs had died, and their cats, apparently driven to distraction by hunger, were put down.

With each additional site cordoned or specialist deployed the people of Wiltshire and a watching world looked on with disbelief. Operators in bright yellow hazmat suits were at the cemetery, while up at the hospital the army was wrapping ambulances up before taking them away on low-loaders. Rumours were flying, some widely reported such as the one that they were about to exhume Sergei's wife and son (no matter that only an urn of his ashes was there), others reaching the police and army such as that scientists had asked everybody to keep an eye out for dead birds, which would be collected for analysis.

Initial advice from Porton experts did little to resolve the confusion. Manuals on VX nerve agent, for example, said it took anything from 'a few minutes' to eighteen hours to do its work. Unlike a gun or knife attack, instant in its effect, this gave investigators a wide window to look at. In following up that timeline, the detectives followed a standard procedure in backtracking from the bench in the Maltings.

If the nerve agent had been inhaled or ingested it would work fast, so they should be looking at passers-by in the Maltings, or others in Zizzi's restaurant or the Bishop's Mill pub where Sergei and Yulia had been earlier. Even this set of possibilities produced an enormous workload. CCTV would have to be harvested from many places in the city centre, and hundreds of people tracked down. All kinds of techniques were employed in this, from mapping credit-card usage to seeking images from bank ATMs of those making cash withdrawals.

Other agencies were drawn into this too, for example number-crunching thousands of mobile phones present in Salisbury that day to look for suspicious activity. To give one example: a woman who had been in town that Sunday found the police on her doorstep a few weeks later after she had returned from working abroad. She had left the UK the day after the poisoning and her phone had been switched off for weeks as she was working at sea, with no signal. For the algorithms processing data, this was enough to flag her number, for she had left the country and 'gone dark' just after the assassination attempt.

In addition to those trawling CCTV, and working through thousands of mobile numbers, there was a third investigative team examining journeys in and out of the country around the weekend of 3–4 March. Had an assassin even been on Yulia's plane, for example? This investigative route, like the others, however, did not produce any rapid results. However over time it was to be these data-based routes of inquiry, combining information from phones, CCTV, and airline passenger details, that would prove particularly fruitful.

As detectives worked back from the bench to Zizzi's to the pub they got to Sergei's BMW. He had parked in the centre at about 13.40. Early tests revealed nerve-agent contamination in the restaurant and pub, but it was his car that proved particularly significant. Traces of Novichok found on the door handle and steering wheel, touched by Sergei's hands, led investigators definitively away from the possibility of inhaled or ingested contamination and towards absorption through the skin. This fitted too with the poison residues on keyboards at Bourne Hill police station. Scientifically, the absorption route also helped explain why it had taken hours for the Skripals to fall ill.

So had the car been contaminated and if so when? Appealing for public help on 13 March, the police tried to pin down where it had been in the hour before the car park in Salisbury. They were having problems tracking the Skripals' movements. As I knew from arranging meetings with him, Sergei did not usually carry a mobile phone – he told me once that he had one but that it was pay-as-you-go and he couldn't be bothered to top it up. Yulia had either left hers at home that morning or switched it off, perhaps to avoid roaming charges.

It became clear to police that the Skripals went out that Sunday morning to visit Liudmila's and Sasha's graves at the London Road cemetery, came home briefly and then went out again at about 13.00. In as much as Sergei had a regular 'pattern of life', a Sunday-morning visit to the London Road cemetery was often part of it. So had the poison been delivered while he was out by somebody who knew he would not be back for a while? Or maybe during the night, after Yulia had arrived but before they went out? The absence of contamination at the cemetery gave some weight to the idea that the Novichok was placed while they were there, not before.

By around three weeks after the attack, suspicions were finally focused on the front door. At Porton, the technicians running items and swabs through the GC/MS equipment reached an important conclusion; concentrations of A234 were significantly higher on the front-door handle than anywhere else. It was 'ground zero'. When tests for contamination on Ross Cassidy's Isuzu pick-up, used to collect Yulia from the airport, were negative they realized they need look no further back.

This news was greeted by detectives with a mixture of relief and dejection. It was good that there was a firm theory at last about the place and approximate time that the poison was delivered. But on the other hand it meant that weeks of work, scanning thousands of hours of CCTV from the town centre and talking to hundreds of witnesses, might well have been a wasted effort. And if the person or people who targeted the Skripals had avoided the centre altogether, made their way direct to 47 Christie Miller Road, contaminated the door handle, and then left Salisbury, the search would become a great deal harder. There were no CCTV cameras outside Skripal's house that could provide images of someone approaching his front door.

With the door as ground zero the investigation took a different turn. The police statement of 28 March downplaying the likelihood of rapid progress also heralded a renewed emphasis on the area of Christie Miller Drive. 'We are therefore focusing much of our efforts in and around their address,' Deputy Assistant Commissioner Dean Haydon, in overall charge of the National Counter-Terrorist Network, announced. 'Those living in the Skripals' neighbourhood can expect to see officers carrying out searches as part of this.' Additional vans arrived, bringing more police and search equipment into the area.

So, twenty-four days after the poisoning, they went around door to door again, and deployed search teams to comb the back gardens, footpaths, and all the rest. It wasn't exactly a return to square one, but it was hardly very reassuring either that this fine-focus search was being conducted at nearly three and a half weeks on. The hope was that they would find a distinctive footprint, a discarded item of clothing, or maybe even the container used to dispense the Novichok onto the door handle. Clearly the chances of turning something like that up were diminished by then.

Another resident in Christie Miller Road, recalling the chaotic early weeks of the investigation, revealed:

> The police came to us and asked the same questions four times. First time it was the Wiltshire CID, the Regional Crime Squad, then people from the Met, one lot after another, they didn't seem to be talking to one another.

From the outset, those looking at the crime had regarded Yulia's arrival as an important moment in the initiation of the attack. She had arrived in London on an Aeroflot flight from Moscow the previous afternoon, Saturday 3 March, had been collected by family friends Ross and Mo Cassidy as well as her father. Ross was the former neighbour who had moved away in 2012 but remained on very good terms with Sergei, and they had enjoyed many a drink together. They had chatted on the way back, hearing of Yulia's plans. She was intending to stay with her father for two weeks.

Some of the instant theories about her arrival – like the 'poisoned gift from Russia' – had soon fallen by the wayside because the evidence in the house didn't support them. But other ideas, voiced early by intelligence people and investigators, proved more persistent. Had Yulia been used to 'fix' a time and place when an attempt on her father's life might be made? Could intercepted emails or calls before her departure from Moscow have provided a broad indication of when might be a good time to strike? Could tracking her phone have provided a finer vector on Sergei's location and even their planned excursions?

Yulia had arrived in a very positive mood. She felt optimistic about her relationship with a thirty-year-old Muscovite, Stepan Vikeyev. They had been an item for well over a year and maybe she was hopeful that marriage might be on the cards. But he seemed to disappear after the attack, friends telling reporters that he was lying low. He had made no attempt to contact the hospital either. Was he just frightened or was there something more sinister going on?

There was a host of questions for Yulia and it was late in March that her health was sufficiently improved for detectives to want to question her. Doctors had experimented with reducing her ventilation as soon as ten days after the attack. In court papers submitted on 20 March, Sergei Skripal is said to be 'unable to communicate in any way', whereas Yulia is described as 'unable to communicate in any meaningful way'.

Within a few days of these proceedings (connected with

the taking of samples by international observers) she was sufficiently improved, and sedation dialled back, that she was becoming 'meaningful'. Sister Sarah Clark described the gradual process of waking her, noting, 'It wasn't something that just happened.' And as Yulia became more aware, she began to recognize the sister, so like any patient awaking in such an alien environment, she began asking questions.

The nurses had been warned not to tell them anything that might be prejudicial to the criminal investigation. They could not, for example, say, 'You were poisoned with nerve agent'! Instead they were to stick to informing them where they were, how they were being looked after, that they were making good progress, and other general information.

This preoccupation on the part of the investigative team, safeguarding any future trial by keeping the patients ignorant of the wider furore, narratives, and counter-narratives that surrounded their case, became something of an obsession with the police. It was drummed into medical staff but it was also, initially at least, used to isolate the Skripals from friends and others who might have helped them through their recovery. Ross Cassidy was one of those, for example, who asked to visit them in the hospital, and as he informed *Sky News* on 28 March, 'I was told quite categorically that we were not allowed.' For the detectives it was vital to test Yulia's memory before anyone could influence it.

With conversations under way the police posted outside Yulia's room on Radnor Ward became frustrated. They could hear talking inside, why couldn't they interview Yulia? Sister Clark and her colleagues wanted to be sure that she was sufficiently aware and strong to have such an interview. 'We had a duty of care to protect them and also we were acting as their advocates,' she explained.

By 29 March, Yulia was formally taken off the critical list, the public announcement following on by a day or two the moment that detectives were able to begin talking to her. Although these long-awaited interviews did not provide them with a Litvinenko-style breakthrough, they were useful in talking through the hours leading up to the poisoning, eliminating the possibility that it was someone the Skripals might have met on the Sunday morning who could have harmed them.

While she had been under sedation an enormous amount had happened: Yulia and her father stood at the centre of a row between the country where their lives had been saved and Mother Russia, still so dear to them both. When sedation is being reduced, the intensive-care team on Radnor Ward normally put the radio or TV on for their patients. It is a way of bringing them back into the conscious world, and helping them adjust to the days or weeks they have missed. In the Skripals' case, however, following consultations with the police, they did not do this.

Yulia, who dated her own return to consciousness from about 24 March, was picking up information fast once the interviews started, and she became able to switch on the TV for herself. Once the key initial interviews had taken place, she was able to communicate more widely, online, with friends and family.

Ross Cassidy and his wife Mo saw her several days later. Perhaps stung by his appearance on *Sky*, police called him, suggesting a time and day. The Cassidys' visit was not detected by the press. When he told me about it later, 'I was pleasantly surprised by her condition,' he said, 'she was a little thinner, with a plaster on her neck, but her spirits were good.' They were not able to talk to Sergei that day, perhaps he was not feeling well enough, or maybe because the police had still not done their initial interviews with him.

Yulia had soon discovered that her country's embassy in London was pressing for access (saying her Russian passport gave them the right to consular visits). A welter of theories had been circulating in the Russian press also, suggesting everything from that she had died soon after the poisoning to that she was being kept prisoner by British intelligence. These were, as we will see, just a small part of the information war unleashed in the wake of the poisoning.

There is no doubt that the Kremlin was hungry for information about the Skripals' condition in order to adjust its information campaign and wider narrative. It was fascinating therefore that Yulia's cousin Viktoria (the daughter of Sergei's late brother Valery) should, after many days of being unresponsive to Facebook messages from one of my colleagues, Olga Ivshina of the BBC Russian Service, reply to her on 23 March. She was desperate to visit Yulia and Sergei in Salisbury Hospital, but said the British Embassy in Moscow had not responded to her calls. Could Olga help?

Here I must briefly reinsert myself into the story. Olga came to me and asked for my assistance. Could we get Viktoria into the hospital? Having closely read the court judgement (about the taking of blood samples by international inspectors) published on the 22nd, just the day before these conversations, I had been struck by its statement that no next of kin had been in touch with the hospital. It specifically mentioned Sergei's mother and Yulia's boyfriend in that regard. This saddened me. Knowing that Viktoria lived with Sergei's mother, of his devotion to Yelena, and that Viktoria must be the closest alternative relative, I decided to help.

Contacting the hospital, I had a conversation where I was

told repeatedly that Viktoria must go 'through diplomatic channels'. But she had already tried, I replied, wasn't there some way we could facilitate this, or simply enable her to get some information? There was no way that this exchange was going to be conducted via the BBC, came the answer. I understand that entirely, I reassured them, but if you could just give me a name and number of someone for her to talk to, an email address even, I will simply relay it, then remove myself entirely from the conversation. 'She must go through the correct channels,' came the answer again.

I told Olga it was no-go, explaining they were probably just being bureaucratic, wanting to do this in the prescribed way. But I confessed to her that it was also possible that the hospital had become conscripted in the information war, and were going to make it as hard as possible for Viktoria to get to her cousin and uncle. And this is how things turned out.

Olga flew to Moscow a couple of days later and on 26 March interviewed Viktoria Skripal. She told of her horror at the poisoning, and how Yelena was so old and frail that she daren't tell her the truth. 'I just wish that there could be some sympathy for us, for the fact that his mother is ill, diabetes, and that she's ninety years old,' Viktoria told Olga Ivshina. As for the long-term prognosis, 'Out of ninety-nine per cent, I have maybe one per cent of hope,' said Viktoria. 'They say they've been given an antidote which has kept them alive, but if they survive it sounds like they'll be invalids for the rest of their lives.'

The British Embassy said they had no record of Viktoria calling them when my BBC colleague asked, though she was able to show Olga the calls on her phone history. Soon afterwards, though, Viktoria did undoubtedly apply for a visa to visit Britain.

Knowing what Sergei had told me about his arrival in Britain in 2010, and how stressful it was, being unable to speak to his mother for one month, I felt deeply for Yelena's situation. There were others though, in the intelligence services of each country, who could see all this in less sentimental terms. Suspicions were rising on the British side that Viktoria was being used to obtain information. Her statements, for example in her BBC interview, that she was assuming her relatives would die and there might be an antidote that could easily have been formulated to trigger disclosures from British officials or indeed Yulia herself. It is quite likely that the FSB or GRU had become aware, through monitoring communications, that Yulia was emerging from her coma, then, a little later, starting to communicate online, and this sharpened their interest in what was really going on.

After Olga's interview with Viktoria, the *Daily Mail* followed suit, and then very swiftly after that she was signed up by Russian state TV, the First Channel. Her comments then assumed a more overtly political character.

Yulia's minders from Counter-Terrorist Command were aware that she might also become anxious about her grandmother Yelena. The hospital staff were sensitive to her predicament too. The result was a phone call early in April when Yulia phoned Viktoria from Radnor Ward. This was the conversation recorded and broadcast by Russian TV:

Yulia: Hello.
Viktoria: Hello.
Yulia: Do you hear me?
Viktoria: I hear you.
Yulia: This is Yulka.
Viktoria: Oh, Yulka, I can tell by the voice that it's you.

I didn't understand. So this means they gave you a
telephone?

Yulia: Yes, yes, yes.

Viktoria: Well thank God. Is everything OK with you?

Yulia: OK, everything is OK.

Viktoria: Look, if I get my visa tomorrow, on Monday
I will fly to you.

Yulia: Nobody will give you a visa.

Viktoria: Well that's what I think too. If they give it to
me, when asked if I'm able to see you, I need you
to say yes.

Yulia: Well, I think no, the situation right now is—

Viktoria: Look I know everything and—

Yulia: Later, let's talk later. In short everything is OK.

Viktoria: Is this your telephone?

Yulia: It's just temporary, you know.

Viktoria: Got it. Is everything OK? You can see it on TV,
you know, what the situation is like here.

Yulia: Everything's OK. Everything's OK. Everything
can be solved, everything can be healed, everybody's
alive.

Viktoria: Is everything OK with your dad?

Yulia: Everything's OK. He's resting now, he's sleeping.
Everyone's health is OK. Nobody has had any
irreversible [harm], I'm being discharged soon.
Everything is OK.

Viktoria: Bye, take care.

Yulia: Take care.

It was a businesslike exchange – after such shocking
events one can hardly say it communicates any great emotion. People though speak of Yulia's reserve and self-control,

and it's clear that she and her cousin were not that close. Also, it might be inferred that they had already exchanged messages online, since the fact that Yulia is conscious and communicating hardly seems like a revelation to Viktoria. There is the uneasy sense listening to the recording and reading it on the page that both women have been deployed for a purpose by their respective sides.

Yulia, not using her own phone for it had become a crucial piece of evidence and presumably had to be decontaminated also, has been given one to make the call. She has one message, communicated nine times in a short conversation, that 'everything is OK'. But she also tells her cousin quite plainly and without sentiment, 'nobody will give you a visa', that it's just not going to happen.

For her part, Viktoria, after the initial surprise that her cousin can call, sets about trying to move things her way, and extract information: whose phone are you using; I need you to support my visa application; and what condition is Sergei in? Curiosity, particularly about Sergei, might seem entirely natural under the circumstances, but Yulia appears to suspect her agenda and keeps it all very brief. And of course Yulia was right, Viktoria was not going to get a visa.

The British side, from its monitoring of communications, and from episodes like Viktoria's attempts to contact the hospital via us at the BBC, had come to its own conclusions. And Yulia appeared to share them. Whatever latitude she might earlier have given to her cousin, the recording and broadcast of their conversation was a stark lesson.

A few days later, on 9 April, and as predicted in the call, Yulia was discharged from Salisbury District Hospital and taken by her police guardians to a house not far away. It was a remarkable victory for the medical team treating her. Yulia issued a statement saying she was already missing the doctors and nurses as well as thanking the passers-by who had helped her and her father in the Maltings.

As for her relative, Yulia added these choice phrases:

> I thank my cousin Viktoria for her concern for us, but ask that she does not visit me or try to contact me for the time being. Her opinions and assertions are not mine and they are not my father's.

Set aside the damaged relations between states, this estrangement between the Skripals seems one of the saddest aspects of the whole affair. They were, after all, by the time of the poisoning, a family that had already been whittled down by the vicissitudes of fate. Viktoria would later bring Sergei's mother more explicitly into the picture, saying that Yelena was distraught that her son had not called her.

What Sergei's emotions must have been, once he became fully aware of the situation, one can only guess. But Russia was now deploying all of the means at its disposal to defend itself, casting doubt on the British version of events.

2 1

THE INFORMATION WAR

April passed slowly for Yulia: released from hospital, housed in a peculiar place with its government furniture and fittings, protected around the clock by armed police. Although she was out of hospital, taking blood and other samples from her did not stop. There were more conversations with detectives, and people who came to give counselling, help her through the dislocation of time, space, and expectation.

When she flew to London on 3 March she was in an upbeat mood. She would be reunited with her father, he was going through a tough time after Sasha's death but she had put her Moscow life on hold to be with him. And she could give him hope, and take some for herself too, with the promise that there were brighter days coming.

She felt confident about her relationship with Stepan. Perhaps they would settle down. Yulia's flat in Moscow was being redecorated while she was away, and she had put her beloved black mongrel, Nuar, into boarding kennels for the duration of her trip to England.

All her plans were derailed by the poisoning. Stepan was staying out of the public eye, not even contacting the hospital (though it's possible Yulia may have got through to him after her release), and her father was still seriously ill in hospital. How could she return to normality? The Salisbury house was contaminated, a crime scene, being investigated by the police, and there was no way she was just going to jump on a plane back to Moscow. Her father still needed her, and of course the advice of those around her was that she would not be safe going back.

Little wonder that in a statement released on 11 April, Yulia wrote, 'I find myself in a totally different life than the ordinary one I left just over a month ago, and I am seeking to come to terms with my prospects, whilst also recovering from this attack on me.' She was well aware also by this point that the Russian state was asking for access to her, citing its rights under consular law to give assistance to a passport-holder.

The campaign for consular access, like the interviews being given by her cousin Viktoria to Russian media, were aspects of an information war that were intensely personal to Yulia. She must have resented this but she also knew that her future, inasmuch as she could see one at that moment, involved going back to Russia. 'I have been made aware of my specific contacts at the Russian Embassy who have kindly offered me their assistance in any way they can', her statement continued, 'at the moment I do not wish to avail myself of their services, but, if I change my mind I know how to contact them.'

Russia had hit on the issue of campaigning for access to the Skripals a couple of weeks into the affair. It was a way of simultaneously doing the right thing, in terms of looking after their citizens, while trying to find out more about their condition, and make the British look bad. But of course these appeals also played another role, as part of the international battle to set the narrative of what had happened. By emphasizing their inability to get consular access they could suggest the British were hiding the Skripals, imprisoning them even, as part of a sinister plot. Inasmuch as there was a coherent single counter-narrative – rather than many different ones – this version suggested the British had carried out the attack, with material made at Porton Down, in order to discredit Russia.

It is not always easy to distinguish the official aspects of the Kremlin information war here. For in the febrile social-media battleground there were rival claims from Salisbury 'truthers' or indeed their opponents, Putin-haters, that were quite unconnected to the official strategies of the Kremlin or Downing Street but might occasionally borrow a good line from them.

British internet users claimed that Russia had murdered Skripal's son or brother, or the whole list compiled by Buzzfeed of thirteen who had died in suspicious circumstances. These charges, often made anonymously on social media, had nothing to do with the official narrative or briefings we were getting. Indeed you could argue they were a distraction from the main event – Skripal – in that officials or ministers had to address them.

This unofficial speculation soared after the discovery on 12 March of the body of Nikolai Glushkov, a friend of the late Boris Berezovsky. Glushkov, found murdered in his home in a southern London suburb, had also been a critic of Putin's and it was quickly established that he had been strangled. He had been a director of Aeroflot, and was, up until his death, involved in a long-running legal battle with them. The action had nearly bankrupted him, and friends accused the airline of pursuing it for political reasons.

The idea of a link with the Salisbury attack just a few days before seemed to some to herald a general onslaught on Russians in the UK. From the start though the police cautioned against making any link with the Skripal affair.

On the other side of the social-media battlefield there were many who had nothing to do with Russia expressing scepticism that Russia had targeted the Skripals. From the supporters of Labour Party leader Jeremy Corbyn decrying the similarities with Britain's journey to war in Iraq to those who could see some connection between Skripal and the Trump dossier compiled by Christopher Steele, many of those rubbishing the Whitehall version of what had happened were not following Kremlin talking points. Having said all that, there were clearly information strategies deployed by the opposing governments that fed into the wider arena, with lines even being used unwittingly by many who debated the issue.

Some of the most revealing Russian responses came in the initial aftermath of the attack. They followed a similar pattern to those after the murder of Litvinenko and some of the high-profile killings in Russia itself. They suggested that Skripal knew only old secrets and wasn't worthy of assassination, or that things never end well for traitors. The Russian Ambassador to Ireland for example told British radio listeners on 8 March, 'For some reason, the British territory is very dangerous for certain sorts of people.' First Channel presenter Kirill Kleymyonov noted, 'The profession of a traitor is one of the most dangerous in the world,' adding that there seemed to be something odd about Britain. 'Maybe it's the climate, but in recent years there have been too many strange incidents with grave outcomes there.' If the aim of attacking

Skripal was to send a message to Russians, well, there it was right there: spy for Britain and it will end badly.

During those last days before the election other ideas were planted too, and they were very helpful to a president, so long in office, who might have feared that a combination of apathy and domestic economic concerns could undermine the fresh mandate he was seeking. His campaign was worried that Putin would not win 70/70, which meant 70 per cent of the vote with a turnout of 70 per cent. Russian political analyst and former Putin speechwriter Abbas Gallyamov argues that the Salisbury poisoning succeeded admirably in creating a distraction from domestic concerns while reinforcing long-standing messages about Western Russophobia. 'Among Russian political experts it's common knowledge that this high result of this last election happened due to this conflict with England over Skripal,' he told the BBC, 'foreign policy again dominated the agenda so all these domestic issues again found themselves at the backstage.'

As Gallyamov's analysis suggests, his fellow citizens drew certain conclusions from Salisbury, even while their government denied it and propagated so many counter-theories. Reading between the lines and making deductions from what's not said are skills any politically aware Russian learns. Someone I've known for many years, a European who had done Russian government work over the years and is therefore not quoted here by name, told me this about his contacts with Russian foreign policy and security officials in Moscow in the days following Salisbury:

> Sometimes, like after the murder of [opposition leader Boris] Nemtsov, there seems to be genuine surprise and things are said about needing to get to the bottom of it.

With Skripal there was no pretence or attempt to deny it at all.

While the Kremlin-friendly media gave airtime or column inches to all manner of alternative theories, the one story you do not see in their output during the weeks after Salisbury is coverage suggesting Russian intelligence agencies did indeed poison Skripal or the 'how we did it' sort of feature. In a British tabloid, by contrast, a successful drone strike against a jihadist in Syria would generate copy about unpiloted aircraft, the war against the militants, and various other topics. You will look in vain in March or April for the Russian story interviewing former KGB operatives giving their take, exploring past examples of poisoning (even the well-attested ones from the Soviet period), and so on. It's understood by Russian journalists that you don't go there.

At the political level too there were certain messages that were notable by their absence, for example, 'We take these charges seriously and have ordered urgent inspections of our chemical laboratories in order to rule out the possibility that any nerve agent was stolen.' Even simple expressions of sympathy for the Skripals, which did come later from President Putin or the Russian Embassy in London, were largely absent at the beginning.

While the messages given or not given are undoubtedly important in the way Russians process a story they can hardly be said to constitute evidence and from an early stage the Russian response aimed to expose the weakness of the UK's case, even poking fun at it. When Theresa May suggested in the Commons on 12 March that it was 'highly likely Russia' that was responsible she was relaying the intelligence she'd received and evidently stating a view formed just a few days into what was obviously going to be a long police investigation. However the Russians seized on the term and #HighlyLikely and #HighlyLikelyRussia became internet memes – a joke about how their country got blamed for everything.

Early on the Russian method seemed to be one of releasing as many counter-theories as possible. It's a tactic that had been seen before, for example after the shooting down of flight MH17. Officials at different times suggested that a dizzying number of nations might have possessed Novichok and used it in this case: from the UK to the Czech Republic, Slovakia, Sweden, and Ukraine. None of these alternative theories generated much traction, but each gained some life among people with a particular agenda.

It was when Putin made his first detailed remarks about Salisbury, on 18 March (election day), that a new and potent Russian argument aimed at undermining the UK version took off. Describing the poisoning as a 'tragedy' that he had read about in the media, Putin argued, 'The first thing that entered my head was that if it had been a military-grade nerve agent, the people would have died on the spot.'

This pulled the rug from under several previous counter-narratives, in that, by the same presumption, any British, Czech, Slovak, Swedish, or Ukrainian use of a nerve agent would also have killed the Skripals on the spot. But no matter, because it is a hallmark of Kremlin messaging in these situations that consistency is far less important than generating numerous alternative theories.

The 'if it was really a nerve agent, they'd be dead' idea touched a chord with many people. It was self-evident that the Skripals hadn't perished. Tragically, the Salisbury Novichok did later display its lethality, as we will see, but in March and April this was a useful talking point. Put out by Kremlin news channel RT and re-tweeted by Russian embassies in the UK and South Africa, as well as by sympathizers on social media, these remarks by Putin immediately gained around a quarter of a million 'impressions' on social media.

In some ways this story was helped by the British government's own language, from 12 March onwards, in using the term 'military-grade nerve agent'. Whitehall signed up to this because it wanted to get ahead of Russian denial by emphasizing that the A234 used in Salisbury was the product of a sophisticated laboratory, not something that could have been cooked up in someone's kitchen. The OPCW, more wisely, simply referred to the nerve agent's high purity.

The term 'military-grade' was, though, both meaningless, in that the stocks of VX or sarin held by armies are often not especially pure, and misleading. It caused many commentators to assume that the results of contamination with this poison must be fatal. When it wasn't, that just helped President Putin to cast doubt on Downing Street's version.

In fact the Soviet Army doctrine for using agents like VX assumed both huge quantities – scores of litres of agent to soak an area the size of a football field – and limited casualties: 10–30 per cent among enemy troops equipped with protective gear. So this 'military' frame of reference, promoted by British language, was hardly useful. Salisbury was a completely different kind of case in that just a few milligrams would be used in a covert operation against one target.

Evidently there had been successful poison plots against defectors – and the curious case of Ivan Kivelidi, a Moscow businessman murdered with Novichok smeared on his phone in 1995, apparently as part of a business dispute. It was also true that a nerve agent was suspected in the 2002 killing of Ibn al Khattab, a Saudi jihadist who fought in the north Caucasus. With Khattab, the FSB was suspected of lacing a letter delivered to him by a previously trusted courier. However, not all the poison plots had achieved their intended aim.

Others had survived attempts by Soviet or Russian intelligence: from Nikolai Khokhlov, poisoned with thallium in Frankfurt, 1957; to Vladimir Korczak, injected with ricin in the US, 1981; Ukrainian politician Viktor Yushchenko, who ingested dioxin in 2004 with near-fatal results; or former Prime Minister Yegor Gaidar, struck down by an unknown substance in Ireland in 2006. All fell seriously ill, but came through.

Whether the Salisbury poison proved fatal would depend critically on issues such as potency and dosage – rather chancy when smearing a thick liquid on the target's door handle. Nevertheless, the 'they'd be dead' narrative, with its implicit, 'if it was really us, we would know how to take care of these things', seemed credible to many. And for as long as Britain pinned as much of its case of the identification of this obscure Russian-developed nerve agent, that continued to be a target of the Kremlin's counter-blasts.

A few weeks after Putin's remarks, on 14 April, Foreign Minister Sergei Lavrov, citing 'confidential information', dropped a bombshell. The international inspectors who'd gone to Salisbury had turned up something else: 'the samples had traces of toxic chemical BZ and its precursors'. Russia had never made the agent BZ, an incapacitant, he said, rather it was a NATO type of chemical weapon. He suggested that the Spiez laboratory in Switzerland had discovered the BZ in samples sent to them by the international watchdog, the OPCW. Yulia had been discharged from hospital by then, perhaps it hadn't been a nerve agent at all but this lesser poison BZ?

The initial RT report of Lavrov's remarks gained 144,000 impressions on social media. But of course the effect was multiplied as truthers or pro-Kremlin users put the same idea into their own posts. This 'story' was though so blatantly dishonest that even the normally mild-mannered OPCW staff and Spiez laboratory came out to rubbish it.

The Spiez lab tweeted, 'We have no doubt that Porton Down was right in identifying Novichok as the poisoning agent.' The OPCW followed up. 'There was no other chemical that was identified by the labs' other than Novichok, said the OPCW's Michael Blum, explaining that some BZ was used 'in the control sample prepared by the OPCW lab in accordance with the existing quality-control procedures. Otherwise it has nothing to do with the samples collected by the OPCW team in Salisbury.' Far from being an alternative, the BZ was in control samples as a means of keeping the lab accurate and honest.

Of course it is a truism much loved by those in the information-warfare business that a lie will travel round the world before the truth has got its boots on. So corrections to Lavrov were shared by far fewer people than the initial reports.

Even so, Lavrov's story was counter-productive in that it triggered accusations, for example from the Swiss government, that Russia was undermining international institutions – namely the OPCW. The British decision to bring them in soon after the poisoning was a deft move, one that the Kremlin had struggled to counter.

Initially, and tellingly given the original purpose of the Novichok project, one Russian official had claimed such agents were not subject to the Chemical Weapons Convention. This view was swiftly squashed by the OPCW itself. Once the inspectors were Salisbury-bound the Russians had suggested they wouldn't accept the findings.

That was problematic too. Casting doubt on the probity of what the organization or its affiliated labs were doing sat ill with Russia's other arguments – for example that it had already got rid of all its chemical weapons, a milestone certified in 2017 by, yes, that same OPCW. But once again, in the febrile atmosphere on social media, few people were marking the Russians on consistency.

As for the British government's Strat-Coms (Strategic Communications), coordinated through Downing Street, they followed an altogether different pattern. The dynamics of the two information campaigns were almost negative images of one another. Britain wanted to maintain a single, streamlined thread: that the Russian state had used a nerve agent to poison Skripal on the streets of Salisbury. Russia by contrast used a highly decentralized approach in which all manner of players circulated any number of alternative narratives with the aim of undermining the UK story.

In the early weeks, driven by the Downing Street Strat-Coms grid, the story found focus on the expulsions and OPCW inspectors' visit. After that, they moved to minimize the story, and even by late March I and others covering it found that calls were not being returned, and there was a desire to move on to other matters. The police, the hospital, Foreign Office, you name it, all became markedly less communicative.

In late March or early April it was still not possible to confirm even quite basic facts about what had happened. Where had Nick Bailey become contaminated? Was Yulia conscious?

Were they in isolation? Had Porton Down been able to confirm the origin of the Novichok?

The information vacuum created its own risks. How come Yulia had phoned her cousin Viktoria, sounding healthy enough, when we had no reason to suppose anything other than that she was seriously ill? That eroded trust in the British version of events. The absence of pictures from the hospital also fed doubts in many quarters, creating a vacuum in which the rumours that the Skripals were already dead or, later, that they were effectively prisoners to gain some currency.

Of course there were tensions within the information machine between those who favoured saying as little as possible and those who wanted to contest Russia's lines more energetically. The 'minimizers' felt remarks by the director of Porton Down on 3 April proved their point. He told *Sky News* that his labs had not been able to trace the Salisbury Novichok samples to Russia, still less a particular Russian facility. This interview also prompted suggestions that Boris Johnson and the Foreign Office more generally had exaggerated their case, implying that the origin of the Russian agent was known to them.

All of this was manna to the Russian media, and prompted some defensive remarks from the British Ministry of Defence along the lines that Porton had never been tasked to make such a determination.

Contrary to the director's public remarks, Porton might actually have come to such a conclusion, based on previous, clandestinely obtained samples of Novichok. If you have an example of the original, made in the Shikhany complex in southern Russia, you should in theory be able to match it by means of its molecular composition to those found in Salisbury. Why not do so, then?

The arguments against making any such determination public were both old and new, I was told. Traditionally anything obtained by clandestine methods, as German intelligence had in the 1990s, effectively bribing a scientist to bring over a sample, is going to be highly classified and therefore must remain under wraps. The more modern reason relates to information warfare: a revelation that the Salisbury Novichok could be matched to that made in Shikhany, but in the possession of a Western country, could soon have prompted Russian counter-claims that if Germany's BND or the CIA had stolen the agent, then they equally well might have used it to frame Russia.

In my view the case that the UK could tie the Novichok to a specific Russian facility, but chooses not to for various reasons, is unproven. Though who knows, some new disclosure may emerge to change that. Certainly, I've heard it said that the determination that Russia had produced the Novichok used in Salisbury involved highly sensitive intelligence material and that this proof while not made public was, in broad terms, shared with allies when the question of expelling diplomats was being discussed.

The information battle was though simply part of the bigger arc of Anglo-Russian relations, and everybody knew that the argument could not be maintained long term at the same pitch. In mid-April a Foreign Office official told me he thought the Russians were seeking to de-escalate the crisis. Certainly the *British* were. But he had a point about the Russians also: taking one crude metric, tweets by the Russian Embassy in London, there were one hundred and twelve about the Skripal affair in the first half of April, thirty-five in the second. In May there were a third of the number of tweets about the crisis than there had been in April. Of course during this time other issues were coming to preoccupy the social-media person at the embassy: the chlorine attack in Douma near Damascus on 7 April triggered Western missile strikes on Syrian government installations, a move loudly opposed by Russia. And on a more upbeat note, by May the Russians were starting their media build-up to the football World Cup.

Having engaged the OPCW to such advantage initially, the British took their foot off the pedal. Chemical-warfare experts have told me of their surprise that the UK did not swiftly move to invoke 'clarification' procedures under Article 9 of the Chemical Weapons Convention. This would have allowed them to ask the Russians certain questions formally: Where is your single facility permitted under the CWC? Has it produced any Novichok-type agents in recent years? Has it made the A234-type agent?

Instead the UK campaigned diplomatically on the Syrian chemical-weapons issue, and at a special session of the OPCW in The Hague in June 2018 pushed through rules to increase the organization's ability to fact-find and attribute blame. Russia tried unsuccessfully to bar these changes. Although the Skripal affair was helpful in convincing some nations to vote for them, it formed a minor part of the British diplomacy at this event.

So while the Salisbury poisoning produced a far greater reaction – whether measured by diplomats expelled or social-media impressions generated – than that of Litvinenko in 2006, there were certain realities that were bound to reassert themselves. The Anglo-Russian relationship still involves so many businesses, families, interactions, and exchanges that neither side can live with a return to Cold War-style restrictions, still less a complete severance of ties. And as that applied to nations so it did to the Skripals.

Yulia had until 3 March assumed her future lay in Russia. The trip to Salisbury was only meant to last a fortnight, after all. While she had spent years living and working in the UK, she was more comfortable within her own culture, and having met Stepan, was happy there. Recovering from the attack, as the April days dragged into May, she found herself working on a statement that would be issued to the wider world. The police were still uneasy about her giving an interview – questions about how much of 4 March she remembered or who she blamed for the attack might be considered prejudicial if a perpetrator was ever put on trial. But she had things she wanted to say, and the authorities knew that this was also a way of addressing some of the wilder rumours and Kremlin counter-narratives.

She was helped in some of the phrasing of the message that was eventually recorded on 23 May in woodland near London by a team from Reuters news agency. But in order to put beyond doubt that these were her own thoughts, she had also prepared a handwritten, signed version, rather in the manner of a police statement, and of course delivered her message on camera.

Yulia expressed gratitude to Salisbury Hospital but noted also that 'the clinical treatment was invasive, painful, and depressing'. Perhaps the most poignant part of it concerns her re-evaluation of her own situation since the attack and its complexities.

My life has been turned upside down as I try to come to terms with the devastating changes thrust upon me both physically and emotionally. I take one day at a time and want to help care for my dad till his full recovery. In the longer term I hope to return home to my country.

And in that last statement her hope for a future relationship with Russia was clear. As the summer wore on it emerged
that she had been in touch with the builders renovating her
flat in Moscow, that a friend had come over from Russia in
June to visit her, and that her relationship with her cousin
Viktoria had gone from bad to worse. In a difficult phone call
(recorded by Viktoria and given to the media early in July),
Yulia insisted she was free to come home at a time of her own
choosing and that she would have done so already but for her
cousin's appearances on Russian media.

At times Sergei had longed for home too but had been
forced by circumstance to accept perpetual exile. Recovering
as he was in hospital from the poisoning he couldn't see any
way he would ever return. But his daughter embodied the
hope for something better and brighter, for a future despite
everything.

22

THE LONG ROAD TO RECOVERY

In Salisbury Hospital doctors took Sergei Skripal off the critical list on 9 April. It happened just before Yulia's discharge, and it reflected the medical assessment that he could breathe without the help of a respirator just over one month after the attack. The gradual 'wakening', through careful reduction of sedation, had brought him back to consciousness.

Their battle, we remember, had been in two main phases. Until they were taken off the critical list it was a matter of survival. In the weeks that followed it was about recovery, most importantly restarting the body's production of acetyl-cholinesterase so that its muscles and organs got working again properly. Experts thought that might take months, but it happened much faster.

When we were filming at the hospital in May 2018, Stephen Jukes, one of the intensive-care consultants, told us candidly, 'We were exceptionally surprised, a pleasant surprise to see the recovery happen at such a pace when it did begin to happen that I can't easily explain.' Discussing it with his senior colleague, Dr Duncan Murray, he did however speculate about a new therapy that was tried on the Skripals at the suggestion of Porton Down.

We were discussing 'heroic medicine', using techniques or drugs untried before and possibly risky to the patient. Dr Murray said, 'The sort of more heroic untested things were clearly key to the recovery of these individuals and exactly how much they contributed to the course we will probably never, ever know.' That said, he argued, 'The vast majority of the improvement and the success, if you like, of the clinical outcomes in these things, these individuals, were attributable to the very good generic basic critical care.'

It is clear that Porton Down did not as such have an antidote to Novichok, but it did have some ideas for novel ways to restart the production of the body's 'off switch' enzyme. Perhaps we should give the casting vote in this medical debate to Dr Christine Blanshard, the medical director, with whom I had some discussion about the Skripals' recovery. It was, she said, 'simplistic' to talk of an antidote, though some novel therapies were tried on the suggestion of Porton Down. As for their precise effect this was hard to say because, as Dr Blanshard pointed out, the time they might have been expected to take to resume normal production of acetylcholinesterase was very hard to predict.

'It's variable,' she told me, 'depending on the way the agent was administered or acquired, the dose of the agent, and there's an individualistic response as well.' Here she pointed to issues that were quite key to the patients' survival and to the rejection of the 'if it was really Novichok they'd be dead' meme favoured by Vladimir Putin.

In going for an agent like A234, which would be absorbed through the skin, and in deciding a dosage that might do the job but not be so big as to cause huge contamination problems, the would-be assassins had to make a fine judgement. That being the case, the rapid help given to the Skripals that day in the Maltings and their swift passage into critical care had made the difference between death and survival. It would also be key to their recovery. The likelihood that Sergei and Yulia may have washed their hands between touching the door handle and falling ill – for example before eating lunch at Zizzi's – may also have had an important effect in reducing the dosage.

So in the latter part of April, Sergei was improving rapidly, able to talk to detectives and to start moving about. Word reached us at the BBC that he had been seen walking gingerly up the corridors, in the company of a nurse, and later, as that long winter gave way to a warm spring, sunning himself in a garden near the main hospital block. He had some difficult psychological adjustments to make also, being initially reluctant to believe that he might be the target of a Russian government murder plot.

The poison had hit Sergei harder than either of the others, and his road to discharge was longer. He left Salisbury District Hospital nearly six weeks after his daughter. As April stretched into May, nursing sister Sarah Clark could see him becoming impatient. 'I'm sure he would have wanted to have been discharged earlier, if he could have been,' she told us, 'but he recognized . . . that there were ongoing issues that needed to be addressed and he . . . was very dignified and accepted the advice that was given to him.'

During these weeks of waiting, Sergei remained on Radnor Ward, the intensive-care part of the hospital. By May, he was certainly well enough to be moved to another ward but it was simpler to keep him where he was, remaining under armed guard in a single room, and under the care of the same people who had treated him since 4 March.

Coming into his room from time to time Duncan Murray and Sergei would engage one another – each with their accented English – and the doctor couldn't help thinking his way into his patient's shoes:

> I certainly found myself . . . very, very conscious of how I would've felt had I been in a similar situation where you're in a foreign country, and, particularly as information starts to come into your possession that the circumstances by which you've arrived there are clearly way outside the normal. And for me that probably more than the immediate [medical] condition was what the future holds and where I might be going and how my life might look at that point. I found that very sobering, and really quite difficult to come to terms with . . . that's a very vulnerable and isolated place to find yourself in.

At last, on 18 May, more than two months after the poisoning, discharge day arrived. The police helped Sergei gather up his things, he got dressed, and headed out of hospital to follow his daughter to the safe house. Dr Murray was not on duty that day, but he'd made sure to say goodbye to Sergei when he knew his departure was imminent, just as he had with Yulia. 'We develop some sort of bond with all of our patients and there was something particular about these two that made that last meeting slightly more poignant,' he felt. Where would they fetch up? How complete would their recovery be? Those basic questions were surrounded by more uncertainty than with any usual patient.

There had been suggestions from Downing Street, while

the Skripals were in hospital, that they might well end up in America or another English-speaking country, and be given new identities. Neither of them, I hear, particularly liked this idea. But even if the arrangement of safe house and police protection could go on for months, a year even, it could not go on for ever, and the question of where they would live would re-emerge.

A few days after Sergei's discharge, the Russian First Channel stepped up the pressure on him and Yulia. His mother Yelena, approaching her ninetieth birthday, was seen on camera tearfully pleading for him to call. A finger of blame, implicitly at least, was pointed at the British authorities. 'Why don't they allow him to phone, why, what is the reason?' she implored. 'After all when he was at home we used to talk every week, and now for some reason we are not allowed to talk.'

Viktoria also appeared in the segment, staging a one-woman demo outside the British Embassy in her quest for a visa. Yelena called on them to give her one, but the embassy refused once again. It was quite uneasy viewing.

More than that, knowing how important Yelena is to Sergei, I found this Russian TV piece disturbing. It was another turn of the screw in the information war, another ploy at the expense of the Skripal family. Viktoria had done a few appearances on the First Channel by this point and I presumed they were paying her. But for poor Yelena to be drafted in also must have made it so hard for Sergei.

And the question arises, why – at the time of writing at least – hasn't he called his mother? The recording of Yulia's previous call had clearly created distrust. The feeling among those looking after Sergei was apparently that a further call might be used to push him into saying things prejudicial to the investigation or to make political statements. There were two sides in the messaging battle, and in respect to Yelena one could see toughness on the British side also. Late in July, Yulia called Yaroslavl and spoke to Yelena, telling her what had been going on medically, and explaining that Sergei was not yet able to talk to her direct.

In their safe house Yulia and Sergei had access to TV, the internet, and a phone. They were in contact with some friends but even so it was a form of isolation. They could not simply head up to London to have dinner and see a movie.

There were many reasons why the police and intelligence people sought to keep it that way, even if ultimately they recognized the moment would come when the Skripals, particularly Yulia, might want to move on. There was still a sense of guilt in British officialdom that he had not been properly protected on 4 March, nobody wanted to be accused of that again; they didn't want any trial jeopardized by public statements; while they were still recovering they didn't want father and daughter doorstepped by the media; and lastly, if Sergei Skripal was to opt for long-term 'witness-protection'-style security he would have to disappear, severing many contacts he had with his old life, maybe moving to another country.

While Sergei and Yulia weighed decisions about their future, the police investigation moved on. Early in June, Assistant Commissioner Dean Haydon reported, somewhat plaintively, 'We continue to deal with a number of unique and complex issues in what is an extremely challenging investigation.' But it was to be the fusion of data by the intelligence agencies and detectives that would turn the investigation around. By early July this had brought a handful of individuals into sharp focus; Scotland Yard had subjects of interest.

The type and quantity of Novichok used had been guided by a number of considerations: they had wanted it to enter Skripal's body slowly, by absorption through the skin, in part to give the poisoner time to escape; the A234 was applied as a viscose liquid so it did not blow away when applied to the door handle; the quantity used was very small, not least because they did not want an operation that might kill many bystanders; such factors as the temperature and some of the liquid dripping off the door handle onto the ground could further have limited its effectiveness. In the matter of dosage, the experience of the hospital, Porton Down's tests, and the police investigation all dovetailed nicely.

With regard to the perpetrator, the early assumption that they would have been part of a team of two or three grew as analysis of phone data caused them to narrow focus on a few people who had entered the country just before the poisoning and left the following day. A team was needed for the operation because one person might have been keeping watch while the Novichok was used, another possibly driving a vehicle to take them away. The contamination trail and the Skripals' movements before they headed into town on 4 March had allowed the police to narrow down a couple of time windows for when the key perpetrator approached the front door. This led detectives to try to identify every-body who had been moving about in that part of Salisbury during those periods, a process that by early June had involved checking the identity of 14,000 vehicles and 2,500 pedestrians.

As for the people responsible, attention was focusing by July on a few who had left the country soon after the act. So the question was whether the police could tie anyone identified in Salisbury during those time windows to later transit through an airport or port. Initially investigators assumed that anyone with the backing of an organization like the FSB, SVR, or GRU would be very hard to spot.

Looking, by way of example, at the protocol used by Russian illegals in the West to return home for their occasional debriefs or during an emergency extraction, they are designed to thwart investigators. The hallmarks of these secret journeys were multiple identities, different countries, and switching forms of transport. But as investigators combined the datasets from Salisbury, the pointers suggested a more straightforward itinerary. And indeed there were precedents also for simply catching a flight straight back to Russia.

Andrei Lugovoi, the prime suspect in the Litvinenko case, took a plane directly back to Moscow, using his own name. There's one other case worth remembering: Ruslan Atlangeriev, the man suspected of coming to London in June 2007 to murder Boris Berezovsky. Journalists' attempts to track him down once he was deported back to Russia failed. He simply disappeared.

When journalists from the Press Association, a British news agency, revealed in mid-July that several suspects had been identified and that they were Russians, it prompted the security minister to condemn the story as 'wild and ill-informed speculation'. As I heard it from my own contacts, they considered the PA report unhelpful because it was premature. Detectives had indeed by then identified suspects, and they had left the UK on Russian passports, but the identities they had used were believed to be false. Until they could find the true identity of those poisoning suspects, Scotland Yard didn't want to say anything. After all, if they weren't genuine identities, and the UK authorities hadn't worked out the real ones, the possibility remained – however remote in the view of Whitehall – of a false-flag operation designed to tarnish Russia. They wanted to nail down the real identity of the hit team before any public naming of suspects.

This narrowing down of focus on subjects of interest coincided with a quite separate development – the identification of twelve GRU officers by the inquiry into Russian meddling in the 2016 US elections led by former FBI boss Robert Mueller. In this instance the US indictment revealed in remarkable detail the activities of a cyber-operations team that had presumably assumed it could operate from its offices in Moscow with complete anonymity. The US indictment named the GRU units, their physical locations, leading staff members, and their places within the organization. The relevance of this to the Salisbury investigation is threefold: it is another instance of a Western country calling out Russia (and specifically the GRU) for illegal activity; there was a presumption that the Kremlin would never agree to the delivery of these twelve officers for questioning in the US; and the Mueller investigation, by exploiting for forensic purposes cyber techniques normally kept highly secret, showed how the British might gather further information on the Salisbury operation, once it had discovered the true identity of its suspected perpetrators.

It comes as little surprise then that many of those I've spoken to since the poisoning assume that it may never be possible to try these people in a British court. Instead there could be charges levelled, arrest warrants issued, and further investigations conducted.

For the view of intelligence people is that the two or three member poisoning team were not the only elements of this operation.

Among them there is a belief that Skripal was likely under

some physical surveillance before the attack in order to establish his pattern of life and check for CCTV coverage (or the lack of it) in the environs of his house. Although this means going back weeks or maybe even months, and therefore involves a potentially vast pool of people, the likely existence of a surveillance team suggests a larger operation.

Just as the search for a possible surveillance team added to the size and complexity of the investigation, so the shocking events in Wiltshire in June 2018 would both open new paths of inquiry and resolve some questions that detectives had struggled with since March. Four months after Sergei and Yulia found themselves fighting for their lives, another couple were in exactly the same predicament in Radnor Ward of Salisbury Hospital. Dawn Sturgess fell ill on the morning of 30 June in nearby Amesbury, and a few hours later her boyfriend, Charlie Rowley, also fell victim, with the telltale symptoms of sweating, pinpoint pupils, and a frothing mouth. The emergency services found drug-taking paraphernalia in the house.

By Tuesday, with the usual therapies for narcotic overdoses having little effect, the same intensive-care team that had saved the Skripals was sending samples from these new patients off to Porton Down. That evening they heard it was nerve-agent poisoning, and by the following day it was confirmed to be Novichok of the same type that had hit the earlier victims.

The police, taking action to cordon the places where they knew the couple had been during the twelve hours before falling ill, declared a major incident and the media interest took off. It didn't take long for detectives from the Counter-Terrorist Network who were working the Skripal case to switch to the new incident. For this new poisoning seemed to offer some vital answers that had eluded them. Where had the March poisoner disposed of the Novichok container? How could they better focus their searches of CCTV and witness statements to find the suspects?

It was soon apparent that the new victims had been living on the margins of society. Ms Sturgess had lost custody of her kids and was staying in a hostel. Mr Rowley was a hard-drug user on a methadone prescription. The two, both in their mid-forties, had become an item a few months earlier. The day before falling ill they had been with friends in a park on the southern fringes of Salisbury, Queen Elizabeth Gardens.

The couple were known to 'skip dive', searching through bins for items they might sell, or indeed discarded drugs. Police soon formed the view that they had found what appeared to be a normal perfume bottle, with some Novichok still inside it, and took it with them, initially back to Sturgess's hostel in Salisbury, and then on to Rowley's house, several miles away, in Amesbury. Swabs carried out in hospital showed that they had become contaminated through handling something. Dawn was believed to have applied the thick liquid inside the bottle to her wrists, giving her a dosage of poison estimated at ten times that what Sergei Skripal had received.

It wasn't initially clear to investigators whether the perfume bottle was simply a clever way to get the poison through an airport, and that some was subsequently put into a syringe-type applicator for use on the Skripals' door handle, or whether the bottle found in Amesbury was the device used to squeeze the viscose liquid onto the door handle in Christie Miller Road. For months they had been frustrated by their failure to find either a transport container or a syringe-type applicator during their earlier searches. These two poor people, one of whom had died, had done that for them.

While the new crisis shook public faith in the clear-up operation, and to a certain extent the police investigation, it did offer the detectives a new opportunity. Earlier assumptions that the perpetrator was picked up by his or her driver quite close to the Skripal home could be re-examined. If that person had walked down from Christie Miller Road, through the city centre, to the Gardens just to the south, discarded the applicator, and then got into a vehicle to leave Salisbury, then the CCTV footage harvested earlier in the investigation could be looked at afresh, with this new hypothesis in mind, and matched to the known locations of their subjects of interest.

On 8 July, eight days after being taken ill, Salisbury Hospital announced the death of Dawn Sturgess. With this tragedy the investigation became a murder inquiry. Government ministers made it clear that they would not be stampeded into new steps against Russia. The new poisoning was, after all, believed to be a consequence of the original act and therefore also fitted with their priority of avoiding further conflict with the Kremlin.

The Amesbury postscript reminded us of something we saw during the Litvinenko affair. Complex investigations of this kind can go quiet for long periods during which diplomats or businesspeople might assume that relations are getting back to normal. But a new police announcement can suddenly reopen the wound. For the UK government, trying to manage its relationship with Russia, these months showed how everything would become subject to the interplay of two opposing forces: on the one hand a stream of consequences from the Salisbury attack periodically inflaming the situation; on the other a recognition that the two states still had such extensive complex ties that it was essential to get on – or try to.

As the Skripals convalesced that summer, life more widely seemed to be on the road to recovery. Wild talk, early in the poisoning crisis, about a European boycott of the World Cup tournament, perhaps even a drift to open conflict with Putin, had been put to bed. Instead, an England team and its fans set off for the football in Russia – enjoying a successful tournament too – firms announced new contracts, and Russian tourists by the thousands still arrived weekly in London. When Dawn Sturgess died, ministers sought to cool the political temperature rather than further inflame it.

The British government knew it would be fighting diplomatic headwinds if, for example, it tried to go for a second round of Russian expulsions at that moment. European allies didn't want to take further action, and indeed earlier in the summer Jean-Claude Juncker, President of the European Commission, told a public audience, 'I do think we have to reconnect with Russia . . . this Russia-bashing has to be brought to an end'. As for the UK intelligence agencies, elements in MI6 made emollient rather than bellicose noises.

British spooks appear at this time to have leaked their own counter-narratives designed to limit the damage to relations with Moscow and get things back on a calmer track. Certainly the notions that Putin may well not have known about the attack or that Skripal might have been the victim of some sort of feud with former airborne or GRU colleagues were around, and made it into a couple of Britain's national newspapers during the summer months.

In an echo of the earlier Litvinenko and Berezovsky crises, the 'better to keep channels open' faction among the alumni of MI6's Russia operation found themselves on a different side of the argument to the leadership of MI5, the Security Service. After clearing out most of Russia's spies in March, the domestic counter-espionage people took a tough line with visa applications for replacement staff at the embassy, refusing point blank to agree to those of known intelligence officers. Having gained an advantage over the SVR and GRU London stations, MI5 did not intend to give it up.

Just as these arguments for and against normalizing relations with Russia ebbed and flowed in Whitehall so Washington's decision-makers could not easily unite around a common policy. The Trump administration oscillated from a tough initial response with sixty expulsions, to the president suggesting in June at a G7 economic summit in Canada that Russia should be readmitted to their club; him tacking still further in the Kremlin's direction at a meeting with Vladimir Putin where Mr Trump suggested that the Russian leader's word carried greater weight than that of his own intelligence chiefs; to a dramatic move in the opposite direction in August when the US announced sanctions against Russia under a 1991 statute banning chemical and biological weapons use.

This last measure set in train an escalating series of possible steps if Russia did not comply with American demands for on-site inspections. Thus almost everyone, from presumably those who conceived the original Salisbury operation to the many NATO and British decision-makers who discussed its possible consequences, apparently overlooked the possible effects of the US Chemical and Biological Weapons Control and Warfare Elimination Act. At the Kremlin, where perhaps they had assumed like many in the West that relations were back on the road to normality, a shocked spokesman lambasted the American move as irrational and illegal while Moscow financial markets tumbled.

Even if the State Department had not unleashed this retaliation by late summer everyone in Whitehall was expecting Scotland Yard to name and charge suspects from the Russian poisoning team, following up with an extradition request. While many predict the Kremlin will refuse, the expected battle of wills looks set to give hardliners on the Salisbury issue the advantage over those who want Anglo-Russian business to get back on a more even keel.

And what of the man who was the original target of all this? What was to be done with him? From the British government perspective it was better that he remain quietly out of view, even if a statement like Yulia's might follow. In theory he was free to do or say anything, whether that be launching a blistering attack on the British government for failing to protect him from Putin's assassins to pleading it had all been a terrible misunderstanding and could he go back to Russia now please.

Viktoria Skripal though had shown them how, even starting with the best intentions, going public carried the risk of creating untold family pain as well as serving the Kremlin's interests. Sergei and his daughter were so dependent on the British government at this time that there was every reason to follow the advice of those around them.

They were still receiving medical treatment, and benefited from police protection too. They were not in a position to work, and their home remained a quarantined crime scene. Even once it was clear, the idea of Sergei just going back to Christie Miller Road was out of the question. Instead the British taxpayer stepped in to acquire the property. Clearly, his life in that street was over. While the months passed and they considered the future they were dependent on the British government for almost every part of their daily existence.

Perhaps he thought back to that fateful meeting in el Retiro park back in 1996. On that day, twenty-two years earlier, he had reached a resolve, his agreement to work for MI6, that had defined the rest of his life. It had been such a long, hard road from Lefortovo, to IK 5, and even the safe house where they found themselves whiling away the summer days. Sergei though is not a man for regrets. That much was clear from my meetings with him. Once resolved, he entrusts himself to providence, like the paratrooper hurling himself through the door of an aircraft. Sergei Skripal had taken the plunge, first as a spy for his own country, and then for Britain, at a very particular point in history. His recruitment by MI6 came at a time when the intelligence services of Western countries were triumphant and, it is clear, signed up dozens of new Russian sources. As Vladimir Putin sought to exercise control of the state, curb corruption, and reimpose discipline in the military and espionage services, he knew he would have to make examples of agents of foreign powers.

While the FSB, through the late Nineties and early 2000s, produced impressive-sounding figures for how many foreign spies it had arrested, the truth is that it had only limited success in blunting the efforts of the CIA, MI6, or other countries' agencies. This was shown most clearly in the 2010 Vienna spy swap, when the US traded ten Russian agents for just four people (including Sergei) – and two of them were not actually Western spies at all. There were simply no others in Russian custody to make the exchange more even. The trial of Sergei Skripal, and quite likely the attack upon him in Salisbury, grew out of a determination to send messages – that treason against the Russian state would be punished severely. And arguably, having caught so few real 'hirelings' of these foreign agencies, the Russian organization that targeted him may have decided that a more extreme sanction might have to be the substitute for elusive convictions.

Gazing on the house in Christie Miller Road that summer, it is a place robbed of life. The front door, along with many fixtures and fittings, was removed, both as evidence and a source of potential danger to the police there. In its place, wooden panels have been used, creating a new front porch, through which forensic officers in protective suits go in and out. There were things Sergei and Yulia had touched on 4 March, and there were places their shoes, having trodden on the contaminated threshold that day, spread the Novichok also.

On a shelf in the living room the little model cottage that Richard Bagnall gave to Sergei back in 1996 still sits. Even after everything, it carries its promise of a better future, a happier one in that mythical place where a man's home is his castle. This English Eden is a vivid, imagined world, where an old colonel might while away the days of his autumn, relishing happy memories of Kaliningrad, Fergana, or Malta, free from the ugly brutality of those who rule his mother country.

INDEX

INDEX